Far left
Thomas Koster, winner of the 1976 Dutch International at Arnhem, about to launch.

Center left
Speeds of 80 or 90mph are common with models of this type.

Left
Andres Lepp, a famous glider flyer, holds Russian teammate Sergy Samokish's model. A disc protects the propellers from a broken rubber motor during the winding of the clockwork timer mounted at the extreme nose of the model.

Below
Revell's 1/32nd scale McDonnell Douglas F4E Phantom built by Ted Taylor has been given the super detail treatment. Of the many modifications, the most notable are rescribed panel detail, plenty of additional cockpit detail, pitot tubes on fin and nose from old hyperdermic needles, sway braces to rocket rails, and reworked armament.

THE WORLD OF Model Planes

Martin Hedges

CHARTWELL BOOKS INC.

A BISON BOOK

The Hawker Typhoon MK1B was built as a stripped-down display model by Cyril McCann.

Contents

Published by
Chartwell Books Inc.,
A Division of Book Sales Inc.
110 Enterprise Avenue
Secaucus, New Jersey 07094

Produced by
Bison Books Limited
4 Cromwell Place
London SW7

ISBN 0 89009 247 8

Library of Congress Catalog Card Number 79 87906

Printed in Hong Kong

Produced in collaboration with Colourviews Limited

Author: Martin Hedges

Designer: Mike Wade

First Models and Machines

Aviation historians have invariably disagreed about the date of the first model airplane, largely because there is an almost total lack of authenticated documentation on the subject. There are numerous theories and claims to give rise to reasonable suppositions but there is virtually no firm evidence. Further confusion arises because, all too frequently, writers fail to make the distinction between static models made to investigate or demonstrate a theory, display models made just to look at or to illustrate a design feature, and actual flying models.

There is another type of flying model which must enter the discussion although it is not an airplane. Even so, the whirligig or helicopter toy plays a part in the story. It is, strangely, depicted in a 15th century painting of the Christ Child which is in the Musié du Mans at Le Mans, the infant Jesus being shown clutching one. It is also shown in a marginal illustration made a century earlier in a Flemish psalter which is now in the Danish Royal Library in Copenhagen. In this the 'Moulinet,' as it was known, is held by a monk.

Such toys first appeared in Europe in about 1320 and can still be bought today. They depend upon the pull of a string wound around the shaft of a propeller to give the rotor arms sufficient lift to fly briefly into the air.

Leonardo da Vinci (1452–1519) built a number of spring-driven models based on this same helical screw principle which, in turn, was based on the design of Chinese toys. Da Vinci also designed several different types of aircraft, almost all of them relying on the idea – which man was unable to shake off for so many centuries – that to fly humans must emulate the birds. Almost certainly – and here supposition comes in – he would have built models of some of them, as he did of the helical screw. What is certain is that, genius though he was, Leonardo did not invent the airplane and was not the first person to make model aircraft. What he did do was to suggest that muscle power was insufficient in itself to propel man into flight and keep him there.

Historians and writers of the Middle Ages have recorded that a Greek builder named Archytas of Tarentum constructed a wooden model dove 'with such mechanical ingenuity and art that it flew,' according to Aulus Gellius. 'So nicely balanced was it, you see, with weights and moved by a current of air enclosed and hidden within it.' It seems possible that the bird did not achieve free flight but was hung from a counterbalanced arm and propelled by a jet of steam (the 'current of air'). This was the method employed some four centuries later in AD 60 by Hero of Alexandria to drive a copper sphere, the eolipile, which was part-filled with water and spun on an axis, propelled by the jets of steam which resulted when the water was heated.

The Englishman Robert Hooke, who was a pupil at Westminster School, recorded in notes he made in 1655 that he had 'contrived and made many Trials about the Art of flying in the air . . . and at the same time made a Module which, by the help of Springs and Wings, rais'd and sustained itself in the Air.' He, too, came to the conclusion that muscle power was not enough and turned his attention to contriving 'a way to make artificial muscles.' However, he recorded that in many of his trials he was 'frustrated of my expectations.' Sadly, no drawings of his work have survived.

A pair of Frenchmen named Launoy and Bienvenu designed a helicopter in 1784 which was powered by a wound bowstring to turn the twin rotors on their model: this again was the principle of the 'moulinet' toy.

Left
A model of the spring-driven helicopter designed by Leonardo da Vinci (1452–1519), now in the Science Museum, London.

Below
Da Vinci also designed a number of ornithopters intended to fly with a flapping mechanism. This model is in the Science Museum, London.

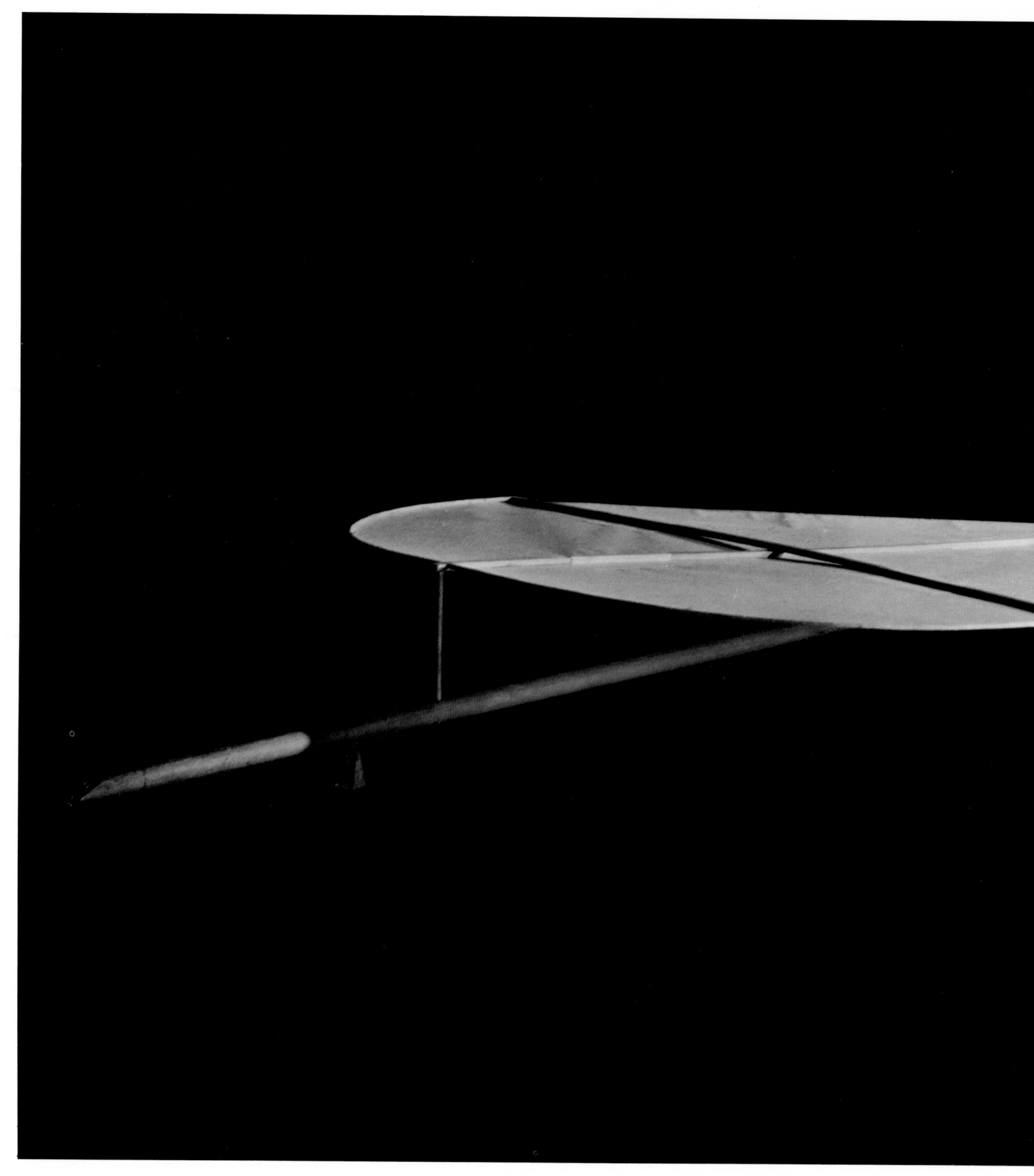

Between 1799 and 1809 another Englishman, Sir George Cayley (1773–1857), a Yorkshire baronet, made significant progress in the field of aeronautical research and used models to further his work. He had already designed a helicopter using feather rotor blades in 1796 when, in 1799, at the age of 26, he designed an aircraft which – at last – dispensed with attempts to emulate the birds' flapping wings and instead established the principle of a fixed wing, a fuselage to carry the pilot and a tail section. His design included a tiller to move a cruciform tail as a means of controlling the direction of flight. Using models, he found that, although a cambered rigid wing was better than a flat wing surface to gain lift, sail-type wings that curved to the flow of air gave the best results for his purposes. He also studied the effects of different configurations and discovered the advantages of the 'flat-V' or dihedral wing shape to improve stability and of streamlining.

To test his theories Sir George built the first successful glider in 1804. Essentially it was little more than a kite

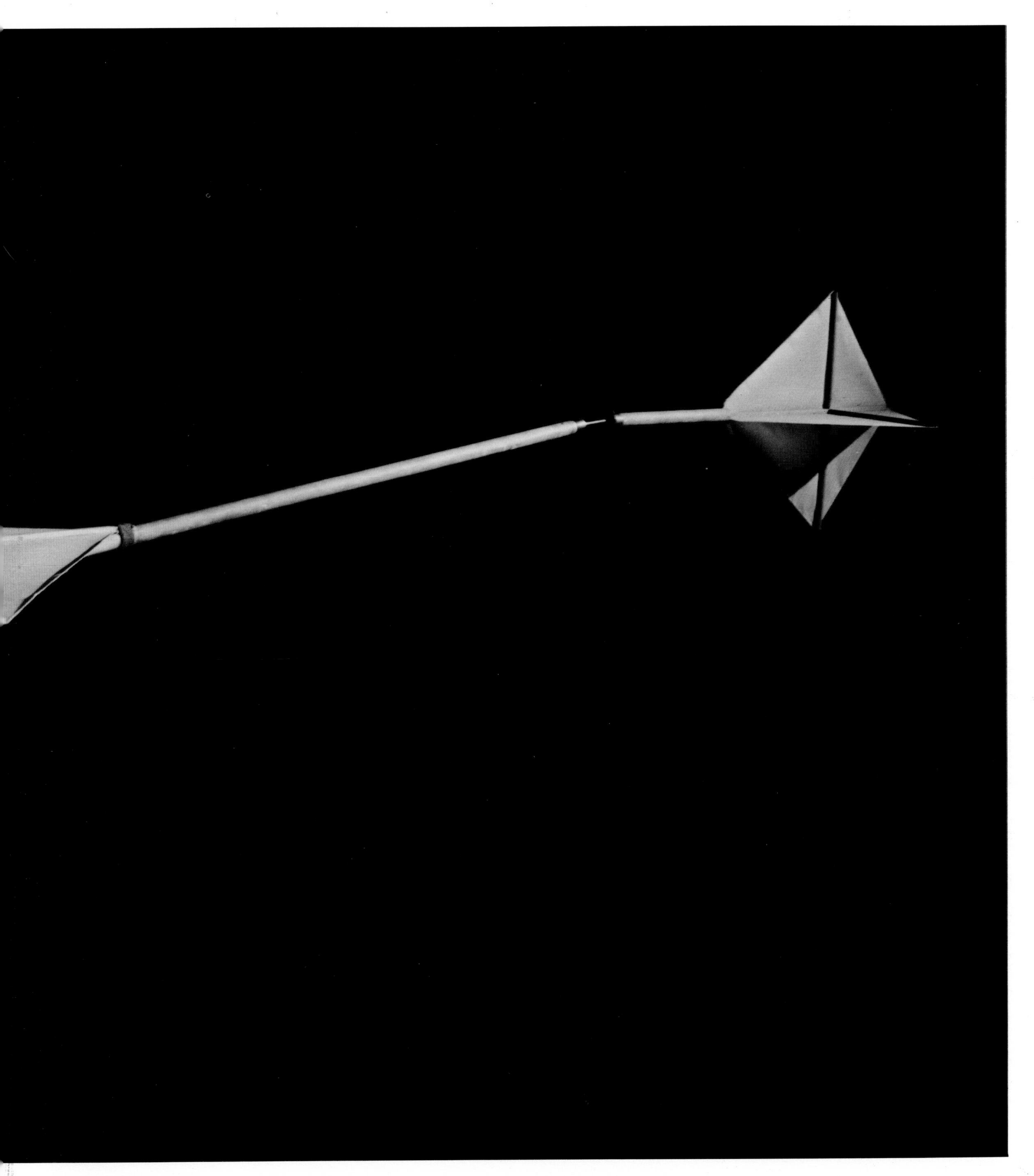

The Yorkshire baronet, Sir George Cayley, made significant progress in aeronautical research between 1799 and 1909. He produced his first glider, of which this is a model, in 1804.

with a tail attached to a rod. The paper kite formed the wings and was attached at the rear end to the rod, while the front was lifted above the rod at an angle of six degrees by a peg. The tail was a cruciform fastened at right angles to a rod which, in turn, was attached to the main fuselage by a universal joint. This joint was used to set the tail at any angle, vertical or horizontal, to control direction of flight. He even used a weight at the nose to adjust it to the center of gravity by sliding it fore or aft.

Five years later Cayley built a full-size version of the glider with a wing area of 300sq ft (2787sq dm) and this flew successfully in ballast as well as when carrying small boys individually on short glides. Cayley then devoted himself to other matters including airship design, and it was not until 1849 that he built another glider. This time it had triplane sail wings which were flapped – for some reason he reverted to the bird principle – and a wing area of 338sq ft (3140sq dm) weighing only 132½lb (60kg). Cayley did not consider it a success and it only carried one passenger, a boy.

Cayley's extraordinary 'convertiplane' was basically a boat fitted with wheels and a superstructure supporting pairs of rotating discs. This model is in the Science Museum, London.

In 1846 Cayley produced a model of a 'convertiplane.' This was a boat fitted with wheels and a superstructure supporting four large discs arranged in two pairs and set at dihedral angles for lateral stability. The intention was that, having raised the machine off the ground by acting as rotors, the discs would be closed to form circular wings. Propulsion forward then would be provided by a pair of pusher propellers. The design did not get beyond the model stage. Then in 1853, when he was almost 80, he built his 'new flyer' which he launched downhill with his reluctant coachman as the passenger. The craft took off and floated across a valley to become the first man-carrying aircraft in history.

Meantime other work had been going on among men eager to take advantage of Cayley's earlier work and to continue their own research. In 1842 W H Phillips designed a model helicopter which flew successfully, propelled by jets of steam from the tips of its rotor blades. The model, which flew across two fields, contained a combustion chamber in which gypsum, saltpeter and charcoal were combined to produce steam.

In the same year William Henson and John Stringfellow collaborated to produce the design for their 'Aerial Steam Carriage,' which was patented and published in 1843. The craft included a deep gondola-type fuselage slung below a fixed monoplane cambered wing – possibly influenced by Cayley's research – and movable tail unit. It had a wing span of 150ft (46m), two pusher propellers and a tricycle undercarriage.

The model of the design which Henson built had a 20ft (6m) wing span and still survives in the Science Museum, London, Unfortunately it never flew and the pair did not go ahead with the full-size version. When tested in 1847 the model ran down a launching ramp and shot into the air under its own impulsion but the steam engine it contained was too heavy for sustained flight.

Henson had foolishly been carried away by the prospects of success before the design had proved itself, and had formed a company, the Aerial Transit Company, to run passenger services. His literature showed the Aerial Steam Carriage flying above London and Paris but when the model test flight failed he fled to America to escape the ridicule.

The more cautious Stringfellow continued with his research and produced a number of small steam engines. He fitted the one he had designed for the ill-fated Steam Carriage into a new 10ft (3m) wing-span model in 1848 and attached this to a wire running the length of a long room in a disused lace factory in Chard, Somerset. The model flew along the wire and into a canvas sheet at the end. It was this event which gave rise to the claim that Stringfellow built the first engine-driven model in the world to fly.

In 1954 the author, as a junior reporter on a Somerset weekly newspaper, discovered what was believed to be part of the first airplane engine built by Stringfellow – a belief supported by a visit from a member of the staff of the Science Museum. Along with Stringfellow's original single-cylinder, double-action steam engine, the aircraft engine was languishing among scrap in a garage in

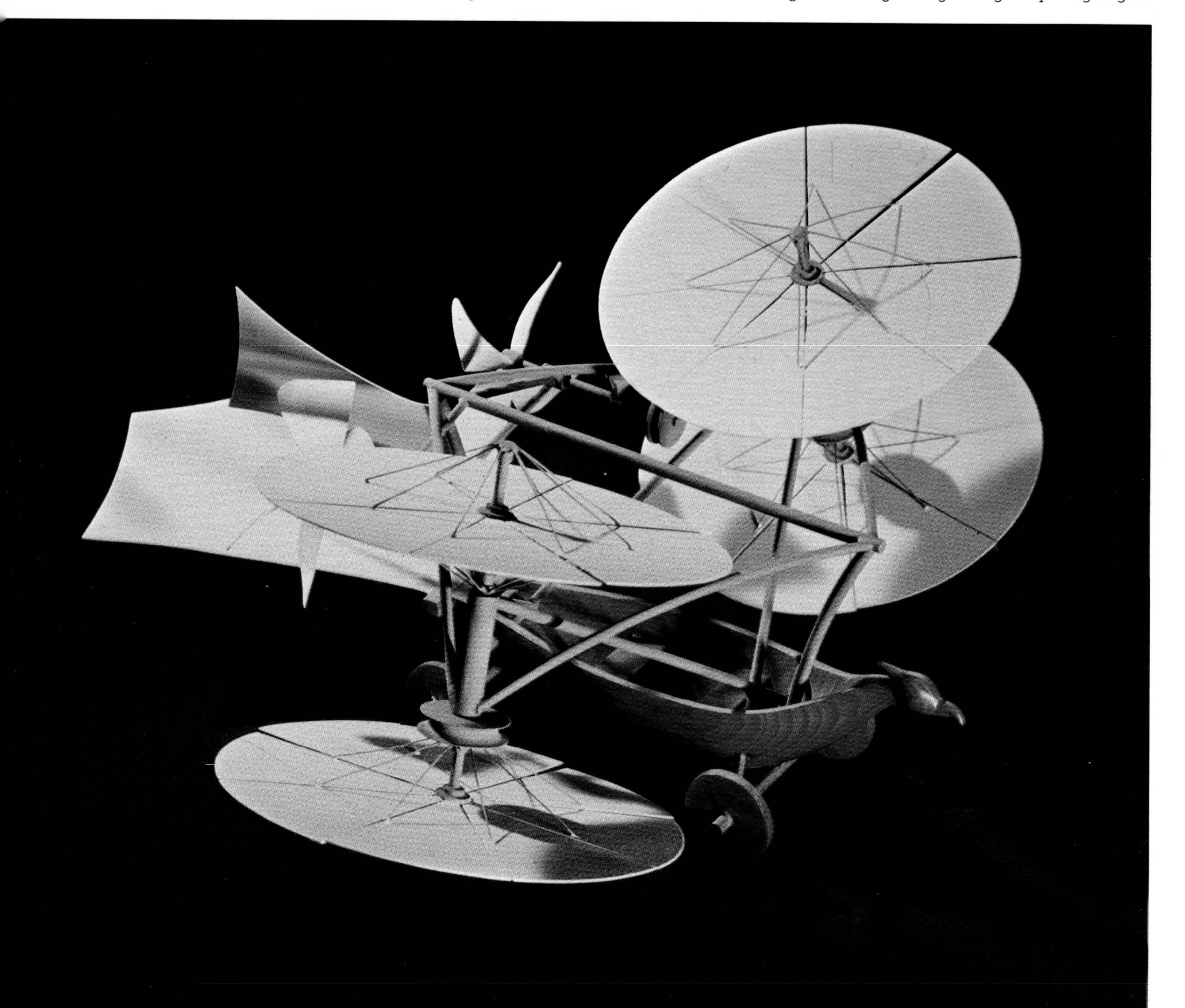

Left
The original model made by William Henson of his 'Aerial Steam Carriage' of 1847 still survives in the Science Museum, London.

Below
In posters advertising his planned passenger services in the 'Aerial Steam Carriage,' Henson let his imagination take flight and showed it sailing above the pyramids.

Crewkerne, Somerset. An approach by the Science Museum to the owner at the time, who had not known what the engines were, proved unsuccessful. However, shortly before the garage was demolished in the early 1970s, they were acquired by the Levens Hall Museum near Kendal, Westmorland, where they are now exhibited.

Short of money, Stringfellow apparently did no more aeronautical experiments until after the Royal Aeronautical Society was founded in 1866. With encouragement from the Society he built a small model triplane with a wing area of 28sq ft (260sq dm) and two pusher propellers. Interestingly, the model retained the same basic fuselage shape as that in the Henson design of 1847 and Stringfellow's of 1848, and all would have accepted the tall, narrow configuration of the engine found in the Somerset garage.

The triplane was shown at the Royal Aeronautical Society's first exhibition at the Crystal Palace in 1868 and there Stringfellow demonstrated it to the Prince of Wales – later King Edward VII. Once again he used a wire support and it is doubtful whether the machine ever maintained true flight from its own power.

Eleven years earlier a French naval officer built a steam-powered model which made what was probably the first successful flight by a powered model. Felix du Temple de la Croix patented his design for this steam-powered monoplane in May of 1857. It had wing dihedral, tail control surfaces, a tricycle undercarriage and a twelve-blade forward tractor propeller. It flew first under clockwork-power and then 'in steam' and succeeded in taking off, maintaining height and landing. In 1874 du Temple built a full-size version powered by a hot-air engine and, with a young sailor aboard, it ran down a hillside ramp at Brest and achieved a short hop. Although this was not the first sustained and controlled flight, it was at least the first powered man-carrying flight.

Meanwhile in 1870 Gustav Trouve pressed the claims of those who persisted in following the belief that man must flap to fly. He built a model which was powered by twelve blank revolver cartridges discharging successively into a Bourdon tube. The detonation straightened the curved tube, thereby pulling down the wings. As the tube returned to its natural curve, the wings flapped back up. Despite the apparent incongruity of the design, Trouve's model flew for over 200ft (60m).

Considerable research was being carried out in France and was published in the most authoritative aeronautical journal of the time, *L'Aeronaute*. In 1871 the journal showed the sketch by Alphonse Pénaud of his stable model and in 1876 it carried his patented design for a full-size monoplane which was, in essence, a natural extension of the principle of his first model. The 1871 model was the first aircraft to be driven by the twisted rubber band method beloved of generations of aeromodellers. A member of the Societé de Navigation Aérienne, Pénaud demonstrated his model in the gardens of the Tuileries, where it rose to a height of about 50ft (15m) and flew for some 131ft (40m) in stable flight for eleven seconds.

The model measured only 18in (46cm) in span and about 20in (50cm) in length and was propelled by a pusher propeller made from two stiffened feathers. Like Sir George Cayley, Pénaud angled the tips of the wings upwards to assist lateral stability. The tail was set at a negative angle in relation to the wing to give longitudinal stability. Pénaud was stricken with tuberculosis of the hip and died at the age of 30 before he could build the planned full-size version of his 1876 monoplane. However, his contribution not only to aeronautics in general but also to aeromodelling is commemorated in the Pénaud Trophy awarded to the team winning the World Championships for rubber-driven model aircraft. In addition a half-size replica of his original model made by Charles Magrath, the American aeromodelling writer of the 1920s, was presented to the *American Aircraft Modeler* magazine.

In 1874 Thomas Moy demonstrated his giant model at the Crystal Palace. This had a wing area of 114sq ft (1059sq dm) and was powered by two 3-hp steam engines driving 6ft (1.8m) propellers. It weighed 120lb (54kg) but succeeded in rising to 6in (15cm) above a circular track and flying around the base of a fountain to which it was tethered.

A model powered by a compressed air engine and measuring 6ft (1.8m) in wing span was the achievement of Victor Tatin, yet another Frenchman involved in the scramble to get airborne. In 1879 the engine, mounted above a tubular fuselage on the monoplane, was used to drive two forward propellers, with four paddle blades, by belts. Tethered to a post, the model flew for some 50ft (15m) and received considerable publicity at the time.

The English mathematician Horatio Phillips is a considerable figure in the history of aeromodelling as well as in the development of aeronautics. The importance of wing shapes in section – now known as airfoils – was investigated and stressed by Cayley but it was Phillips who first published the results of his research in testing wing shapes. To carry out the work he built his own wind

Left
Stringfellow produced his first airplane in 1848. Note the similarity in design to that of Henson, with whom he worked.

Below
A model of the multi-wing pusher aircraft designed by Horatio Phillips in 1893 during his experiments on airfoil sections.

tunnel and used models for all his tests. The first involved a model with 42 narrow wings, one above the other and spanning 19ft (5.7m). The multiplane was powered by a steam engine, and when tethered to a post it flew around at a height of 3ft (about 1m) at 40mph (64kph). In 1884 Phillips took out a patent for 'blades for deflecting air,' which were double surface airfoils of various shapes developed as a result of his wind tunnel research. His second patent was published in 1891.

At about the same time Lawrence Hargrave, an Australian, was working on the construction of box kites, rubber-driven models with flapping wings and the world's first rotary engine, a three-cylinder machine working on compressed air. Hargrave is credited with inventing the box kite, which he perfected in 1893. A year later he was lifted 16ft (5m) by four such kites, which provided lift and stability vastly superior to previous 'mono-kites.' His work had considerable influence on the design of wings for powered aircraft. His rubber-powered models had rigid forward wing spars but flexible rear surfaces so that as the wing beat up and down the flexible surface twisted to provide thrust.

One of the most controversial figures in a field which is still bedevilled by historical controversy was Clément Ader, born in Muret, Toulouse, in 1841. Even today he is believed by many – misled by some historians – to have made a controlled flight of some 980ft (300m) in 1897 – that is, six years before the Wright brothers' successful flight. He is also believed in some quarters to have invented the wing-warping method of roll control and to have been responsible for the Wrights losing their court case for breach of patent on control systems brought against a group of French aircraft builders in 1910–11.

In fact all these points were put about by Ader himself and are entirely false, as is made plain by the distinguished aviation historian Charles Gibbs-Smith in his excellent book *Clément Ader, his Flight Claims and his Place in History*. That is not to say that Ader does not have a place in our story or in aviation history. In 1873 after studying the flight of birds and bats, he built a full-size 'bird-craft' with wings of goosefeathers. This he tethered with ropes, nose to the wind, and, lying in it was lifted from the ground by a stiff breeze. He did not, as has been suggested, make any free-gliding flights, either then or later.

In 1882 he started to build his first powered airplane, an extraordinary bat-winged craft named *Eole* powered by a single 20hp four-cylinder engine. Surprisingly in view of the amount of published research available to him, he reverted to the flapper idea at a time when today's basic concept of fixed, double-surface wings was already established. The *Eole* had single surface wings which could be moved in four different ways,

A museum reproduction of Stringfellow's triplane of 1868, still retaining the gondola-type fuselage. The airplane was demonstrated to the Royal Aeronautical Society.

'none of which movements could be effectively or safely utilised in flight,' writes Gibbs-Smith. Also involved in the process of flight 'was the separate manned turning of no less than six cranks and the working of two foot-pedals in addition to the operation of the engine controls.'

Despite the extraordinary construction of the *Eole* and the fact that it lacked an elevator and probably a rudder, the machine actually took off and covered a distance of 164ft (50m) at a height of some 7–11in (20–30cm) on 9 October 1890 at Armainvilliers near Gretz. The test was not over a great length because of lack of space and also, more importantly, because of the *Eole*'s insufficient stability.

If we accept that 'flight' must be both *sustained* and *controlled* it is clear from the evidence of Ader himself and of observers that this was not the first powered flight by man. On the other hand it was undoubtedly the first successful powered, man-carrying takeoff without the assistance of any launching device.

Ader started to build *Avion II* in 1892 but abandoned it and instead built *Avion III*, a refinement of the *Eole*, with two 20-hp steam engines driving two tractor propellers. On 12 October 1897 he made the first test of this craft at Satory, near Versailles, but *Avion III* failed to leave the circular track and take to the air.

Two days later he made a second test with the machine running along the track. *Avion III* ran off the track, through rough ground, slued around and came to a halt *without leaving the ground*. Even so, years later in 1906 Ader claimed that it had flown for 980ft (300m) in controlled flight; yet witnesses of the event recorded no such flight. Despite this his claim is even today often repeated and is even recorded as fact on a monument erected at Satory in 1950.

Ader's claim to have invented the system of wing warping used by the Wrights was decisively dismissed by a French court in 1911, which found that his system of bending bore no relation to the Wrights' warping. The same court, the Tribunal Civil de la Seine, far from dismissing the Wrights' claim for breach of patent, upheld it, and stated officially that the Wrights had been the first in the world to fly and had invented the system of control which made it possible for men to fly. Even though the French manufacturers appealed against the court's decision, the Paris Court of Appeal supported the verdict in 1913. In spite of the fact that Ader made some contribution to aviation he does not seem to have done so in modelling except at secondhand, in that there exist some excellent model replicas of his machines, such as that of the *Eole* in the Science Museum, London.

Models played an important part in the work of Professor Samuel Pierpoint Langley, Secretary of the Smithsonian Institution in Washington, DC. His early work included building a 'whirling-arm' rig on which he mounted wings of various configurations, and even stuffed birds with wings outstretched. These studies and analysis of other people's work on wing configuration, together with tests on numerous rubber-band-powered models provided him with sufficient data to embark on building a series of steam-powered models. Launched by catapult to give them initial impetus, they were flown from the roof of a houseboat moored on the Potomac River below Washington.

Most of the models exhibited stability problems and many rolled and slid sideways into the river. However, in May 1896 he produced a model with tandem wings – using the configuration adopted back in 1873–74 by D S Brown on his gliders – of some 14ft (4m) span. Powered by a steam engine developing about 1½-hp,

Right
A close-up of the bat-winged *Eole* model with which Clément Ader attempted to revert to the theory of 'flapper-flight.'

Below
The *Eole* designed by Clément Ader in 1882 and reproduced in model form in the Science Museum, London, never achieved true flight.

which drove two pusher propellers, the model weighed 30lb (13.6kg) and was 16ft (4.8m) long. Langley called it an 'Aerodrome,' a name he gave to several of his machines.

The 'Aerodrome' was, like his other models, launched out across the river and it flew for some 90 seconds, covering a little over half a mile (0.8km). Encouraged by this success and backed in 1898 by $50,000 from the US War Department, Langley and his engineering assistant, Charles M Manly, set about building a full-size, man-carrying version of the model.

In 1901 the two produced a quarter-size model of the 'Aerodrome' which was powered by a lightweight gasoline-burning radial engine built by Manly after he had studied a rotary engine of S M Balzer. It was the first gasoline-powered engine to propel any aircraft.

By October 1903 Langley had completed the full-size version of the 'Aerodrome' and Manly had installed in it a 52-hp, five-cylinder radial engine. Again it was decided to launch the machine by catapult from the houseboat roof, this time with Manly, who had never piloted any aircraft, in the open cockpit. However, as the catapult thrust the craft forward the 'Aerodrome' hit a post and plunged into the river. Manly was not injured and the machine was repaired and ready for its second test on 8 December 1903. Yet again the catapult launching was a disaster: this time the tail smashed against the launching gear and the 'Aerodrome,' once more piloted by the luckless Manly, took another ducking. Sadly, the authorities now refused to support Langley any longer and he was ridiculed by the press. In fact his theories and design principles were correct and years later the 'Aerodrome' was repaired and flown as a seaplane by the aircraft designer Glenn Curtiss.

Despite the setback to all Langley's hopes of achieving the first sustained, controlled and powered flight on that December day, aviation history was in the making across the Atlantic in North Carolina. Once again it was a series of exhaustive tests on models and on gliders which set Orville and Wilbur Wright on the flight path. Among other things, they had studied the results of work by the German, Otto Lilienthal, in building and successfully flying gliders. He was the first to sustain consistently good, controlled performances in a man-carrying glider in the course of thousands of flights in a variety of gliders, using the movements of his body for control. However, on 9 August 1896 he lost control of his bird-like craft, crashed and died of his injuries next day.

Right
A museum model of one of Otto Lilienthal's experimental gliders of 1895. He was killed a year later in one of his monoplanes.

Above
A close-up of the power plant for Langley's 1896 'Aerodrome' built by Charles Manly.

Preceding page
Model of a Voisin biplane of 1908.

Below
A diorama of the Wright brothers' first flight from Kill Devil Hills, Kitty Hawk, North Carolina, in 1903 in the Science Museum, London.

The Wright brothers, who ran a bicycle business in Dayton, Ohio, also carefully weighed the evidence presented by the American Octave Chanute in his book *Progress in Flying Machines*, in which he detailed all the useful research work achieved in aeronautical design. After that, they decided to aim for a powered airplane which they would build themselves and to work toward that objective painstakingly. Over the course of the next five years they built a wind tunnel to test various wing models and control surfaces and then progressed to flying gliders. In 1899 they built a biplane kite which was an important step toward controlling flight other than by body movements. The 5ft (1.5m) span biplane glider incorporated control wires which they used to warp the wingtips to alter direction.

Next they built a full-size glider with a 17ft (5.1m) span and this they flew, both unmanned and piloted, from Kill Devil Hills outside Kitty Hawk, North Carolina. Two further gliders, No 2 and No 3, followed in 1901 and 1902, each incorporating improvements either designed as a result of tests on the previous glider or from their continuing wind tunnel research.

They added a forward elevator to give controlled climbing and diving, and a movable rudder for steering and stability. Then, satisfied with the results of their work on No 3, the Wrights built their own 12-hp, four-cylinder gasoline engine which was fired on the hot wire principle still popular with model builders today. The engine was

designed to lift an aircraft with a span of 40ft 4in (12.3m), weighing just 750lb (340kg) with two propellers driven by bicycle chains and fitted with two launching skids which rested on a trolley. They named it *Flyer*.

On the first take-off attempt on 14 December 1903 Wilbur took the controls, but as the *Flyer* trundled along its launching track and Orville released the restraining wire, he raised the nose elevator far too soon. The aircraft went briefly nose up and then tipped on to the ground. However, on 17 December, with Orville as pilot the *Flyer* left the ground and flew under power and control for twelve seconds. Brief though it was, the flight covered 120ft (36.5m) and was sufficient to put the brothers into the history books. In fact, later that same day Wilbur achieved a flight of 59 seconds, covering 852ft (259.6m) before the *Flyer* was overturned and wrecked.

It is worth repeating here the words of Charles Gibbs-Smith in his book on Clement Ader: 'Having solved the various problems of control in roll, the Wrights could rightly claim that they were the first in history to establish – first in a glider, then in a practical powered aeroplane – full three-axis control. This was their greatest contribution to aviation and *every aeroplane today derives its flight-control system direct from the Wright brothers, and from them alone.*'

Strange as it may seem now, the Wrights' achievements received very little attention and less acclaim at the time, even though they continued flying and improving their design. In October 1905 their *Flyer* No 3 covered over 24mi (38.6km), yet later that month the US Army's Board of Ordnance and Fortification had told the brothers that the Army would not be interested in aircraft until a machine could be produced that was shown to be able to produce horizontal flight and to carry an operator!

Below
Closeup of a model of the Wright brothers' biplane of 1907–9.

Ironically, particularly in view of the false claims advanced by and for Ader, another Frenchman attained far greater recognition for lesser achievements than the Wrights'. On 23 October 1906 Alberto Santos-Dumont flew his *14-bis* 200ft (60.9m) to win 3000 francs for the 'first' powered airplane to fly 25m. The following month this strange craft flew 722ft (220m) and averaged 25.657mph (41.2kmh) to set up the first official speed and distance records. Based on the box-kite designs of Australian Lawrence Hargrave, the *14-bis* was a 'back-to-front' machine which flew tail first. Santos-Dumont stood in front of the 50-hp engine which was mounted between the box-kite wings with a pusher propeller at the back. Though it was a crude machine it achieved widespread recognition and in effect marked the start of flying in Europe.

Even in those early days of flight there were people who made a hobby and a sport of aeromodelling and model flying clubs started to be formed almost as soon as the Wrights had achieved their first flight. Inevitably, where two or three modellers are gathered together there grows a competition; where two or three thousand modellers are about, there grows a publication.

The first competition in Britain was organized by the *Daily Mail*, a newspaper which did much to support pioneer aviation, and the Aero Club. Performance trials were held on 15 April 1907 at the Alexandra Palace, London, where 130 modellers entered for prizes worth £275 and some 7000 people paid one shilling (5 pence) for admission. At the same time an exhibition of models was staged at the Agricultural Hall, Islington.

The winning model was built by Mr Alliott Verdon Roe. It was a biplane with a wing span of 8ft 6in (2.6m), 8ft (2.4m) long and weighing 6lb (2.7kg) and built by him to replace a 3ft (0.9m) model he originally intended to enter. This, like Santos-Dumont's *14-bis*, was a 'back-to-front' machine, with its tail at the front and the rubber-band-powered propeller at the rear. The model, which competed against others driven by clockwork, petrol and even rocket, won both the indoor and outdoor trials and with the £75 prize money Roe went on to build the first full-size A V Roe-designed plane, powered by a 24-hp Antoinette engine. Soon he had founded the famous Avro company from which came generations of famous aircraft. Roe, incidentally, was at this early stage of his career so determined to devote all of the little money he had to aircraft design that he lived on 25 pence (50 cents)-worth of food a week. He used aeromodelling techniques for his 1909 triplane which was powered by a tiny 9-hp JAP engine and had a wing span of only 20ft (6m); the wings and fuselage were covered with sheets of brown paper.

The Kite Flying Association of Great Britain was formed in 1909 and in 1911 was renamed the Kite and Model Aeroplane Association. It had eight affiliated clubs and among the members were such people as Sir Sydney Camm, Colonel S F Cody, Michael Desoutter, Sir Geoffrey de Havilland, Sir Richard Fairey, Sir Frederick Handley-Page, Sir Thomas Sopwith – all

Right
Samuel 'Bill' Cody's first official military airplane, the 'Army Aeroplane No 1' of 1908.

Below
A model of the 1911 Avro biplane built by one of the pioneer aircraft designer-manufacturers, A V Roe.

illustrious pioneers of aviation. In 1922 the Kite and Model Aeroplane Association merged with the London Aero Models Association to become the Society of Model Aeronautical Engineers, which is affiliated to the Royal Aero Club.

In the United States one of the earliest modellers' clubs was the New York Model Aero Club, founded in 1907 by Edward Durrant. It staged the first local flying competition in the States in a drill hall in 66th Street, near Broadway, which was 200ft (60m) long. When it is recalled that man had only recently achieved controlled flights of a few yards, it is worth noting that the drill hall rapidly became too small for the models, which tended to crash into the end wall. Soon the club had to move outdoors, to Oakwood Heights Airport, Staten Island.

While model-making was to continue as a means of research and development, it also developed rapidly as a recreation and a sport.

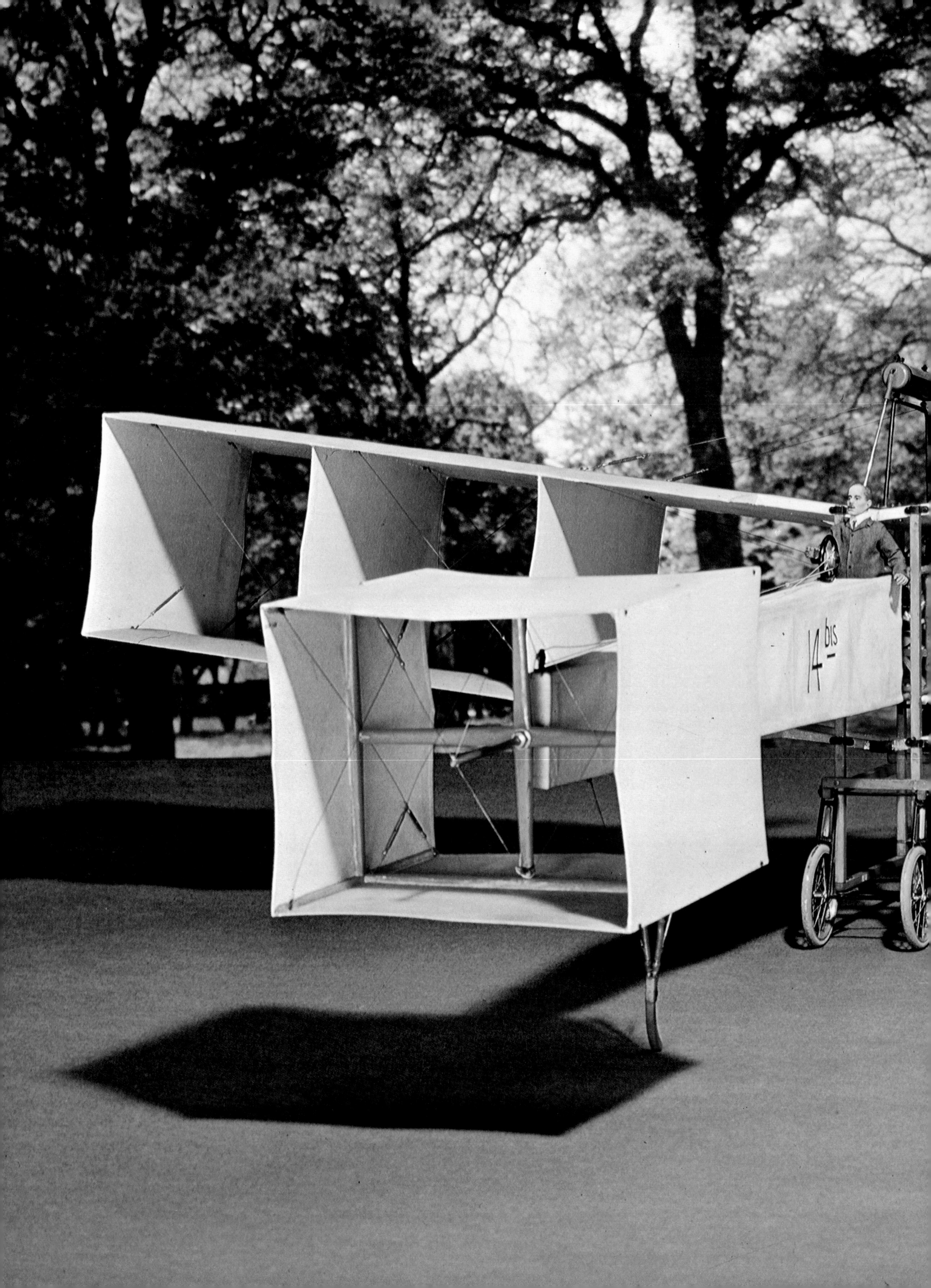
14 bis

A museum reproduction of the *14-bis* biplane built by Frenchman Santos-Dumont in 1906. The back-to-front design was based on the box kites of Australian Lawrence Hargrave.

Materials and Tools

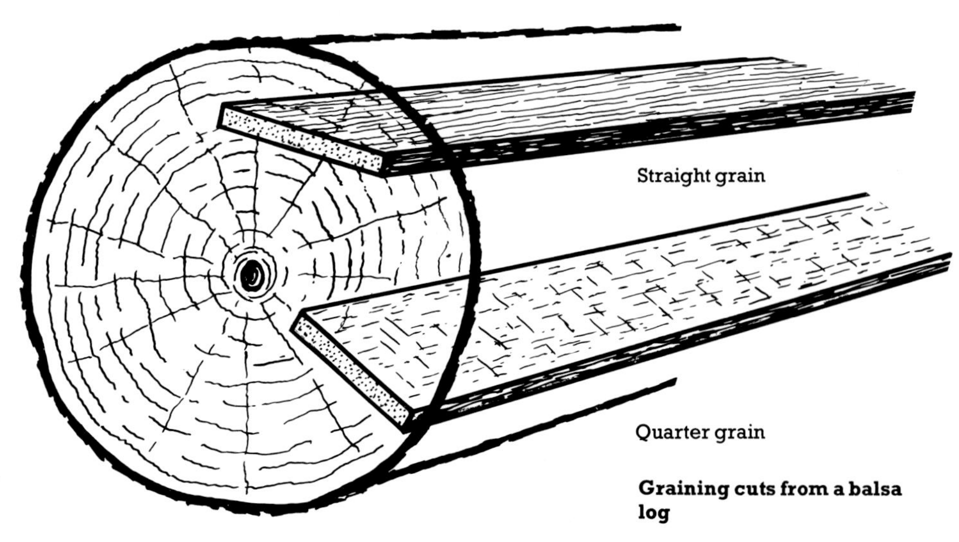

Graining cuts from a balsa log

Can there be any aeromodeller who has not at some time used balsa wood? It seems unlikely, for this material is still the most popular among those who are building from scratch. It is light, strong and relatively easy to work with, assuming that the wood has been chosen wisely and is not expected to tackle jobs for which it is unsuitable because of the manner in which it has been cut.

In the early days of the development of aeromodelling as a sport and hobby, serious modellers tended to use exactly the same materials as the builders of the full-size airplanes which they were copying. Principally these were spruce for airframes, oiled silk or paper surfaces and wire for crossbraces. However, thin sheets of spruce or of birch veneer were also used in place of silk or paper for some surfaces. The disadvantage of this sort of structure was that it was heavy, particularly in relation to the limited power that could be generated by the twisted rubber motors which predominated at the time and which suffered from a lack of strip rubber of reliable quality.

Early in the 1920s modellers in the United States were delighted to 'discover' a new modelling medium in balsa, a natural wood which grows principally in the Central American state of Ecuador, where it thrives, and also in Nicaragua and Peru. It is very fast growing in the humid climate and is imported as lumber and available usually in pieces of not much more than 36in (91cm) long and 6in (15.2cm) square. Its great advantage is that it is extremely light yet strong, and though it is botanically classified as a deciduous hardwood, it is soft and spongy and, therefore, easy to cut and shape. The remarkable properties of balsa were seen by Spanish Colonists in the 16th century who found Indians using logs of the wood for their rafts and were amazed to discover how easy it was to lift one of the craft.

Perhaps because of its lightness – a cubic foot (28.3cu dm) of balsa can be as much as one-third or one-quarter lighter than most other woods – balsa is sometimes thought not to be strong yet, so long as the correct cut is used, the wood can bear very considerable loads. Tests in the United States have found that pieces of the wood could accept loads of over 4500lb per sq in (316.3kg per sq cm). This is a property well worth bearing in mind when considering the load placed on an airframe – and particularly a nose cone – by a fully wound rubber motor.

In general balsa is graded as hard (14–16lb per cu ft; 224–256kg per cu m), medium (10–12lb per cu ft; 160–192kg per cu m) and soft (8–10lb per cu ft; 128–160kg per cu m). For the purposes of flying models where weight-to-strength is so important it is worth adopting a finer form of grading extending, in particular, below the basic 'soft grades' down to an ultra light grade of 4–6lb per cu ft (64–96kg per cu m).

Balsa is available in sheets, strips and blocks and when purchasing any of these cuts it is as well to go shopping around with a reasonable knowledge of, at the very least, what job you require the wood to perform. However, few shop assistants or owners have the knowledge or the time to go into the question of weight and density. It is, therefore, even more sensible to know *exactly* what you require: for example, a medium grade block of 2 x 2in (5 x 5cm) with a weight of 16oz (0.453kg) or a medium light strip of 1/4in sq (1.9cm sq) with a density of 21oz (5.9g).

The standard lengths of sheet, strip and block balsa are all 36in (91cm). With sheet balsa the standard width is 3in (7.6cm) but it is also available in 4in (10cm) and 2in (5cm) and even 6in (15.2cm), although the latter often has to be specially ordered and is, therefore, inclined to cost more than two 3in-width sheets which can be cemented together. Standard sheet thicknesses are 1/32 in (0.76mm), 1/16in (1.5mm), 3/32 in (2.38mm), 1/8in (3.17mm), 3/16 in (4.76mm), 1/4in (6.35mm), 3/8in (9.5mm) and 1/2in (12.6mm).

Balsa can vary widely in stiffness depending upon the way it was cut from the virgin log. A sheet of wood which has been cut radially to the rings of the log will be stiffer across its width than one that is cut tangentially to the rings. The former method of cutting gives a finish generally known as 'quarter grain' and a sheet which is virtually unbendable from edge to edge or end to end (it will crack rather than bend); the latter cut is known as 'straight' or 'normal' and provides a sheet with considerable flexibility. However, the vast majority of balsa is random cut so that the grain is neither exactly straight nor speckled like the quarter grain. The result is that degree of flexibility may vary between two sheets which *appear* to have almost identical, even-looking graining.

The thinner sheets of balsa can be easily cut with a sharp blade, using the edge of a metal rule as a guide for straight cuts. When diagonal cuts have to be made a useful tip is to direct the cut in such a way that the run of the grain tends to turn the knife blade *toward* the edge of the rule. If the direction of the cut follows the run of grain away from the rule there will be a tendency for the blade to waver from the straight. When cutting at right angles to the grain always make a cut from both edges to avoid a split when the second edge is reached.

To cut sheets of over 1/8in (3.17mm) it is best to use a fine razor-tooth saw both for straight cuts across the grain or with the grain. Though a knife can be used for with-the-grain cuts, on this thickness of material it requires a greater pressure and increases the risk of damage to the wood or the blade and also the risk of error. A good modelling knife cannot be bettered for curved cuts made freehand on thin sheets. It can be used for thick as well, although if a thickness of more than 1/4in (6.35mm) is being dealt with, a fine fretsaw is advisable.

Strip balsa comes in squares, rectangles, triangles and rounded sections (the last two are useful for trailing and leading edges). The square and rectangle sizes normally available are:

	1/16	3/32	1/8	3/16	1/4	3/8	1/2	1in
1/16	✓	—	✓	✓	✓	✓	✓	—
3/32	—	✓	✓	✓	✓	✓	✓	—
1/8	—	—	✓	✓	✓	✓	✓	—
3/16	—	—	—	✓	✓	✓	✓	—
1/4	—	—	—	—	✓	✓	✓	—
3/8	—	—	—	—	—	✓	✓	—
1/2in	—	—	—	—	—	—	✓	✓

When selecting strips it is important to check that they are of equal hardness and therefore of the same weight and flexibility. The 'bendability' of a group of strips can be easily checked by grasping them together and waving them up and down. Any strip which is less flexible than the others will show up immediately and can be discarded.

In cutting strip balsa one of the greatest pitfalls is in failing to make the cut exactly square, which can result in ill-fitting joints which require building up with balsa cement. For the larger sizes it is useful to have a metal set-square and to score in the cutting line along its edge, around the four sides. Strips of up to $^3/_{16}$ in can be cut with a sharp modelling knife or razor blade while thicker strips are best cut with the razor saw.

The standard sizes for block balsa are:

	1	$1^1/_2$	2	$2^1/_2$	3	4in
1	✓	✓	✓	✓	✓	—
$1^1/_2$	—	✓	✓	✓	✓	—
2	—	—	✓	✓	✓	—
$2^1/_2$	—	—	—	✓	—	—
3in	—	—	—	—	✓	✓

correct shapes and balsa cement was used for gluing. Unfortunately the plastic was extremely prone to warping, a problem which was not overcome in plastics until the introduction of the molded styrene or ABS sheet kits in the early 1950s.

The arrival of expanded polystyrene was also of considerable benefit to modellers. This is a granulated form of plastic which is extremely light at about 3lb per cu ft (48kg per cu m). Most commonly seen as packing for electrical equipment, it comes in blocks or sheets which can be easily cut to shape using a simple hot wire cutter. The major advantage of this form of plastic is as a strengthening packing for wings and fuselage, thereby dispensing with the need for cross-members or bulkheads. A disadvantage of this material is that it is affected by engine fuels, some types of acetate adhesives,

This is a D B Mascot, another good example of craftsmanlike finishing.

Again, when cutting block balsa a metal set-square should be used to mark all four edges and the cuts should be made with a stiffback saw. A modelling knife will not cope with the thickness without crushing the block. Curved shapes can be cut with a fretsaw or with a coping saw. Cut shapes slightly oversize and trim down to the final shape.

The most basic of all models is the solid balsa model which is carved to shape and sanded. Though the production of homemade scale models from solid balsa is not particularly popular, mainly because models are so easily obtainable in kits which can be more quickly assembled, there is an art in this form of model work. It is also an extremely useful way of gaining modelling experience since it employs many of the techniques which are common to all forms of modelling.

The biggest factor in turning modelling into a growth industry was the introduction of plastic – and particularly of the plastic kit. While some ultrapurists still claim – and have always claimed – that kits take the art and craftsmanship out of modelling, it is also true that they have been the means of introducing millions of young people to modelling and that a high proportion of the youngsters have gone on to extend themselves beyond the fairly limited abilities demanded from kit construction into the exciting realm of scratch-building.

The first plastic kit to come on the market was the Frog Penguin range which used an acetate plastic much different from today's injection molded plastic kits. The acetate plastic components were molded into their

cellulose finishes and heat, and so should not be used where it will come into contact with any of these.

Plastic card has also been a valuable addition to the modellers' armory of materials and can be used as the basic material in scratch-building in place of balsa. The card is available in thicknesses ranging from 5 to 60thou, is easily cut, will soften when heated and so can be molded to shape, and, having cooled, retains its shape. The card can be used as a strong material for forming a fuselage – a sheet of 30thou is best for models of 1:36 to 1:72 scale, using lesser thicknesses for components which are not liable to stress – and for making wings.

There are various construction methods which can be used for wings. The simplest is to make them from a solid laminate of sheets of plastic built up to the required thickness, glued and allowed to harden in clamps or under weight before carving and sanding to shape. Any intakes will need to be cut into the inner laminations before they are sandwiched between the outer layers.

Molded wings can be made by producing male and female balsa wood molds to the exact upper and lower wing configurations desired but allowing approximately $^2/_{32}$ in (0.8mm) clearance between the male and female molds. The warmed and therefore pliable plastic sheet is then placed between the two and molded to shape. The resulting halves are then cut from the sheet and cemented together, the male being left inside as a strengthener.

A third method is to use a balsa core cut exactly to the shape of the whole wing. The outline is then traced on to a sheet of 10thou plastic, holding the underside of the wing down on what will be the inner surface of the bottom of the wing, and leaving sufficient overlap of card for it to be folded over the balsa to form the upper surface. The trailing edge and wing tips of the underwing should be chamfered to accept the upper surface when it is folded over. Now the balsa core is cemented into place on the under surface and allowed to set. The top of the core and the under face of the overlap card are then both coated with adhesive. Bend the overlaps so that the leading edge of the wing can be pressed vertically on to a hard level surface and firmly roll the wing forward from you, turning the core on to the coated plastic card. When the top and bottom trailing edges of the card meet, apply cement to each joint and complete the join.

It should be noted that if wing tip curvature is excessive, then it will be impossible to fix the top and bottom surfaces successfully and 'crimping' or cracking may result. Apart from reducing the curvature – and thereby reducing the accuracy of the model – the only solution is to cut off the wing tip and add a new one made by the lamination method. The ailerons can be cut out and then recemented in position for added realism and the control and panel lines can be scored in lightly – remembering that this thickness of card cuts right through very easily.

Some radical changes took place in model building from the early 1950s to the mid-1960s: not only did injection molded plastic come into increasing use, the period also saw the introduction of grp (glass reinforced plastic), more often called 'glass fiber' or fiberglass. This is considerably heavier than the molded polystyrene but possesses exceptional strength and hardness. Its particular value is in models which are required to perform at speed. Complete fuselages can be made for radio-control models, but the shells must be made thinly because of the weight penalty, and therefore require internal bracing.

Fiberglass is formed from long, thinly drawn filaments of glass which are woven into a cloth or short

This picture illustrates the distinctive color scheme on Rudi Kessel's (W Germany) Control-Line Aerobatic model powered by Veco .45 and flown at the 1966 World Championships at RAF Swindersby. Careful application of the masking tape and use of the paint makes all the difference to the finished effect.

lengths which are bunched loosely and are known as mat. The cloth and mat can be varied in thickness and are identical in terms of weight. A cloth referred to as '1.5oz' (42.5g) would be 1.5oz per sq ft or 4.5g per sq dm.

Once again, in using fiberglass it is necessary to prepare a mold or pattern and to ensure that this is free of blemishes and really accurate. The necessity for this cannot be overstressed for, once the fiberglass has been molded over the pattern, coated with resin and hardener and allowed to solidify it is well nigh impossible to get rid of irregularities. The actual stages of production are: mix the resin and the hardening catalyst in the proportions recommended by the manufacturer; brush the mixture over the mold and lay on the first layer of fiber, firming it down to match the contours exactly. Further coats of the liquid and the fiber are added to reach the desired thickness of skin, each time making sure that the catalyst is penetrating thoroughly and the fiber is well molded down. Because of the problem of imperfections it is advisable to use a female mold: that is, a mold *into* which the fiber is placed rather than, in the case of a male mold, *over* which it is placed. If the female mold has been carefully prepared and finished, the resulting fiberglass molding will have a perfectly smooth outer surface.

It is worth noting that the 'curing' of the fiber will be affected by variations from the recommended proportions for the hardener and also by the temperature and humidity. A dry atmosphere and a temperature of not less than ten degrees Centigrade are recommended.

Although fiberglass can be, and is, used for engine mountings, plywood is really ideal for mounting engine bearer beams and for several other jobs. It has a high degree of strength and stiffness for its weight and 3-ply is excellent for fretted ribs or sound bulkheads. A point worth noting is that plywood is made in *nominal* metric thicknesses which can vary by as much as ten percent, and it is therefore important to check when buying particular thicknesses to ensure that a batch is within acceptable tolerances.

Ply will accept all types of glues and has the advantages of being oil-resistant in its aircraft grades and a good medium for absorbing vibration. Commercial ply is not waterproof but any ply under 2mm thick is likely to be resin bonded and waterproof. Above 2mm it is necessary to insist on this resin bonding. Grades of ply above 2mm include aircraft, marine, exterior, normal and cheap grades. The thicknesses most likely to be of use in aircraft modelling range from 0.3mm up to 8mm. The former is useful as sheeting in small craft while the latter is suitable for bulkhead work in larger models. The majority of ply used for modelling is birch or 'birch-type' with a relatively close grain and coloring which varies from a pleasing honey to off-white.

Other materials which should be mentioned here for use in building actual model structures are bamboo and reed, lime and spruce. Bamboo and reed are long-established materials for repairing and strengthening and for undercarriages and wing tips and also for the frames of large gliders. Lime has the great advantage, particularly for display models, of being close grained and hard, providing an excellent finish. It can also be shaped down to very fine curves and edges. Spruce, used by the pioneer aviators, is still popular for wing-spars of larger gliders – say of a span of 6ft (1.8m) or more and also for longerons in large models.

There is today a wide choice of adhesives available for the aeromodeller, to the degree that it is easy for the inexperienced to become confused by the claims of rival makes, some of which, if the advertisers are to be believed, achieve the impossible. The following is intended as a guide to the advantages and disadvantages of various types; it is for the modeller to decide finally from experience which best suit his method of working or are his favorite materials.

Cellulose cements: These are usually referred to as balsa cements and are nitro-cellulose acetate-based with various additives to provide varying degrees of hardening, plasticity and speed of drying. A 'normal' balsa cement will set in about fifteen minutes while a 'field repair' type will take as little as five minutes and is ideal for emergencies. However, as a general rule it is

The American, Professor Samuel Pierpoint Langley's steam-powered 'Aerodrome' of 1896 adopted a configuration first used in gliders by D S Brown in 1873. This beautiful model is in the Science Museum, London.

fair to say that the longer the drying time, the stronger the resulting joint will be. Balsa cements have a reasonably high degree of penetration and it is therefore wise to apply an initial coat to each balsa surface to act as a sealer in the open grain. After it has dried, a second and final coat is added and the joint held together under light pressure. It has good gap filling qualities and so can be used to disguise poor joins. The cement is slightly flexible but does become brittle with age, and also tends to shrink and therefore to distort under big temperature changes. It is not fully waterproof.

PVA or 'White glues': Polyvinyl acetate adhesives have a high degree of strength and stability and they soak well into open grained wood such as balsa. They are clean to use and when dry usually turn transparent. Drying takes about one hour and PVA therefore gives plenty of time to adjust positioning of parts before pinning or applying the final pressure to secure a join. They are not waterproof but do not cause any distortion. Because of the rubbery tactility of the dried adhesive, sanding can be difficult. An advantage is that they are easily cleaned off hands or clothes before dry!

Contact adhesives: These are not waterproof and do not fill gaps but have an advantage in that they do not warp. Latex-based, they are useful for joining large surfaces of wood. The two surfaces are coated and allowed to dry for a recommended time before being matched.

Epoxy resins: These are excellent in providing strong bonds between nonporous surfaces which can expect high stresses and they can also be used for wood-to-metal joints. Scoring of the two surfaces to be joined is advised. Usually the resins are mixed in equal quantities from two tubes and will cure in five minutes (although a complete curing in normal temperature will take up to three hours). Curing can be accelerated by heat. A slower curing type with an even stronger bond requires up to twelve hours. The epoxy resins are fairly expensive and are therefore best confined to use for joints presenting particular problems.

Urea formaldehydes: The best choice for use on ply and hardwoods, these either consist of a dry chemical powder to be mixed with water, or include a hardener to be brushed on to one surface while the powder-water mix is applied to the other. The finished joints can be regarded as virtually waterproof. An advantage is that they have reasonably good gap-filling properties and are colorless when dry.

Resorcinol resins: Another type of two-part adhesive, these are usually a powder and a viscose liquid which, when mixed, provide an exceptionally durable joint which is completely waterproof and very strong. For the best results a curing time of 24 hours with pressure applied is advisable.

Polystyrene cements: These should be used only for styrene kits, vacuum formed parts and plastic card. The clear, thin liquids act as a solvent on the styrene before hardening and great care should be taken in applying them sparingly to joints; spillage will result in scarring of the parts. Their adhesive qualities with other materials is not good.

Polyester resins: These are used for fiberglass constructions and without the addition of fibers are extremely brittle. They are considerably cheaper than epoxy resins, which can also be used for fiberglass work.

Iso-cyanoacrylates: These are the extremely fast-drying adhesives which set within seconds and require extra care in use. Although they have no advantages for general model construction they are of great help in carrying out rapid emergency repairs – for example during flying competitions. Though expensive, the thin, clear liquid need only be applied in very small amounts to give very strong joints.

Unless it is made completely from balsa sheet, plastic or grp, a model is obviously going to require a final skin. The choice of covering will, of course, depend very much on what role the model is to fulfill, whether it is to be static or flying (powered or glider) and if it is a competition model, whether there are any restrictions which apply. Choice of material will also depend to a degree on the shape and size of the model: a small, light craft naturally requires a thinner covering than a larger machine.

Despite the tremendous strides made in the technology of aeromodelling it is true to say that the coverings used in those first early models and full-size planes that struggled into the air are still used today. Silk, for example, has found popularity as a covering for radio-controlled models, but with the addition of multiple layers of toughening cellulose and varnish.

A V Roe was among the early pioneers to use paper as a covering for powered aircraft, although it had, of course, been used for centuries by the Chinese in their kites. Today Japanese tissue is second only in lightness to microfilm and is particularly useful because it can be applied easily to balsa, does not crease when it shrinks (assuming it has been applied carefully) and accepts clear dope without any problems. Next up in weight, and suitable for larger models, is bamboo paper which can be applied while wet and allowed to dry to the shape of the underframe. Swedish tissue only offers the advantage of cheapness. It is much coarser than Japanese tissue and bamboo paper, will not accept dope satisfactorily and is really only suitable for basic models.

In Britain there is a paper tissue designed specially for covering model aircraft. Named Modelspan, it is similar to Japanese tissue but heavier. It is available now in white only and in a 'wet-strength' which means that it is applied damp and then shrinks tight to the frame as it dries. It requires several coats of clear cellulose dope to seal the pores and give additional strength.

Unlike Modelspan which is not grain directional, Japanese tissue has a definite grain which enables it to be pulled more one way than the other without risk of tearing. Jap tissue is also less porous and therefore does not require many coats of dope to seal it.

The simplest method of applying tissue – though not the neatest or longest lasting – is to paste it on to the wing or fuselage section by section, working root to tip or nose to tail. Ensure that no parts of the frame are left dry of paste, and gently pull the tissue tight as it is laid. Press the tissue down with your finger tips to give a good grip and make sure there is enough tissue to wrap around edges. If the tissue has been applied wet, allow it to shrink as it dries; if it was put on dry, wet it (a perfume spray filled with water is ideal for the job) and allow to dry. Where a small model is concerned, it is important to pin or weight the structures during drying to avoid warping. Once the tissue is dry, trim off any excess material and then apply the first coat of dope.

A slightly more complicated but a neater method is to apply thick grade dope to all the edges to which you wish to stick the tissue. Allow this to dry and then lay the tissue on to the frame. Next brush dope thinner on the tissue but only over the previously doped frame edges. The thinner will dissolve the dope which seeps into the tissue before hardening again. Pull the tissue taut as it begins to adhere. Again,if the tissue was applied wet, it will shrink as it dries; if dry, wet it as before and allow to dry. If two layers of tissue are used for added strength, apply a thin coat of dope to the underlayer before adding the second skin. A final coat of clear cellulose provides the finishing varnish.

Silk and nylon are both strong fabric coverings which are successful on powered models. However, silk is porous in its natural state and must be treated with dope, which then causes shrinkage. Nylon must also be dope sealed but does not shrink as much as silk so it must be applied as tightly as possible to the frame and will require more final coats of dope to shrink it as much as possible. All fabrics should be applied wet. Pin the material to the frame over a thick application of dope, drawing taut as you do so.

Because fabrics tend to develop pock marks, a useful tip is to dust talcum powder over the surface, brushing it into the weave. Then apply a light coat of dope. At least three coats of dope are needed to seal the fabric after it has been applied, and a brush is more effective in working the dope into the material than is a spray, which tends to deposit a film on the surface.

The lightest of all coverings, microfilm, is a homemade chemical deposit which is simple to make and to apply to indoor models. One formula is to mix 2oz (56.6g) of clear dope to 1oz (28.3g) of amyl acetate and twenty drops of medicinal castor oil. This mixture is then poured from a spoon on to a large water area such as that provided by a bath or a good size kitchen sink. The mixture immediately forms a chemical film which can be scooped off the surface with a wire or wooden frame. Moving the spoon rapidly over the surface will ensure that the film spreads quickly and evenly. The film should be hung to dry and mature for a few days. The framework to be covered is pushed on to the newly dampened microfilm while it is still held in its scooping frame. The microfilm is cut with a hot wire cutter or heated blade and finally trimmed down to exact shape.

A commercial high-strength polymer plastic film has proved successful in aeromodelling since its relatively recent introduction. It is available in most good model shops under such brand names as Coverite, Monokote, Solarfilm and Unicote. The colored film is coated on one side with a heat-sensitive adhesive. Cut slightly oversize, the sheet is laid over the frame and the edges sealed to the wood by running a warm (not hot) iron over the surface. Shrinking to achieve the required tautness is achieved by moving the warm iron close to the surface or by playing a hot air gun (hairdryer) over it. The result is an extremely strong skin.

The tools of model making are almost as varied as the methods of construction and in the final analysis their selection depends very much on the personal preference of the builder. Some modellers find that they can make do with a few quite simple tools; others require a collection to meet every contingency and yet another group will enjoy using what we might call 'high technology' equipment such as vacuum forming tools, metal casting techniques, electric power tools and the like.

However, let us start from the basic requirements – and work upwards. It is true to say that armed with only a razor blade anyone could build a model from balsa. What the finished product would be like is another matter since he would be trusting to luck with every cut he made. To aid him in achieving the accuracy that is essential for good model building he must have a metal straight edge which can either be a ruler or a plain cutting edge. If a plain edge is used it can be up to a yard long but a metal rule, marked in inches and centimeters and not less than the 24in–60cm type, will still be required.

While razor blades are perfectly satisfactory as basic cutting implements, they have their limitations. A single edge blade with a backbone is recommended rather than the double-edged, though the latter can be split and used for cutting around curves. A blade broken to shape with a pair of pliers makes a useful fine-pointed tool.

Although it is possible to make do with a single small pair of pliers for most jobs, a set of three is recommended, all with hardened jaws and side cutters: fine pointed, round nosed and square nosed.

A heavy-duty knife, such as a Stanley 199 with interchangeable blades of varied shapes, is useful for cutting thicker materials but you will also require a lighter-handled variety, also with interchangeable blades, such as those supplied by X-Acto and Humbrol. The blades vary from large, for heavy-duty work, to small and fine for more precise work. To avoid having to change from large to small and back again it can be time saving to have two knives of this type. A razor saw, also available from these manufacturers, is extremely useful for cutting large blocks or strips. For fine work a flat-handled scalpel with a choice of blades is a worthwhile addition but must be used with great care as the blades are very sharp.

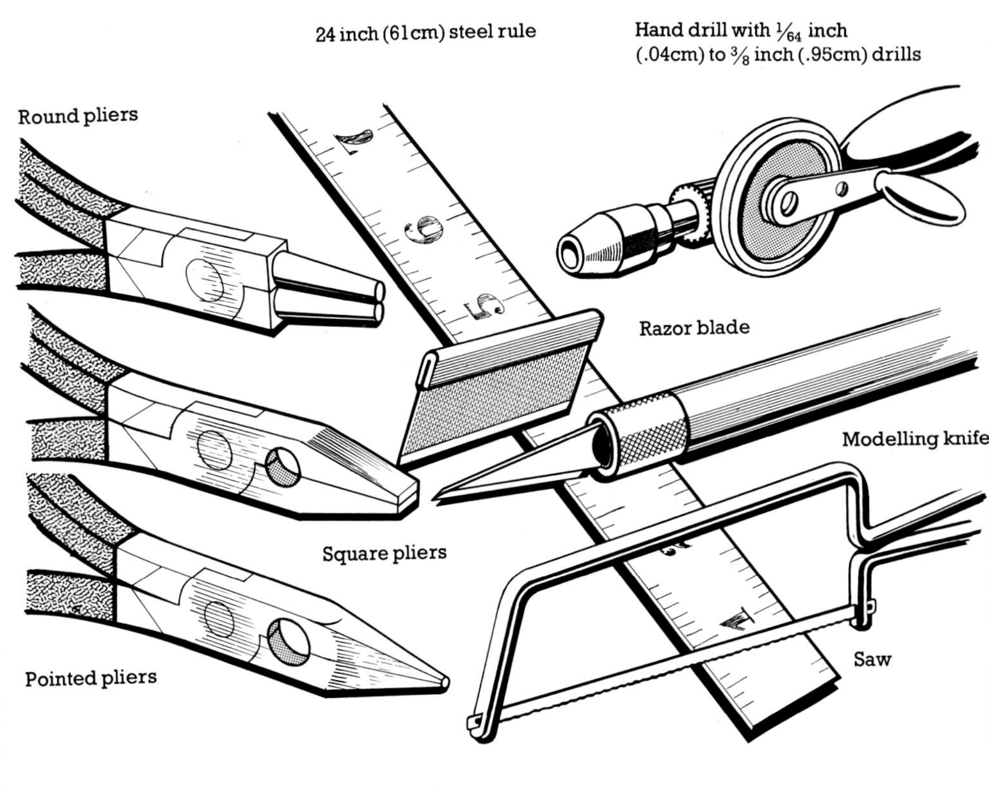

A selection of typical tools for the aeromodeller

Here it is worth making the point that whatever cutting edges are used they should always be kept in a safe place when not in use – particularly if there are children in the house. To avoid accidents while working, a sensible precaution is to make a habit of returning knives to the same position every time you put them down; do not bury them under materials and debris. It should go without saying that blades should be kept sharp – an oil stone for sharpening is another addition – and accidents both to the modeller and the work are more likely with a blunt cutting edge.

A fretsaw has an obvious place in cutting harder woods to shape, such as plywood, and a hacksaw will be required if any metal work is contemplated. Fine file blades can also be useful and a set of hand files, including half-round, round and flat are almost essentials. Though a vice is not essential it is extremely useful in providing a 'third hand' and here a quite small one with a jaw of about 3in (7.5cm) is recommended. Again not essential but worthwhile as an extra, a pair of lady's tweezers can help greatly in handling and positioning small parts.

Small hand drills or miniature power drills are an asset, though the latter might be considered a luxury, with their variety of attachments. The hand drill will require a range of twist drills from $\frac{1}{64}$ in (0.3mm) to $\frac{3}{8}$in (9.5mm).

A metal set-square is a 'must' not only for checking right angles but also, and more important, for accurately scoring round blocks or strips to be cut. The other 'musts' without which it is virtually impossible for a wood modeller to work are garnet paper, which is more effective and cleaner to use than sandpaper, and hundreds of pins.

Two other essentials which, though left to last in this list are by no means of least importance, are a building board and a cutting board. The building board should be soft enough to accept pins without undue pressure, flat and large enough to be able to lay out plans and various parts of the assembly at the same time. The ideal is a table with a softwood top. The building board should never also be used as a cutting board since it will become scored with use. The cutting surface should be hard, firm and flat; a panel of hardboard or of hardwood is entirely suitable for the purpose.

What Sort of Model

The biggest mistake that any would-be modeller can make is to think to himself or herself, 'I want to build a model' and then to plunge in with very little thought, no plans and only a few of the materials which are going to be needed.

My own first model aircraft was just such a mistake, begun at the age of eight or nine on the spur of the moment with only the vaguest idea of what would be required. It was supposed to be a Gloster Gladiator and it was constructed from cardboard, matchsticks, a toilet roll and balsa cement and no plans of any sort. Needless to say, it was never finished and sat in my school locker, wings sagging, balsa cement cracking and fuselage squashing until it finally disintegrated.

The next attempt was more ambitious but also ill-fated: a balsa-wood glider built from a Keilkraft Kit and launched from a catapult rigged unwisely between two Rugby posts. The maiden flight was delayed by a succession of nose dives necessitating repairs to the nose, wings and body framework and adjustments to the power of the catapult. Eventually the thing soared gracefully into the air, climbed superbly to some 80ft (24m) and swooped to rest on the school roof, inaccessible three stories up.

First, then, what sort of model do you want to build? Is it to be a static, display model or a flying model; if the latter, is it to be free flying or controlled; is it to be powered or a glider? What about the scale? And what materials will you use? These are just some of the questions and each can be followed by others. Let us consider the range of models which can be built.

The simplest of all is the static display model built from balsa wood as a representation rather than an exact scale reproduction of a particular aircraft. It is as good a way as any for the beginner to launch himself into the fascinating world of model building. It is better than some, because it allows for a degree of latitude in building and gives the builder an opportunity to gain experience while making mistakes which will not be as expensive to correct as with more ambitious models.

Having said this, it is advisable for the modeller who is a complete beginner to get used to handling balsa wood and to carry out a few trials on off-cuts of sheets and blocks so that he knows what to expect when cutting or shaping for the model itself.

It may be that after this first attempt, the new enthusiast will want either to aim for a homemade solid wood scale or go for a plastic kit. In the first case it will be necessary to decide on the scale (a subject we shall discuss more fully later) and to seek out plans showing accurate drawings of all the components, outlines, cross sections and so on. The Aeromodellers Plans Service is an excellent source for a considerable number of plans and has a catalogue available, while in the United States *Scale Modeler* magazine is a helpful source.

If the static model is to be made from a plastic kit, the job is obviously made easier because the hit-and-miss of shaping the wooden components is replaced by the far greater accuracy of preformed parts. This does not mean, however, that building a plastic kit is plain sailing, a mere matter of cementing the parts together, leaving no room for improvement or a touch of originality. The days have long gone when plastic kits were considered by purists to be looked down upon as cheating, requiring no skill.

Today's plastic kit market is aimed principally at the young buyer and many thousands of one particular model kit are mass-produced to a high degree of authenticity. However, the true enthusiast aiming for the highest degree of accuracy in his scale model so that it relates identically to the full-size original, will never be entirely satisfied with a kit which has been assembled 'straight from the box.' Purely on the grounds of the high cost of tooling-up for a model, manufacturers have to take some short cuts and invariably these will be spotted at once by the experienced eye. It is here that the originality of the builder comes into its own and he can demonstrate his skill. Features that are omitted from the kit can be added either by obtaining the appropriate part from the extensive range of accessories now available, by adapting a part from another model or by making a completely new part on the home workbench. Parts of the kit which are inaccurate – perhaps too thick, wrongly angled or over simplified – can be replaced, altered or fined down with the care of experience.

Fastidiousness is today sometimes regarded as a

A line-up of three unorthodox designs which give their builders free rein in imagination and techniques.

weakness in a person's character but in modelling it is an attribute of which to be proud and which can only lead its possessor further along the road to perfection. The pursuit of that perfection can also be furthered by building up a library of good photographs, not only of general shots of a particular aircraft but also of its finer details. If this seems too expensive an approach there is a vast range of books on aircraft which can be used as references, a fair cross section usually being available in a local library. In addition all the aircraft magazines regularly carry photographs of current and obsolete types and are a useful reference source.

Turning to flying models, the starting point is again balsa wood, for there can be no simpler construction than a balsa-framed glider, be it a 'chuck glider' (one launched by chucking it into the air) or one launched by catapult.

However, we must again pause to decide which category of flying model is to be selected. Having decided on that, the next question is: which subdivision of that category interests you? Broadly the categories of flying models are: free flight, control line and radio controlled. Each of these can be subdivided as follows:

Free flight – glider, indoor flier, rubber-driven, power-driven, unorthodox.

Control line – aerobatics, combat, speed, sport flier, team racer, unorthodox.

Radio controlled – sport flier, contest type, combat, pylon racer, unorthodox.

This is not the end of our classifications. The free-flight glider can be hand launched, catapult launched or slope soaring and it can be microfilm or tissue covered, built to scale or to the most appropriate flying design. The indoor flier may be a microfilm or tissue-covered model.

The unorthodox in each class leaves the field wide open to imagination, ingenuity and whatever degree of aeronautical design engineering the individual may possess. The power-driven free flier can be a sport flier or built for duration competition flying.

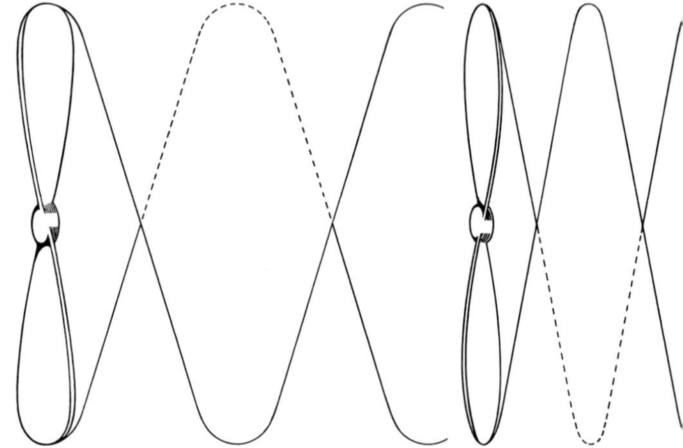

Whether the power-driven model is free flight, control line or radio controlled, the power source itself presents another range of choices; shall it be Jetex (no longer available in Britain), internal-combustion diesel, fired by glowplug driving a conventional propeller, or working a ducted fan, or shall it be battery operated? It could even be a real jet-propelled model but these are expensive, difficult to make because of the very intense heat generated, very noisy and dangerous in the wrong hands. Places in which they can be flown – they can reach speeds of 190mph (305kph) – safely and without complaint are difficult to find.

In many respects control-line flying is the easiest form of powered model flying because of the degree of control that can be exercised over the model by the simple means of adjusting the tethering lines. It does not require the air space of a free-flight model and is not as expensive (or as sophisticated) as a radio-controlled craft. That is not to say that there is no art in control-line flying: competition in the various categories for this sort of model demands a high degree of skill.

Top left
Ken King of the Cosmo Club flew this APS plan U-2.

Above left
Frog North American Super Sabre in the Hasegawa range.

Above right
Theoretical forward motion of a coarse pitch (left) and a fine pitch propeller and the paths taken by the tips of each

Top right
The famous Ted Evan Jaguar, winner of the 1948 Wakefield Trophy.

Below right
This free-flight scale model by Tom Stark is powered by a fast Cox glowplug engine.

Today's technique of control-line flying was developed by an American, Nevilles E Walker and introduced in the early 1940s by the American Junior Aircraft Company or Portland, Oregon, as the 'U-Control.' Though it was not the first system of control-line flying to be marketed – that distinction probably falls to a Texan, Victor Stanzel, who marketed the 'G-line' in January 1940 – it introduced the degree of sophistication in control that is common today.

Aerobatics models commonly use glowplug engines of between 6 and 7cc flying at between 50 and 60mph (80–96kph) and using a propeller with a fine pitch to make the most efficient use of the engine's power. Combat flying has two models in the same flight circle, each attempting to slice a streamer towed by the other. It is an exciting sport requiring intense concentration and fast reactions. Though the engines used for World Championship events cannot exceed 2.5cc with air speeds of around 90mph (145kph), models powered by engines of 7cc and more and capable of 120mph (193kph) are finding increasing popularity.

Speed flying in World Championship events is also limited to a maximum engine capacity of 2.5cc achieving around 145mph (233kph) but different countries have different maximum capacities. In Britain classes range from 0.9cc to 10cc and speeds of over 200mph (322kph) are reached. International rules insist that two lines must be used for control of the model, which is flown with the 'pilot' resting his arm in a pylon yoke as it is timed over a set distance.

By contrast the aim in team racing is to cover 10km (6.2mi) as fast as possible with an engine of up to 2.5cc and a fuel tank which has a maximum capacity of 7cc. The art is in attaining the right balance of speed and fuel economy, in the teamwork involved in refuelling with minimum time loss and in successfully piloting the model in a circle also occupied by two other models.

As we shall see later, each of these categories of control-line flying demands different types of construction to meet the very specific requirements of that particular branch of the sport and also, where official competitions are involved, to comply with the rules.

Radio-controlled flying is the most sophisticated form of model aviating and continuing technological advances in electronics make this a category of modelling filled with promise. Because of its sophistication, this form of modelling is also the most expensive and the newcomer is well advised to temper the first flush of enthusiasm with a considerable degree of caution. He is likely to have caught the radio-control bug from watching others fly their models and they may well have made it all look remarkably simple. But if the beginner believes he can buy, build and fly an aerobatics model quickly, for example, he will be in for a nasty – and probably an expensive – shock.

If the intention is to take the subject of radio control very seriously the beginner would be wise to seek out some instruction and advice and also to choose a relatively simple model to start with, be it in kit form or built

Below left
A world-beating glider: Valerij Ekhtenkov of Russia became 1973 World Champion with this model, flown at Wiener Neustadt, Austria.

from plans. The most suitable model would be one which has high wings fastened to the fuselage by rubber bands so that they collapse rather than break on impact. The model should not be too small since it will be even more difficult for the beginner to see and control and will quickly disappear into the distance. Ideally the aircraft should not have a wing span of less than about 4ft to 4ft 6in (121 to 137cm) so that it can be more easily handled and will comfortably carry a payload of equipment of perhaps 9oz (255g). However, the size of one's pocket may limit the size of the model. The engine – a glowplug type is the most popular – should be open so that it can be adjusted simply. The radio equipment should be of the two- or three-function variety if the intention is only to enjoy the hobby as a weekend sport flyer, but will need to be a multi-function system of six or more functions if the idea is to progress to a more sophisticated pursuit of the hobby such as competition flying.

Electrical power for radio-controlled models nowadays tends to be by nickel-cadmium cells – or nicads – rather than ordinary dry batteries. These have the advantage of a constant voltage output rather than the dropping output of a dry battery and they can be quickly recharged.

It should be remembered that it is necessary to have a license for radio-controlled models. These are now issued by the Radio Regulatory Division of the Home Office at Waterloo Bridge House, Waterloo Road, London, SE1 8UA, and cost £2.80 for a five-year period. Modern systems are tuned to transmit on any one of six spot frequencies from 26.975MHz to 27.245MHz. In the United States Class C licenses for nonvocal radio transmissions are issued by the Federal Communications Commission.

The various categories of model we have touched on in this chapter will be dealt with in greater detail later in the book.

Below
Brian Gagle shows a fine example of a radio-controlled glider with this D-Day troop-carrying 'Horsa' with a 76-inch wing span.

Scales and Plans

If a modeller has settled on building a static model from a kit the matter of scale will have been decided for him by the manufacturer. His choice will be limited only by the amount of working space he has available and, of course, where he intends to display the finished article. The average room will not accommodate many 1:48 scale models, after all.

When it comes to flying models, scale becomes of considerable importance for a variety of reasons. Not least of these is that, however much of a purist you may wish to be, it is virtually impossible to build a true-to-scale model of an actual aircraft which is also capable of reproducing a scaled-down flying performance of the original. One elementary explanation for this is simply that it is not possible to scale down flying conditions: a ten knot wind remains a ten knot wind whether it is being flown into by a full-size aircraft or a flying scale model. Therefore alterations have to be made to the model to compensate.

For example, a true-to-scale propeller on a model would be incapable of performing the duties of its full-size counterpart because the chord of the small propeller blade (its width) would be insufficient to provide the drive or thrust needed to 'pull' the airframe forward. Of necessity, the model propeller must be larger than the original.

Similarly it is necessary to alter the chord of the model's wings to a small degree and even to change the airfoil section of the wing, depending on the type of flying which the model is intended to perform. Here it is necessary to explain, for the benefit of true beginners, something of the basic theory of flight.

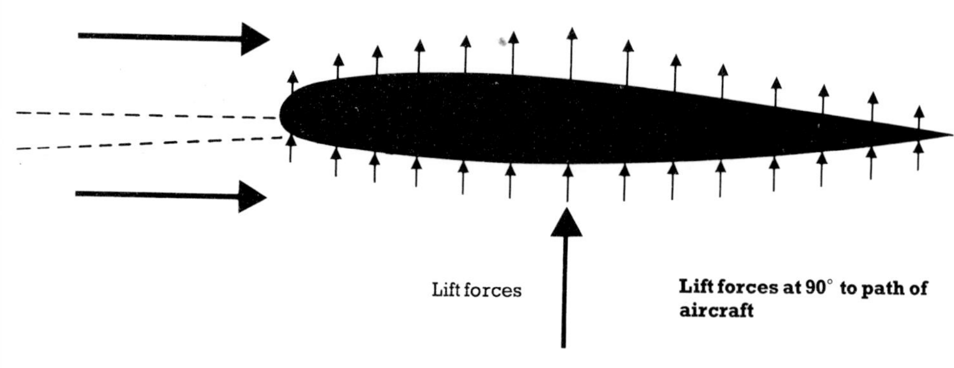

Lift forces at 90° to path of aircraft

Lift is obtained from every part of the wing's surface, though in differing proportions, and all lift forces work at 90 degrees to the direction of the oncoming air. Two-thirds of the lift is from the *top* surface of the wing – a technical point which is often not appreciated by those who think that lift must of necessity be a pushing upwards from beneath the wing. If you take a piece of paper and blow *over* it, the paper will lift. If two pieces of paper are held parallel about half-an-inch apart and you blow between them they will tend to cling together. When a smooth stream of air flows into a constricted passage and out again, the airflow speeds up as the constriction increases but the air's sideways pressure decreases until the flow is at its highest speed and least pressure at maximum constriction. Thereafter it slows down and emerges at its original speed.

If the top of the constricting surface is removed the pressure drop remains, although it is reduced. Imagine the upper surface of the wing as the *lower* constrictive surface and the normal airflow over the wing as the *upper*. The result is still a decreased pressure above the wing, helping to create lift. Slight angling of the wing increases the lift force below and combines with the decreased pressure above to produce positive lift. The amount of lift varies, depending upon the airspeed, the angle of the wing, the air density, the shape of the wing section and the wing area.

The best chance of lift being provided without leaving a trail of turbulence where the upper and lower air flows meet at the trailing edge is for the upper-wing surface to be designed to have sufficient curvature to decrease pressure effectively but not enough for it to interrupt the steady flow of air. In this way the two air flows meet at or behind the trailing edge at the same speed

Returning to our problem of scale, it will be appreciated that if a wing chord of, say, 10ft is reduced to 5in on a model but the same airfoil section is retained, the flows of air above and below the model wing will not have the same opportunity to adjust as on the full-size version. Positive lift is, therefore, reduced on the model.

In a model aircraft, lift is usually created by the angle of attack (the angle at which the leading edge of the wing meets the air) being raised to as much as six degrees to horizontal and by adjusting the airfoil section. The extent of readjustment from the airfoil of the full-size version will depend upon the role which the scale model is expected to perform and the ratio of size-to-weight-to-power.

A glider should be built with the thought in mind that it should be loaded at about 5oz per sq ft (15g per dm^2) wing area while a rubber-powered or a Jetex model will have wing loadings of 6oz per sq ft (18.3g per dm^2). With a control-line model, wing loading can range from 10oz per sq ft to 16oz per sq ft (30.5g per dm^2 to 49g per dm^2) depending upon its role but with a free-flight model the range is from 6oz per sq ft to 16oz per sq ft (18.3g per dm^2 to 30.5g per dm^2), again depending on the performance required. A ducted-fan model requires a wing loading of around 12oz per sq ft (36.6g per dm^2).

Powered models are, of course, limited in weight according to their power sources. For example, a control-line model which is to have reasonable power should have a top power loading of 8oz per cc (226.7g per cc); a free-flight model has a top limit of 20oz (567g per cc); a ducted fan is limited to 10oz (283g per cc).

The weight of Jetex powered models will vary according to the size of the power unit. A model of around 1.5oz (42.5g) should use the Jetex 35 unit; a 2oz (56.6g) the 50; a 4oz (113g) the 100; 5oz (142g) a 200 or Jetmaster; 7 oz (198g) the 350 and an 8oz (227g) a Scorpion. Thrust Augmenter tubes raise the performance significantly.

We return, now, to the question of airfoils: the model's wings must be designed to be of suitable loading and to provide sufficient lift for the performance expected of it, but the vast majority of many hundreds of wing shapes used for full-size aircraft will not meet these requirements. Over the years, from the variety of wing shapes which have evolved, a certain number have become established as the most suitable for various types of flying scale models. Consequently the 'Clark Y' is generally accepted as the best airfoil section for free-flight models and for radio control. The NACA 0012 is good for control-line aerobatics and the NACA 2412 is suitable for control-line and radio-controlled types. Another popular control line section is the RAF 30 type while RAF 32 is favored for rubber-driven models and the RAF 15 and Grant X-9 for biplanes. If fast flying in any of the model categories is intended the airfoil sections should be fined down to about 60 percent of normal.

Once the appropriate airfoil has been selected the matter of scale becomes important yet again since the shape will almost certainly not be that of the original. The wing must therefore be reconciled to the rest of the model so that the final effect is as close as possible to the appearance of the full size. To increase the lift effect of the wing it will be necessary to alter the angle of attack of the leading edge by raising the bottom edge from horizontal by between three and six degrees. Any alteration in the appearance of the model in comparison with that of the original can usually be compensated for by a very small change to the depth of the cockpit for example. Final painting can also be a useful ally in disguising such changes.

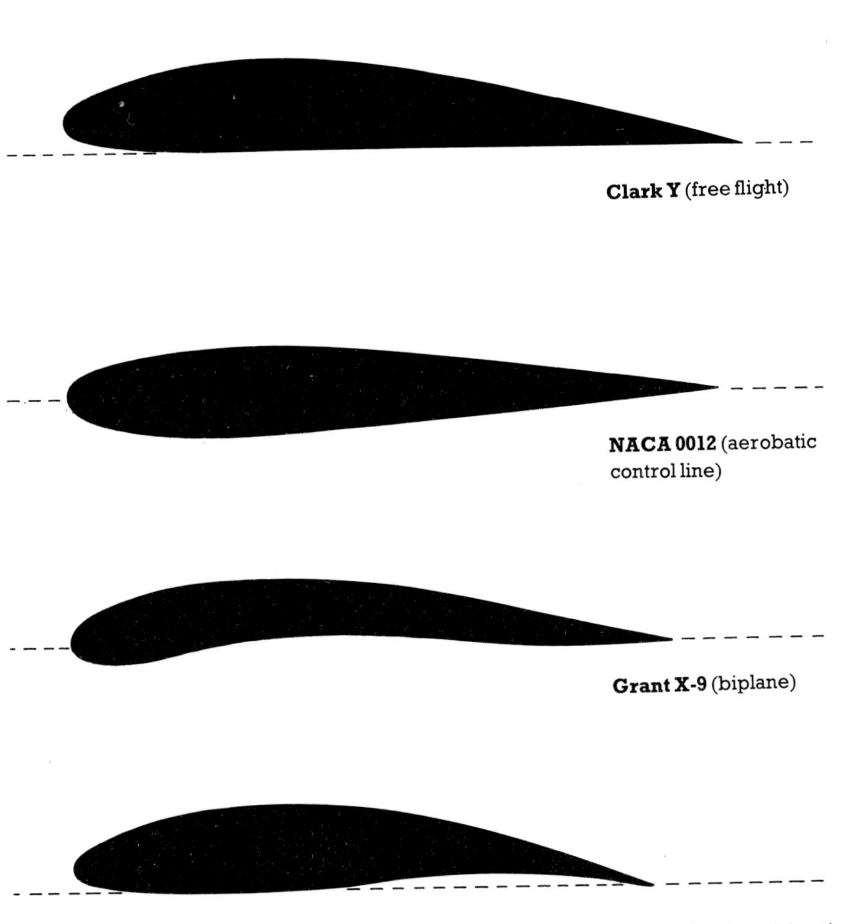

Clark Y (free flight)

NACA 0012 (aerobatic control line)

Grant X-9 (biplane)

RAF 32 (rubber driven)

Before leaving the subject of the wing, at least for the time being, there is another matter to be considered: dihedral. This is the upward and outward sweep of the wing and it governs the lateral stability of the aircraft. On some full-size airplanes virtually no dihedral is necessary because the pilot can retain lateral stability by using the ailerons. However, some models will require considerable dihedral – as much as ten degrees on a high wing and fifteen degrees on a low wing. Again the modeller has to face the problem of reconciling the look of the full-size aircraft he is modelling with the requirements of the scaled-down version if it is to fly properly. The answer is some more subtle adjustment to increase the dihedral enough to give it the necessary stability but not so much as to ruin its appearance. That will limit the increased dihedral to around three degrees on a fixed wing model. The wing struts can be placed so that their angle with the fuselage is decreased and the wing is lifted, but this tends to be a more noticeable alteration than the alternative of extending the struts in length.

Still further additional dihedral can be gained if two-part wings are used. The two sections plug on to dowel stubs at the fuselage and are given extensible struts so that as the model takes to the air the wings lift.

Turning to the tail of the model, it is necessary to go through the same sort of procedure as for the wing in deciding its airfoil section and angle and how much 'cheating' may be necessary to achieve the balance between looks and performance. First the area of the tail in relation to the wing area must be determined. Usually this will vary from 15 to 25 percent of the wing area for a glider, up to 50 percent for a power model. The tail's section can be 'symmetrical,' 'flat-plate' or 'lifting.' The first tends to give virtually no actual lift to the model, the second gives a small lift if it is set slightly at a positive angle and the last gives a tail lift which forces the nose down. For a free-flight scale model it is wise to make the tail removable for initial flight tests so that it can be adjusted easily.

The vertical tail made up by the fin and rudder also plays a part in stability. Too small a vertical tail will tend to make the model rock in flight. If only low speeds are required – as in gliding – a relatively small fin area is sufficient, but as greater air speed is required so more fin area is necessary. Too small an area will result in the model showing directional instability and a tendency to go into spiral dives.

Most engines are offset to the right to counteract the torque of the propeller, which tends to pull to the left. The higher the speed requirement, the greater the need for offsetting. On a full-size aircraft the torque can be compensated for by offsetting the fin but this is not feasible with a model which, normally, will be landing without power. An offset fin would send the model into a spiral dive or a spin. However, directional stability can be aided by the rudder and fin if these are cambered. A 'lifting' airfoil section on the vertical surface will make the tail counteract the torque effect and on a control-line model the rudder can be offset so that the aircraft wants to fly out of its circle rather than into it. This offsetting combined with slight cambering of the fin keeps the control lines tight.

A glider which is launched by tow line requires a different approach so far as the rudder is concerned. If the rudder was fixed in an offset position while the glider was under tow the model would fight to veer off to one side or even crash, but once free of the towline the offset position becomes a useful aid. What is required, therefore, is a rudder which can adjust automatically from straight to offset when the glider is released. This is achieved quite simply with the 'auto-rudder' which is connected by cord to the tow ring through a pivot. The rudder bar is set so that when the glider is under tow the rudder is pulled into a straight position and when the line is released a rubber band pulls the bar to set the rudder to the required offset angle.

The offsetting we have discussed for control line, free flight and gliders is necessary because, ideally, all the types are required to fly in a circling path rather than meandering off over the fields. However, with a radio-controlled model we are as close as possible to the full-size aircraft flying under 'piloted control' and we are dealing with the only type which we can expect to fly straight and level. There is no necessity in these circumstances to offset the rudder; indeed it is in part by controlled rudder movement that straight flight will be achieved.

Obviously an essential to all this preliminary work and all that follows is that the builder is armed with a three-view of the chosen aircraft at the outset and then proceeds to prepare scale plans. There are many possible sources of information about different aircraft types, ranging from the famous *Jane's All the World's Aircraft*, to the growing number of aircraft museums and collections and taking in photographic libraries and, of course, aircraft and aeromodelling magazines. *Jane's* is likely to provide a basic three-view drawing but without sufficient detail, which is where photographs are useful for extra information. Magazines generally oblige with three-views or silhouettes. However, the ideal is a plans service such as the Aeromodeller Plans Service, which supplies thousands of accurate drawings.

Perhaps one of the most difficult aspects of scale modelling is in preparing scale plans from the drawings you have obtained. In doing this it is essential to know the dimensions of the aircraft, the scale to which the drawings have been prepared (even if this is only approximate) and the scale of the model one intends to build. We are assuming here that all these points have been taken care of and that the builder knows what size of engine he will be using and therefore what size of model he will require.

If you can afford it, the simplest method of enlarging plans to the required scale is to use a photographic service such as is widely employed in industry. However, this really is an expensive way of doing the job and it also demands that the original drawings are of

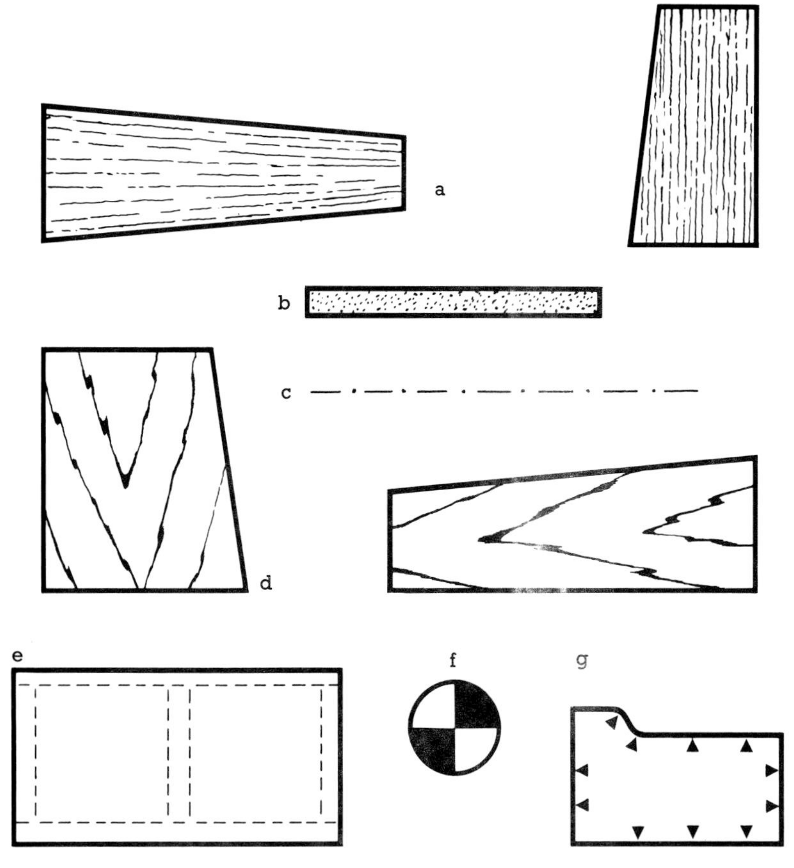

Typical markings found on aeromodellers' plans: (a) Grain direction on sheet balsa; (b) End grain; (c) Datum or center line; (d) Plywood; (e) Hidden detail; (f) Center of Gravity (CG) or balance point; (g) Outline of part picked out from mass detail.

Right
This 1:24 scale LGV CV1 was completely built from plastic sheet, with markings and camouflage hand painted.

excellent quality. Enlargement to any but the smallest degree will show up and exaggerate any faults. In addition, since the photographic paper has to be wetted and then dried, there will be some shrin' age and distortion.

The oldest 'trick' for enlarging is to draw a series of squares over the small drawing to the scale of that drawing. If the plan is 1in equals 40ft, draw one-inch squares, or, better still, half inch squares for every 20ft for greater accuracy. Then, on a separate sheet of paper draw larger squares to your chosen scale and transfer the lines of the smaller drawing on to this sheet, square by square.

Proportional dividers are an excellent and easy-to-use means of adjusting scales. All the measurements made at one end of the dividers are automatically transferred to the other end to the scale selected by adjusting the instrument setting. The dividers are ideal for transferring straight lines and nearly as effective with curves, so long as these are plotted in small sections.

A pantograph can be an extremely successful means of enlarging a drawing, so long as it is used with care. This instrument is simply a four-sided latticework with one side extended as an arm on which a pencil or pen is attached. On the side joining this arm a pointer can be set in various positions depending on the scale required. The bottom corner of the lattice is securely fastened to the plan and the pointer is traced over the outline which is to be enlarged. The pen or pencil moves in a proportionally greater ratio to copy the outline. However, the pantograph copies and enlarges any errors or shakes made in the tracing and it can also be accidentally moved from its locating point.

There are other methods of preparing actual-size plans of your proposed model but one of those mentioned above should be acceptable. If the plans have been supplied by a plans service they will indicate the various parts, joints, spars etc, but if the builder is making plans of his own he will also have to work out for himself the positioning of these.

Any modeller who is working out plans should be equipped with a set of medium-hard and hard pencils, ruler, a set-square or T-square, dividers and sheets of paper large enough to take the full-size plans of the model in every detail.

Once the full plan has been prepared it is necessary to transfer its detail on to the material to be used. Let us assume here that this will be balsa. There are a number of methods or combinations of methods which can be used, but possibly the most effective is to use a sheet of carbon paper laid between the plan and the sheet of balsa. Ensure that you have placed the plan over the wood so that the grain runs in the direction you want it to and then run over the outlines with a sharp, hard pencil so that the detail is transferred clearly. Take care not to apply so much pressure that the plan is cut through but also ensure that the pencil point is not blunt as this will thicken the lines. Damping the plan with turpentine sometimes helps: the paper becomes semi-transparent until it dries and positioning on the wood is easier.

Alternatively, the detail can be pricked through the plan on to the balsa with a pin, the prick-marks being joined up afterwards. There is, however, a greater risk of error in this method. Another method which is particularly useful for parts which are repeated several times is to mark out a template of the shape on 1.5mm plywood or thick plastic card, using the sheet of carbon paper to do so. The template can then be cut out and used over the balsa repeatedly, cutting round its shape with a sharp modelling knife. Care must be taken (a) to pin the template securely in position on the balsa sheet and (b) not to cut into its edge with the knife.

Some modellers make use of paper templates for all but the smallest parts on the basis that these, like the ply or plastic sheet templates, help to save wood because of the care with which they can be positioned close together. However, paper templates are easily damaged or crumpled, can distort or shrink and in the author's opinion do not give a solid enough edge for the outline.

As each part is cut out it should be numbered to coincide with the plan. It is a good idea to keep parts for different sections of the model separate at this stage: for example, collect together the wing pieces in one part of your working area and fuselage components in another.

When all the parts have been cut, lay out the plan on the building board and cover it either with thin polythene cling film, waxed paper or a coating of soap and pin it firmly to the board. This prevents or minimizes damage to the plan and reduces the risk of adhesive sticking a part to the paper. The basic framework can now be assembled over the plan, remembering that parts should be pinned in position on the plan until the adhesive has dried.

L.V.G. C VI
7631/

Balsa Building

Since strength combined with lightness is the most desirable attribute to be considered for any flying model – and an essential when it comes to competition flying – it is not surprising that balsa wood remains the most popular material for building all types of models. Add to that the comparative cheapness of balsa and the ease with which it can be worked and its place at the top of the list, particularly for beginners, is assured.

There are, of course, occasions when balsa is not used either on its own for a complete structure or as part of one, because even its inherent strength will not be enough or simply because the builder prefers some other material, having, almost certainly, gained his initial experience with balsa.

The simplest type of fuselage is the box type built from four longerons with vertical and horizontal spacers and covered with tissue paper. This basic structure, without the covering, can also be used as the foundation upon which formers are mounted to provide a skeleton incorporating curves. The formers can then be covered with tissue, using stringers running lengthways to give extra support, or with planking made from strips cut from sheet balsa for a more solid – but heavier – body.

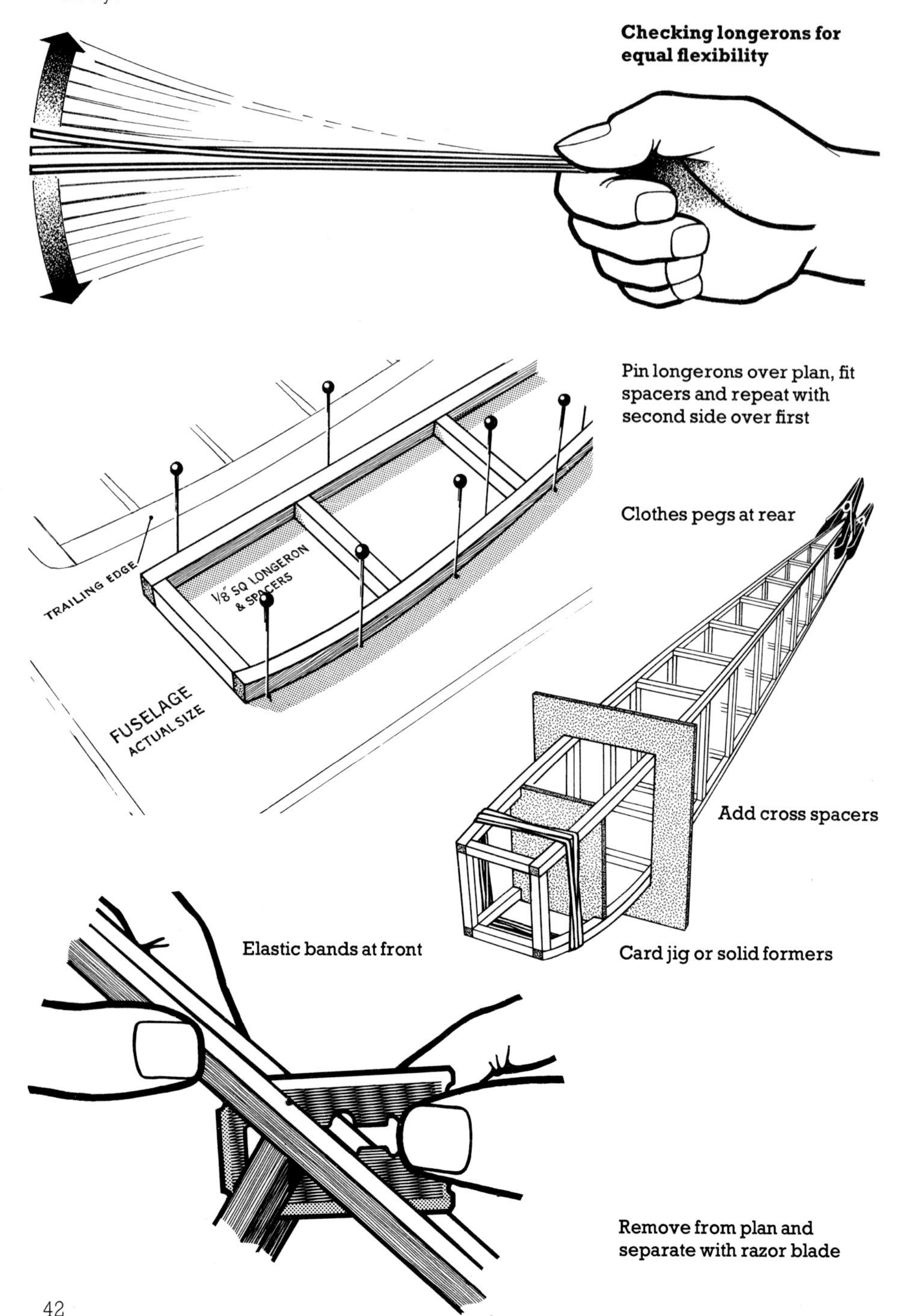

Checking longerons for equal flexibility

Pin longerons over plan, fit spacers and repeat with second side over first

Clothes pegs at rear

Add cross spacers

Card jig or solid formers

Elastic bands at front

Remove from plan and separate with razor blade

Select two pairs of longerons from your strip balsa, checking that they are of nearly equal flexibility by holding them together at one end and flapping them up and down; any excessive difference in flexibility will immediately become apparent. Use pins to position the first pair of longerons on the plan, flexing the lower one to its gentle curve by placing the pins firmly against the bottom face of the wood (*do not* pin through the wood if the longerons are of small cross section). The inside edges of the top and bottom longerons can either be tapered at their tail ends before they are positioned on the plan or when both sides of the fuselage have been made and are ready to be cemented together at the tail.

After locating the longerons on the plan, cement the upright spacers in place, working from the center and ensuring that they have been cut square. Use the cement sparingly and give it time to dry before moving parts. A method of avoiding the messy business of parts sticking to the plan is to rub the paper over with a candle; alternatively, thin waxed paper can be pinned between the plan and the parts which are being assembled. When the first side has been constructed carry straight on with the second, building it over the top of the first to ensure that the two are 'twinned.' If you wish, waxed paper can be placed between the two sides to avoid them sticking to each other but this is really unnecessary, unless you are excessively generous with the cement, as the two can be easily separated with a razor blade inserted at sticking points after the cement has dried.

The two sides are then joined by the cross spacers which reduce in length from the center towards the tail and nose. Work from the center outwards. At this stage it is important to ensure that the structure is held square. For this purpose a card jig is made to fit as a collar over the point of maximum cross section. In addition, extra strength and resistance to warping is provided by adding permanent formers cut from sheet balsa. These also hold the fuselage square and are worth their small additional weight.

After the center spacers have been fixed, add the nose spacers. These can be individual pieces of strip balsa, four pieces which have been previously cemented into the correct rectangular shape and are slotted between the nose uprights of the sides or a single sheet of balsa cut to size and with its center removed.

As the tail is cemented together there will be a tendency for the longerons to pull apart at the nose. To prevent this a further jig can be cut to fit over the nose or the longerons can be held in place by an elastic band. At the same time, clothes pegs can be used to hold the tail end in place as it dries.

For models that are to be rubber-driven – and this kind of structure is most suitable for that type – additional diagonal bracing can be added to the sides as they are made, to resist the twisting effects which result from propeller torque – that is, the force which tends to twist the fuselage in the opposite direction to that in which the prop is rotating. Additional strength will also be required in the nose and this can be provided by making the nose cone from solid balsa, or by reinforcing the nose with sheet balsa or, better still, thin ply which can also be used around the rear motor peg fixing. Extra strength can, of course, be provided by covering the whole framework with sheet balsa.

The greatest danger faced by any rubber-powered model is that of serious damage when the rubber skein breaks under tension. The suddenly released ends of the skein whirling inside the fuselage can wreak havoc. Protection against this eventuality can be provided by wrapping thin sheet balsa into a tube shape which is then covered by fiberglass or nylon laminated with epoxy resin or polyester resin. The rubber strands can run inside this tube with safety.

Another, slightly more complicated, construction method using a balsa frame is the crutch construction which has the advantage of providing improved shap-

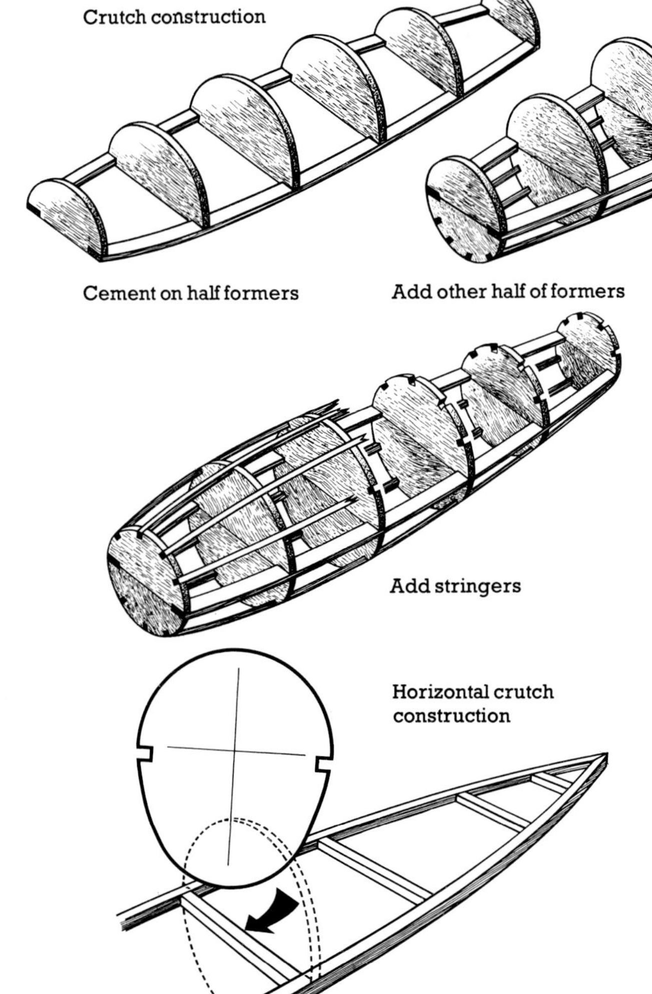

ing for streamlining. The crutch can be as simple as a tube running through a fuselage center or even a solid stick of hardwood on which whole formers are positioned. Alternatively, if the fuselage is nearly symmetrical the crutch can be a vertical or horizontal outline on to which are cemented half formers to the shape of the fuselage. The vertical crutch follows the top and bottom lines of the fuselage from fore to aft and the horizontal follows the plan outline of the sides. In either case the method of construction is the same, except that for the vertical type a space must be left in the top half for wing spaces or a cockpit opening.

The outlines are laid in strip balsa on the plan, pinning the wood in position as before, and the half formers are keyed and cemented in position.

The half formers can be made solid so that they run as a series of bulkheads inside the fuselage, or as arches cut from sheet balsa which become circles when the

Above
Before and after shots of this 19-inch span rubber powered 'Lizzie' (Westland Lysander) illustrate the method of constructing the fuselage in two halves, split along the center line, with stringers added. The model was built by Doug McHard.

halves are joined. The keying should be only to half the depth of the strip so that there is sufficient space left for the second set of half formers to be set in place on the reverse side. A problem with this method is that the keying may not be sufficient to give a secure foundation for the formers; in addition care must be taken to ensure that the formers are positioned absolutely at right angles. Do not move the structure until the formers are dried, to avoid the chance of introducing warping. To avoid these pitfalls there is an advantage in making a matching pair of these skeletons which can be left in position until each is safe to be moved. The two halves can then be cemented together.

Depending upon the type of aircraft being built, planking or stringers are then added to run fore and aft. If the model is of a plane that in full size is metal-covered, planking will give the necessary solid look after finishing; if an older, soft-sided machine is the subject then stringers spaced regularly around the circumference will look right when covered with doped tissue or light fabric. Make sure that the stringers are positioned quickly, one after the other in diagonally opposite rotation to prevent twisting in the fuselage.

If the fuselage shape is elliptical a further crutch method should be used, employing whole formers which are keyed on to a horizontal crutch to abut cross braces which are cemented in position while the outline backbones are laid on the plan. In this case the outline strip balsa and cross braces should be cut from strips of about $^{3}/_{16}$ in square. The whole formers are placed in position by dropping them into the frame at an angle and then turned so that the keys slide over the side members and up against the cross braces, to which they should be cemented.

When a motor tube for a rubber-powered model is used, whole formers can each have a hole cut in them to the diameter of the tube. They can then be slid on the tube in order and fixed in position before main and subsidiary stringers are added.

For gliders there are a number of other fuselages which can be adopted, bearing in mind that a strong structure is required to withstand the stresses of towing, not infrequent crash landings and plenty of handling. At the same time the weight should be as low as possible and drag reduced to the minimum. If realism is not the prime objective, a slim fuselage can be made simply by cementing sheet balsa on to flat section top and bottom longerons of spruce or balsa. The structure, which offers low drag, is strengthened by 'bulkheads' spaced along its length. An even simpler fuselage can be provided by hollow fiberglass fishing rod tubes which can be purchased as blanks and are virtually incapable of being destroyed.

Sheet balsa can also be used effectively to construct more solid types of sports models than those with a skeleton framework. Here the balsa sheet is cut to the outline shape of the whole fuselage – two sides, top and bottom. The sides have slots cut vertically in them to accept keys left on the formers which are placed along the fuselage to add strength at points of stress. A pair of dowels can be inserted right through the fuselage, from side to side just below cockpit roof level to protrude about $^{1}/_{4}$ or $^{1}/_{2}$in to provide points at which the wings can be attached by rubber bands so that they detach in a crash.

Yet another method of fuselage construction with sheet balsa is to use two thin layers for each side, cut so that the grain runs in opposing directions: if the bottom sheets have the grain running vertically, the top should be horizontally grained. This provides considerable extra strength and rigidity and the extra weight is quite small. In both single and double sheeting, girder braces should be added to the reverse faces of the sides. Wooden models which are expected to fly at high speeds will require additional protection at their most vulnerable point – the nose. Here again, double sheeting can be used but thin ply for the inner lining is recommended. It should be used in the small area from the nose tip to the front of the cockpit or cabin. If a high-wing model is involved the outline of the cabin itself can be reinforced with spruce runners and the bottom with balsa strip to protect against extra stress from the undercarriage.

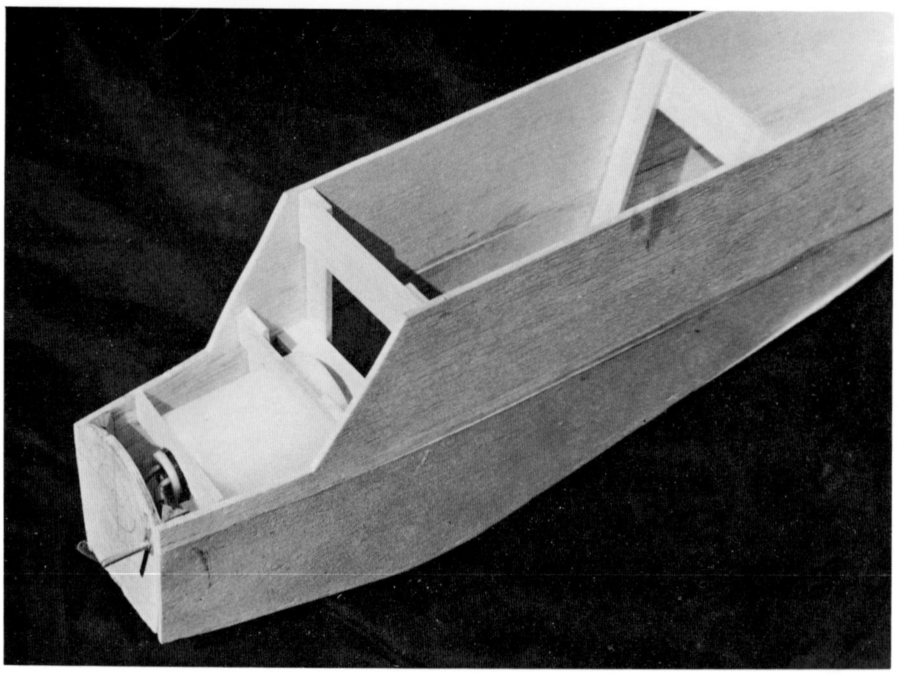

Top, above and above right
Step by step in a basic fuselage balsa construction from the simple box to installation of the tank and offset shaft, to pinning down the cowling.

Below right
Detail of the undercarriage construction for the same model.

A method of balsa construction which provides an extremely strong fuselage is the molded stressed-skin. Though it takes longer in the making than any of the other types we have mentioned, the finished result is well worth the trouble both in the high degree of indestructibility and in the amount of streamlining which can be given to the fuselage. The first requirement is a dummy fuselage carved from block wood in two 'mirror' halves which should be $^{3}/_{32}$ in undersize. A sheet of $^{1}/_{32}$ in straight-grained balsa is dampened to make it sufficiently pliable to wrap around this mold without splitting and is fastened at the point of widest cross section. The sheet can either be pinned at this point or, preferably, bound with flat tape which will not cut into the material.

The sheet will now be too big at the tapering nose and tail. To make it fit, a series of deep Vee cuts is made from the tail point inwards and nose tip inwards, the cut edges being pulled together, glued and taped until dry. Now the process is repeated with a second sheet laid over the first, ensuring that the Vees do not coincide

with those on the bottom sheet. When part-dry the two are covered with cement and placed back on the mold to set to shape. Finally a third layer is added and allowed to dry before being treated for any blemishes and sanded. If it is necessary to have any slots or openings cut in the fuselage (for wings, tail section, cockpit etc) it is advisable to make the cuts when the skin is dry and still on the mold.

These then are some of the construction methods employed in making fuselages. There are others but they invariably involve a variation on the techniques we have mentioned or a combination of some aspects of a number of different methods.

What of the wings? Here there are fewer ways of doing the job which, in itself, is simpler than that of fuselage building because the wing shapes are simpler. The most important considerations in making a wing are that it should be strong enough to bear the strain when it is under the greatest stress and that it maintains the correct airfoil shape. Any twisting of the wing, particularly at the tips, will affect the flying characteristics; the strutures must incorporate anti-warp-and-twist sections while being as strong as possible in their main section and as light as possible at their tips.

To achieve all this is to find exactly the right combination of ribs, spars and covering. The best way to ensure that the correct airfoil section is retained throughout the wing is to use templates of the section to cut out the ribs and to provide as rigid a surface as possible between the ribs. The templates can be made from ply or aluminium and will either be identical or one will be shaped for the tip of the wing and the other for its root. If there is a taper in the wing it will be necessary to position the templates to allow for this, drilling or piercing two holes in each to take a pair of bolts which will run through the sandwich of rib blanks. As the ribs are carved and sanded the taper will be produced naturally.

The number of spars used will have a bearing on the weight of the wing but will also provide greater warp resistance. A basic multi-spar structure will have the spars running, root-to-tip, close together. The greater the number of spars the thinner the rib should be to compensate as much as possible for the extra weight. The thinnest practical thickness for ribs is $\frac{1}{32}$ in cut from sheet balsa and, although this may sound extremely flimsy, a rib of this thickness will still have a remarkable degree of resistance to pressures applied vertically. In addition to the strength provided by the closely spaced spars, there is the extra advantage that if a tissue or fabric covering is used they will prevent sagging in the rib bays.

However, a more realistic finish can be given to the wing by a sheet covering on the leading edge, extending back about 40 percent of the wing chord on top and bottom surfaces. Not only does this dispense with the rather unsightly undulations which tend to appear on a leading edge which is entirely 'soft-covered'; it also provides a means of ensuring that the airfoil section is retained throughout the wing.

One method of guarding against warp is to use just one deep main spar and to construct geodetic ribs as bracing. These are placed diagonally to the main ribs, running from the trailing edge to the spar and then are continued forward with 'riblets' of the same airfoil section. Alternatively two thinner main spars can be placed one above the other and the diagonal ribs can run the full chord of the wing, being keyed into the spars at their intersecting points. For more added strength, greater warp resistance and smoother air flow, the trailing wing edge should be of sheet balsa or shaped from solid balsa. The wing tips are points which are going to be subject to stress and need some attention to make them as strong as possible and to make them conform to the correct shape. If tissue or fabric covering is being used and the tip of the full-size wing is not square but requires tapering off, a lower surface of sheet balsa can be added to overlap from the halfway point of the last rib bay and project beyond the final rib, which is rebated to accept the thickness of the sheet. The tissue can then be glued to the protruding tip and shrunk.

A more satisfactory method is to use block balsa carved to shape and – in the interests of weight saving – hollowed out. This can be cemented to the side of the final rib. A third way is to cut the shape of the wing tip from expanded polystyrene using a hot wire cutter. This can also be stuck to the final rib and will be covered by layers of doped tissue. However, polystyrene is prone to denting and care should therefore be taken not to pick up the model by the wing tips.

Expanded polystyrene can, incidentally, be used successfully as a packing in wings, dispensing with the need for ribs since the polystyrene is cut to the correct airfoil section using templates and hot wire cutter. However, spars should still be used, inserting them in slots of the appropriate size cut into the plastic foam. Balsa should also be used for the leading and trailing edges, and the whole can then be covered with sheet balsa.

The method of attaching the wings to the fuselage depends upon the type of model which is being constructed as well as the role it is to perform. It is always worth bearing in mind that the wings and tailplane are the most likely parts of a model to be damaged in a crash and that the risks can be reduced if these units are made to detach on impact. To the uninitiated this tends to imply that they will also detach in flight! This is not so: there are a number of attachment methods and all, if carried out correctly, ensure that the units remain in correct positions during flight and only collapse on impact or when you wish to break down a large model to pack it away.

With high-wing models or those on which the wings run below the fuselage rather than into it, the simplest fixing method is to construct the two wings as one unit with a sheeted center section. Four short dowels, two on either side, fore and aft of the cabin either at roof or deck level provide anchor points for elastic bands stretched from the leading to the trailing edges of the wings. It is important that the bands are strong enough to hold the wings firmly and this means that under tension they could cause damage to soft-covered wing edges. These should therefore be reinforced at the delicate trailing edge using a ply strip.

To ensure that the wings or tailplane are correctly

Early detachable high wing is held in place by elastic band to the dowel. (Note the need for repairs.)

positioned, small keying blocks should be cemented to the lower (for high-wing) or upper (for low-wing) surfaces on the sheeted center sections. If the under surface of the high wing at this point forms the roof of the cabin, the keying blocks should be exactly fixed to drop into the four corners of the cabin. If the cabin is separately roofed (which is unlikely but possible) and also in the case of low wings running under the deck, rebates should be cut into the fuselage surfaces to accept the keys, having first made sure from test flights that the correct positions have been determined. This method of fixing is not really suitable for powered models but is entirely adequate for gliders.

For free-flight powered models the most popular method of attachment is the tongue-and-box system, which is also suitable for gliders. A tongue is firmly fixed into the center section or wing root to fit tightly into a receiving box built into the detachable unit. The tongue is rounded to the curvature of the arc described if the wing is swung back with the apex of the trailing edge as its pivot.

Some high wing models and biplanes cannot, of course, be constructed with the wings as one piece if, for example, the full size has a clear cabin roof and the wings extend on either side or if the wings are supported by struts. In the first case it is necessary to have the fitting on the reinforced root rib at the end wing rib. The fitting can be a pair of short-radius dowels which key in to holes made at the correct angle for the 'set' of the wing. Another successful means of attachment is in the use of a pair of dress snap fasteners or carpet snaps, the one let into the end rib and the other to the root side, with the added support of wire struts.

Eric Coates with his partly completed BE 126 scale model showing excellent detail of the wing construction.

Construction of the tailplane closely follows the principles adopted for the wings, except where it has been decided that the tailplane should be completely flat, with no curved airfoil section to increase lift. If the size and weight of the model is not too great, this can be made from sheet balsa. Remember that the size and weight of the nose will have a bearing on the area of the tailplane and on whether there will be a need for ballast to give the model balance.

The danger in using sheet balsa for a solid tailplane is that it will be extremely prone to warping, particularly if the wood is cut – as it should be – so that the grain runs spanwise (from tip to tip). Warp will be caused by environmental changes which cannot be avoided: humidity, heat and cold. However, this need not deter you since it is simple enough to let into the tail plane two anti-warp rectangles. These are made from same thickness but harder grade balsa than that of the main surface and are inset so that the grain runs fore-and-aft instead of spanwise.

Another method of avoiding or at least minimizing warp on the built-up flat section tail is to use sheet balsa over the top of a frame of strip balsa. The whole structure is then covered (top and bottom) with tissue or fabric which is doped.

Where tailplanes are made as lifting airfoil sections the same principles as for wings apply exactly, as do the hints we have already mentioned for attachment. However, if tailplanes are eventually to be made a permanent fixture rather than detachable, it is important that they should not be finally fixed in position until test flights have been made to determine the correct angle of incidence.

Plastic Kits

So far we have been chiefly concerned with the construction of models which will fly. Almost certainly anyone who has become involved in the fascinating world of the flying model will have started off by building a static model first and the likelihood, today, is that this will have involved the assembly of a plastic kit.

There is a tendency among some modellers who are interested only in the flying variety to regard the hobbyist whose interest is in making aircraft from plastic kits as being third rate. Yet this form of modelling is a craft in its own right and one which demands just as much patience and attention to detail if the finished article is to appear exactly like the real thing.

One advantage which the static model has over the flyer is that it can adhere far more closely in its reduced size to the detail of the full-size original since aerodynamic principles do not have to be considered. However, the vast majority of the thousands of plastic kits which are now available are designed with the young constructor in mind rather than being aimed at the specialist market.

The economics as well as the design problems of tooling-up to produce millions of moldings or pressings of a particular part for a model mean that what you purchase in the box will not be a one-hundred-percent accurate scale reproduction of the original. The fact that some details are not accurate is no reason for the purist to turn his back on a kit, however. Rather it should present a challenge for him to carry out the necessary alterations himself. Similarly, he may wish his model to be not just of any old Hurricane, Lancaster, Messerschmitt Me-262 or Mustang but of a specific variant which singled it out by reason of marking or modification. It is up to him to carry out the research and make his own alterations to the kit.

As with flying models so, too, with the static variety the matter of scale becomes important, particularly if the intention is to start a collection based on a particular theme.

In the early 1930s the famous James Hay Stevens pioneered his wooden 'Skybird' Kits which were 1:72 (1in to 6ft) or just half the size of the 1:36 scale which was then generally accepted as standard. Modellers who had found that this latter scale was restrictive because of the size of the finished article quickly caught on to the convenience of the 'new' scale and it became standard. In the United States and Japan the 1:48 scale ($^1/_4$in to 1ft) has always been favored and has become popular in Great Britain. One reason for the appeal of this larger scale is that it allows the inclusion of some fine detail without causing the problems of the 1:36 size. (In the late 1960s the 1:32 scale was introduced but the cost of tooling-up for what proved to be a limited market was uneconomic.) Even so, a 1:24 scale series of the early 1970s, though limited in market appeal, could be considered the ultimate in plastic kits, with superlative attention to detail. At the other end of the scale there is 1:144, which, though it may sound tiny, is still large enough to include some refinement of detail but small enough to be able to make a collection representative, for example, of major airlines and including even aircraft such as the 'Jumbos.'

Although it is obviously advisable to form a collection by using a standard scale throughout, there are occasions on which a break from that rule is not only permissible but also worthwhile. The obvious example is when a particular type of aircraft needed to complete a collection is only available in a different scale to the one you have adopted. Another instance is in the construction of dioramas, that is – representations of a complete scene of, shall we say, an aerial combat or an airport. In either case it is sometimes necessary to give depth to a scene by deliberately including in the background aircraft (and ground vehicles, for that matter)

Below
The fact that this view of a plastic modeller's work top is uncluttered is quite deliberate. Space should be clear for proper work especially if undertaking a delicate task such as rigging this Sopwith Snipe vac-form kit. The dividers are used to measure lengths between struts and the tweezers to apply the thin lengths of stretched plastic sprue. Not shown in the picture is the PVA wood glue used as an adhesive and applied in small spots with a cocktail stick.

Below right
The Spitfire is unquestionably the most well-loved and oft-modelled World War II fighter and the 1/32nd scale MkVb from Hasegawa is probably the finest kit available of this classic. This particular model has been converted to a MkVc by changing the armament and rescribing new wing panel lines. This model, with airbush finish and partly hand-painted markings, is on permanent display at the Shuttleworth Collection, Old Warden, Bedfordshire, England.

Right
Monogram enjoy a fine reputation for their 1/48th scale range of warplanes. The mighty Liberator is one of the finest and most impressive of the range and the interior is fully furnished including the bomb bay. Additional detail can be applied to the rear gun positions and cockpit areas as the canopies and openings reveal all too readily the inner surfaces.

Far right
This Airfix Do 17E (now currently out of production) is to 1/72nd scale and features the unique camouflage and markings of a Spanish Civil War machine. The straight edged splinter pattern was painted without the aid of any masking and decals were from commercial Microscale ranges with a little hand painting.

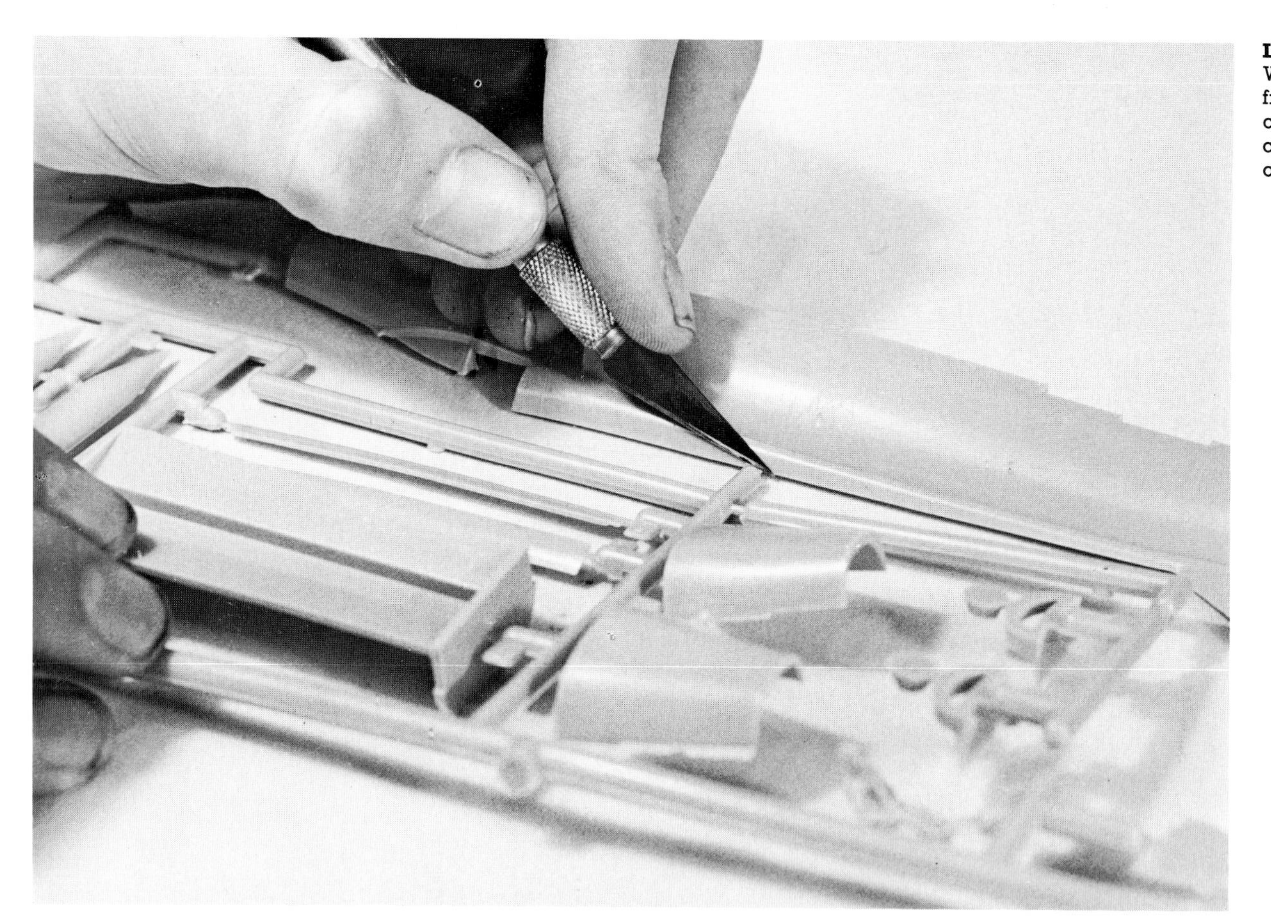

Left
When removing kit parts from the sprue trees *always* cut them away with a sharp craft knife. Do not break them off.

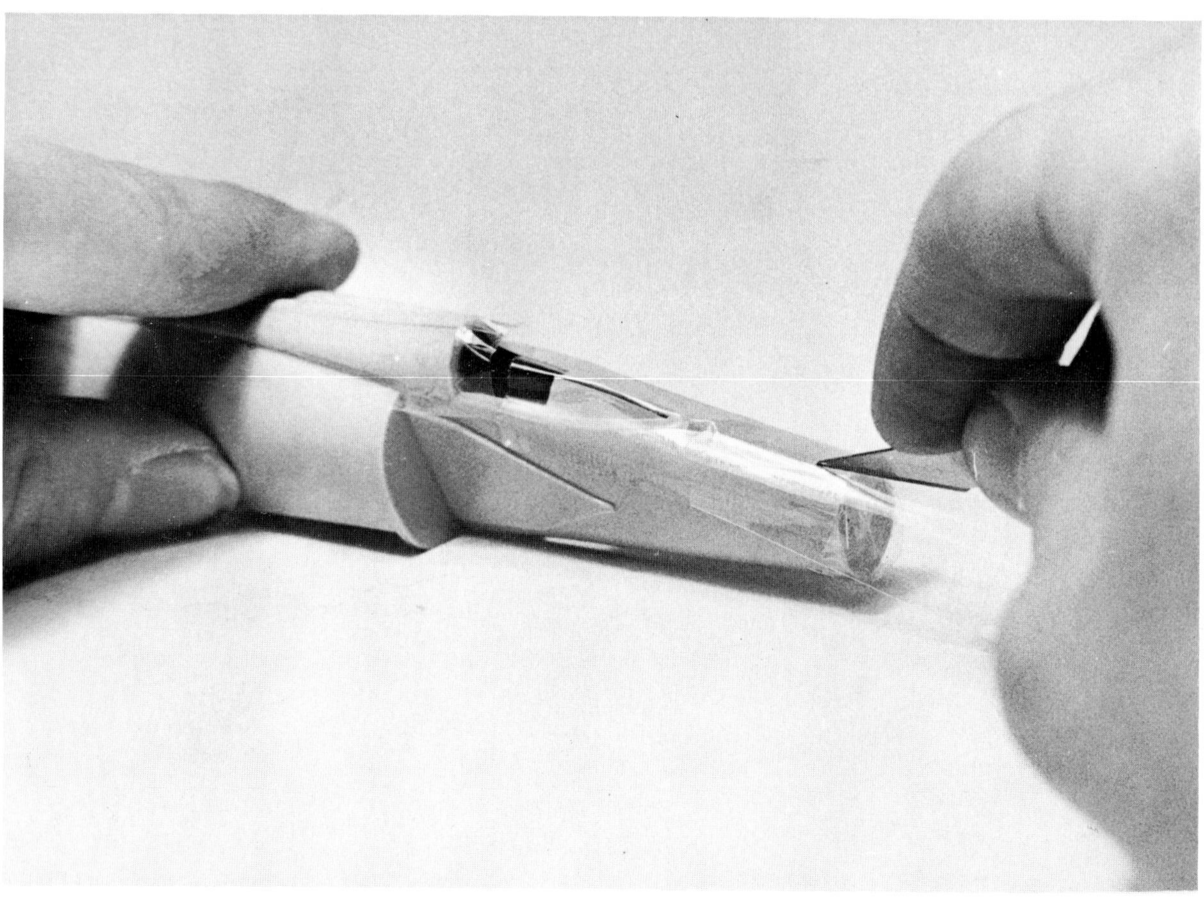

Left
A safe way of gluing two halves is to hold together, run tape all along the join line, then separate with a knife.

of a smaller scale than your 'standard' scale.

Having decided on scale there then comes the problem of which of the many different makes to choose from, since cost is not necessarily a reflection of quality. Here the criterion should be accuracy and the modeller can learn either by experience or through the pages of the modelling press – or by having a look at the completed models of any acquaintances who specialize in the same hobby!

The tools of this adopted 'trade' have already been mentioned although the list was compiled mainly with thoughts of the flying model in mind. However, among those listed are virtually all that is required. To them can be added a pair of scissors, some form of body putty to use as a filler, spatulas for shaping the putty, and toothpicks for applying fine points of cement.

Having purchased your kit the first step is to ensure that it is complete – it is surprising how often one can find that a part has been omitted – and that you understand the instructions. Usually these will present no

Left
Apply cement sparingly to one surface only and ensure that all mating edges are fully covered before joining.

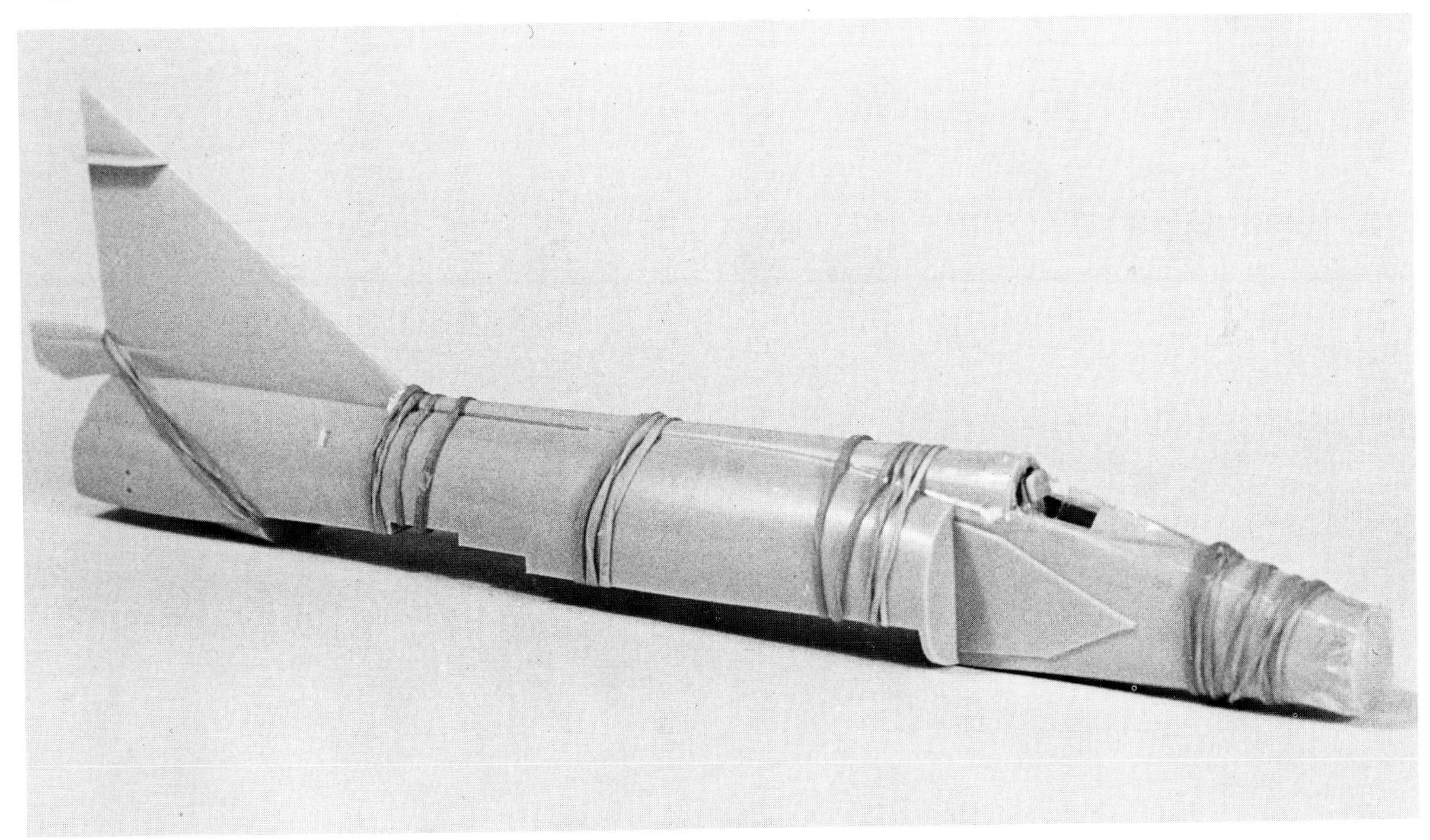

Above
Hold parts together with bands while drying. The tape protects the plastic as squeezed cement oozes from the joint. When dry all this can be removed.

problems but instructions which have been translated can cause some confusion in their choice of English! If a part is missing the box will usually contain a note of the address to which the complete kit should be returned; alternatively, go back to the shop where you bought the model or write to the manufacturers or their agents.

It is a sensible precaution not to separate the parts from the molding racks or sprues to which they are attached until you are ready to start work. That stage should not be reached until you have been through the instructions carefully, decided your course of action and identified any parts which may need to be painted before assembly. In the case of very small parts the painting may best be done before they are cut from the rack, where they will remain until dry.

With experience of working to your chosen scale you will find that errors of dimension in main body parts – fuselage, wings, tail – can be quite easily detected by comparing them with accurate scale drawings

Below
The Revell Beaufighter is an impressive model of this big RAF twin and easily be converted to other marks. This model represents a MkV1 of 603 Squadron and features new exhausts, modified, tail unit, reworked nose, hand-painted markings and extended nacelles. Rear canopy has been hinged open and full interior detail applied.

Bottom left
'Matchbox' biplanes are among the best of a varied range. This 1/72nd scale model (of No 87 Squadron) includes full cockpit detail, rigging and features an airbrushed aluminum finish.

Below right
Heller produced some unique subjects among their range of kits and the Arado Ar 96 is one of the best. The model here is unmodified with kit decals and cockpit area carefully painted, but without additions.

Above right
The French plastic kit manufacturer of Heller produces many fine models including this 1/72nd Polish PZL P11c seen 'taxiing' on a specially created runway. The model was unusual in that it needed no modifications other than detailing in the cockpit, which even by present-day standards in quite rare. This model has also been airbrushed in order to retain the fine detail.

Above far right
Hasegawa enjoy a fine reputation in the plastic kit field – a reputation upheld by this 1/72nd Curtiss P40E Kittyhawk in RAF colors. Camouflage has been airbrushed and decals are Letraset pressure tires. The Sharkmouth motif, seemingly synonymous with this aircraft, has been hand painted using a fine sable brush.

GA Y

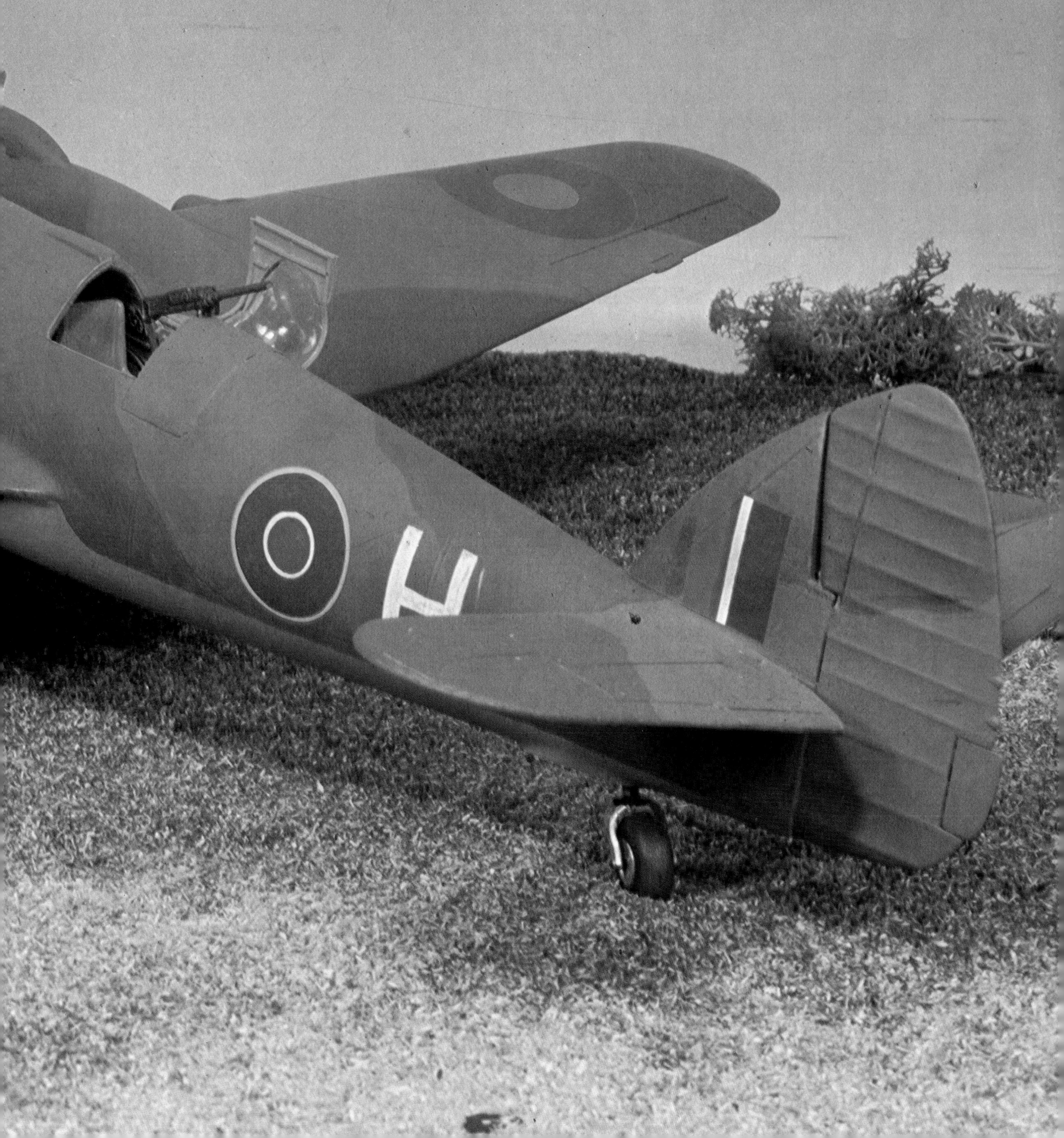

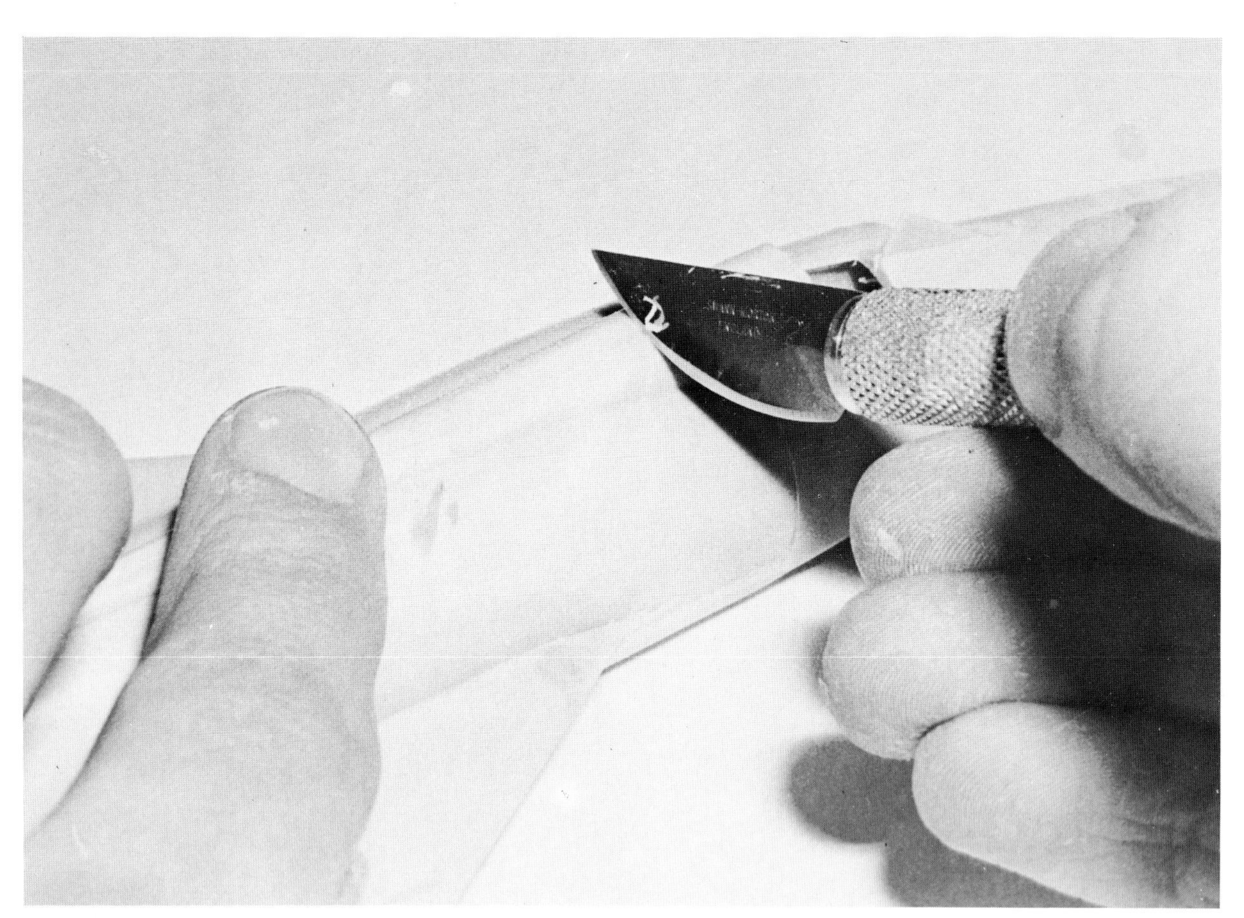

Left
Joint lines can be partly eradicated by paring with a knife blade, but only when the glue has dried thoroughly.

Below
On most aircraft kits, bad joints will need filling and this can be done with commercial filler as shown.

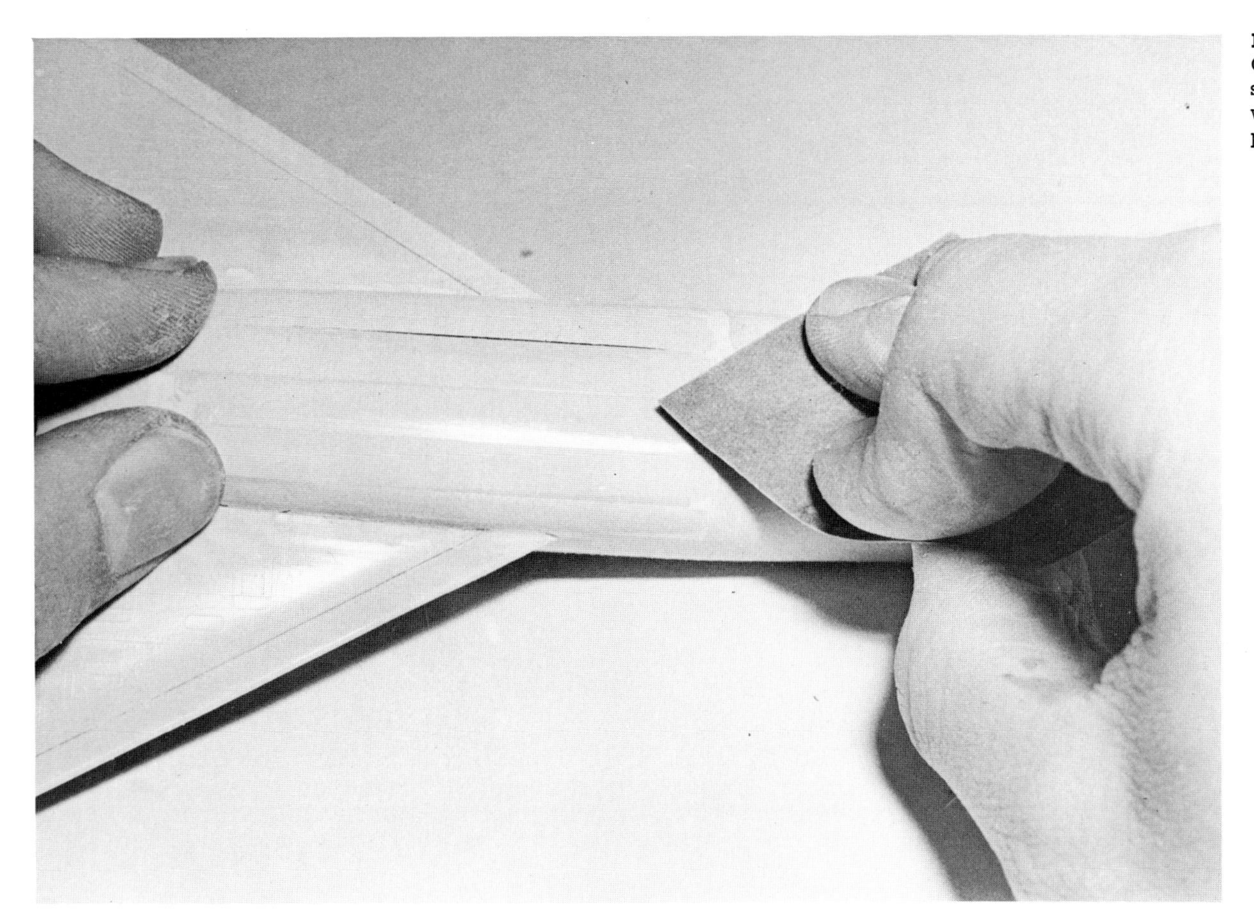

Left
Once the filler has dried it should be rubbed down with wet and dry paper prior to painting.

Left
Larger parts can be held together by tape or clamps while the glue sets. Obviously some filler will be needed here.

which you should possess if you intend to use the kit merely as the basis for your own work. If a part is, say, $^1/_{16}$ of an inch too big in 1:72 scale this will mean that the reproduction would be 9in out in its full-size version. The same error of $^1/_{16}$ in 1:36 scale, though it would represent a distortion of 18in in the full size, will not be as noticeable in the larger model. The problem in curing errors of this sort comes in trying to work out exactly where it has occurred. If complete accuracy is your aim, you will not be happy simply to trim down an oversize wing at the tips or, if it is a matter of the part being under size, adding a piece of plastic card insert at the wing root. In either case this may mean that the dihedral is altered. The only entirely satisfactory cure is to go over your scale drawing – and any additional illustration you may have – with a fine-tooth comb and determine the exact point at which the error has been made. The correction should then be made at that point on the model. All this can be a time-consuming business to correct something which, certainly in small scale, only

Below
Another fine kit currently unavailable is the Airfix Avro 504K which has been improved in this instance by lengthening and deepening the fuselage with plastic sheet. A new cowling has been molded from thin sheet and the model is fully, and correctly, rigged with fine wire.

Bottom left
This 1/24th scale German LVG CV1 was completely scratch-built from plastic sheet and scrap and the airscrew was laminated in thin wood sections and carved to shape just like the original. The multi-colored lozenge pattern on the wings was hand painted using small stencils. The only commercial items are two wheels and a pilot and even these are modified.

Bottom center
The Revell Albatros D-III was one of several fine World War I types produced by this manufacturer. Nevertheless it still requires modification and the model features a partly rebuilt fuselage, reworked flying surfaces and complete cockpit detail. All struts were replaced from fine section plastic sprue and wheels too are substitutes. The result was worth all the effort.

Bottom right
Biplane models always make attractive modelling subjects and the Airfix Handley Page 0/400 bomber of World War I is no exception. Fully rigged and detailed, this 1/72nd scale model is displayed with a Sopwith Camel in order that one can appreciate the large size of the original aircraft.

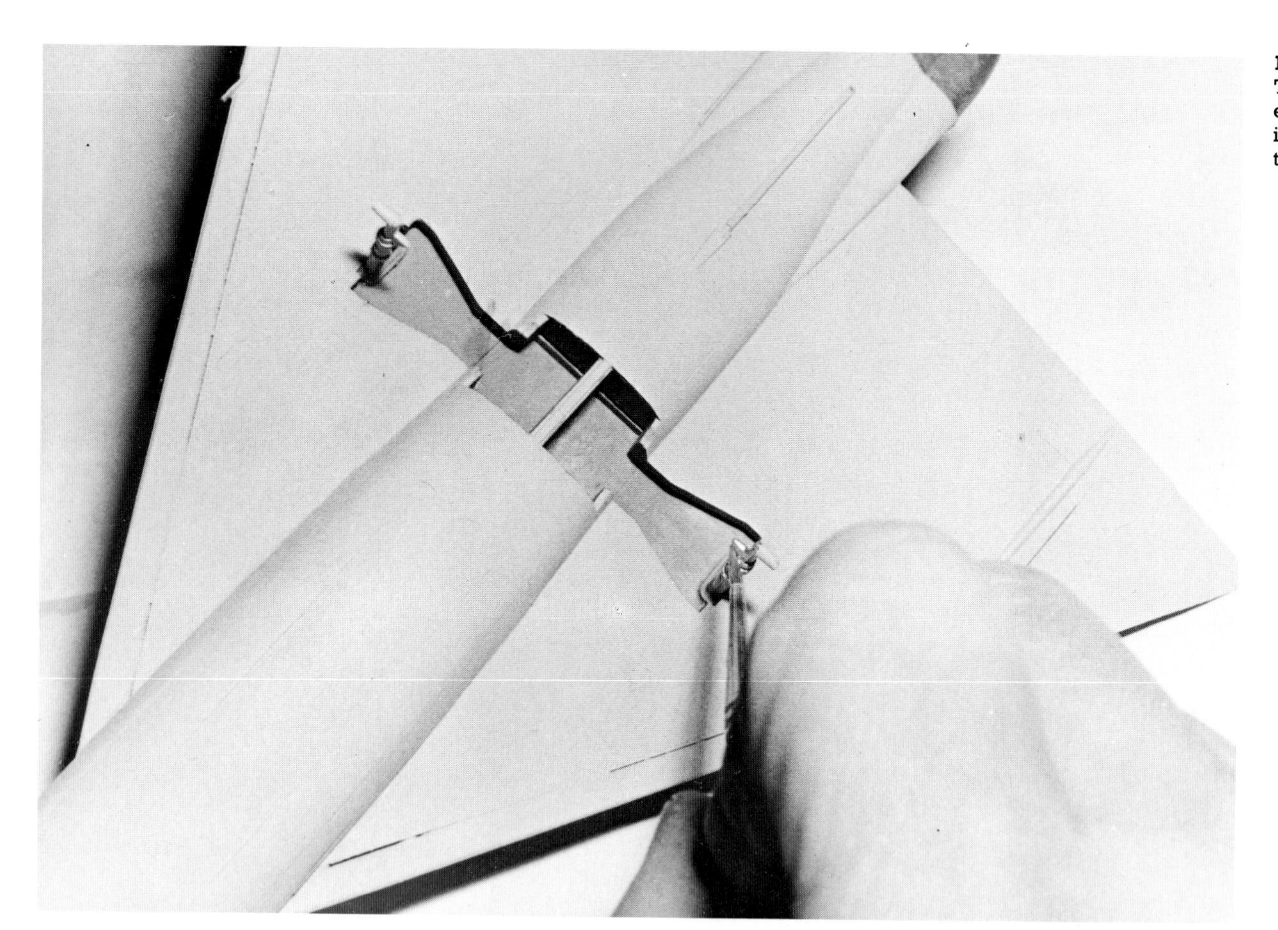

Left
The use of tweezers is essential when adding finer items to the model such as these undercarriage legs.

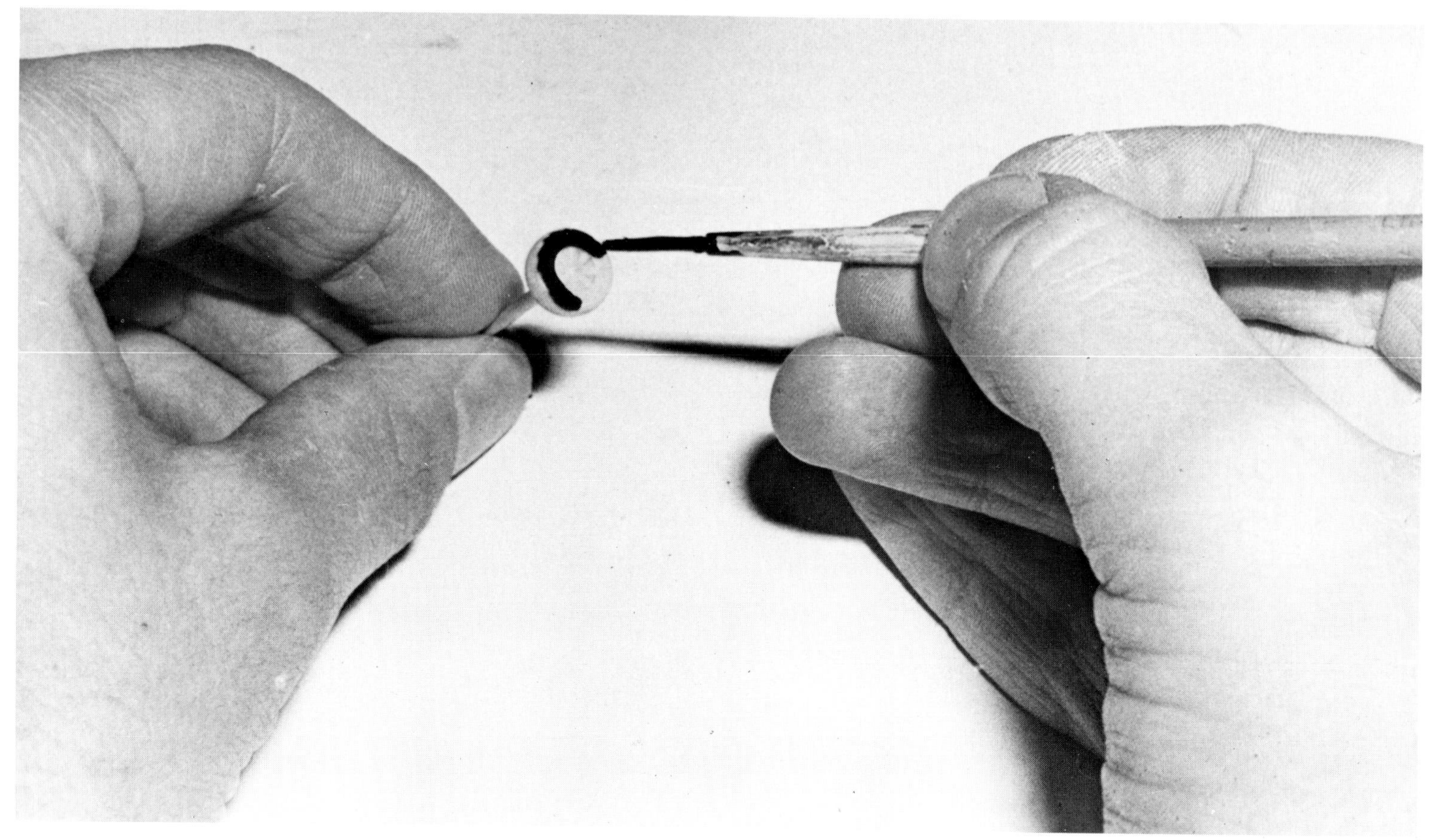

Above
An easy way to paint tires is by rotating them on a cocktail stick and holding the brush close and steady.

you are likely to know is wrong. On the other hand, having put matters right there is a considerable sense of satisfaction to be gained from the knowledge that you have achieved that greater degree of accuracy. I would liken the whole procedure to the home decorator who makes a mistake in matching a wallpaper pattern. No one else will notice the error but his eye constantly strays to the offending point on the wall.

It is inevitable that some of the parts in the kit will have small blemishes such as flashings of waste plastic adhering to an end or mold marks which may be hairline indentations or protrusions or creases in the surface. Any such faults will require either smoothing down with abrasive paper or filling with body putty. The stage at which body-puttying is carried out depends very much on the accessibility of the part concerned: if it is going to be difficult to reach after assembly, obviously the work should be carried out beforehand; if the part is difficult to handle on its own it may be better to wait until after assembly. Where an angle on a

Left
Masking with tape to ensure hard edges when painting is also important, especially if one's hands are very shaky.

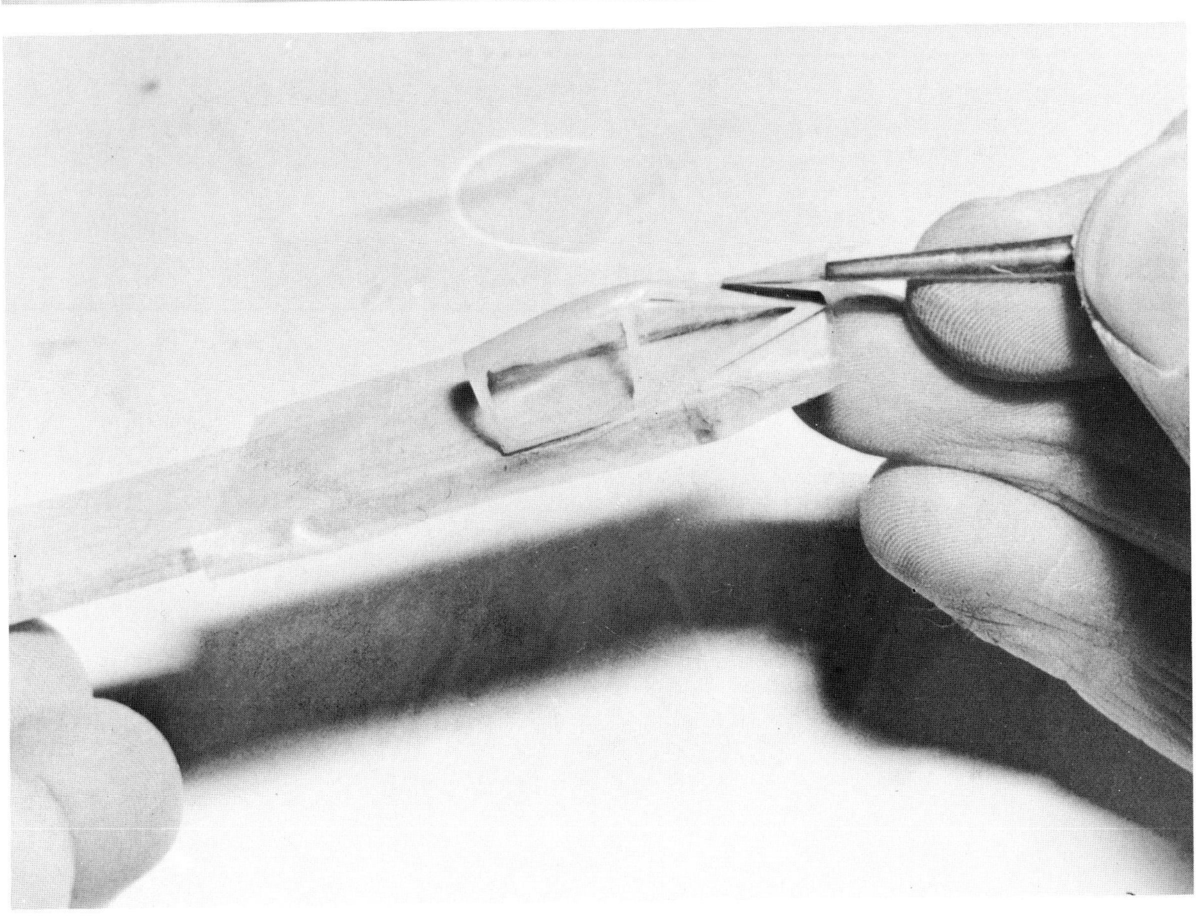

Left
This canopy is held by double-sided tape to a hand hold while carefully painting the fine frame lines.

tongue or groove joint is found to be incorrect, preventing a proper fit, it is best to use the file from your set which most nearly matches the correct angle.

By the time you have been over the model parts carefully to check for accuracy and blemishes and have compared the kit with your plans and photographs you will have had a chance to decide on the extra detail you intend to add to the model. On smaller scales this is likely to include internal stringers, bulkheads, floors and instrumentation in the cockpit. Once again it is important to check your references to be sure that you do not spoil the model by making an addition which is inaccurate. For example, if internal stringers are to be added, are they circular or rectangular? The likelihood is that if they are to run longitudinally they will be rectangular but if they are vertical or diagonal braces they will be round. If the former is the case they can be quite simply made from thick strips of plastic card, heated and stretched with a steady, gentle pull. If rounded stringers are required sprue from the rack

Below
This 1/72nd scale Hawker Hurricane was made by cannibalizing the best parts of the old Airfix and Frog kits in order to obtain an accurate model. Now this work can be avoided by the release of the new Airfix Hurricane which betters its predecessors by far. The markings for the model are a mixture of Letraset and Microscale.

Right
Another classic bomber kit to 1/48th scale is Tamiya's superb Avro Lancaster B1 which incorporates numerous detail parts. The bomb bay includes a full complement of weapons and decals provide markings for three machines. The model was completely airbrushed using paper masks to achieve the upper pattern. After application of decals, the transparencies were masked out and the entire model sprayed in dulled polyurethane varnish.

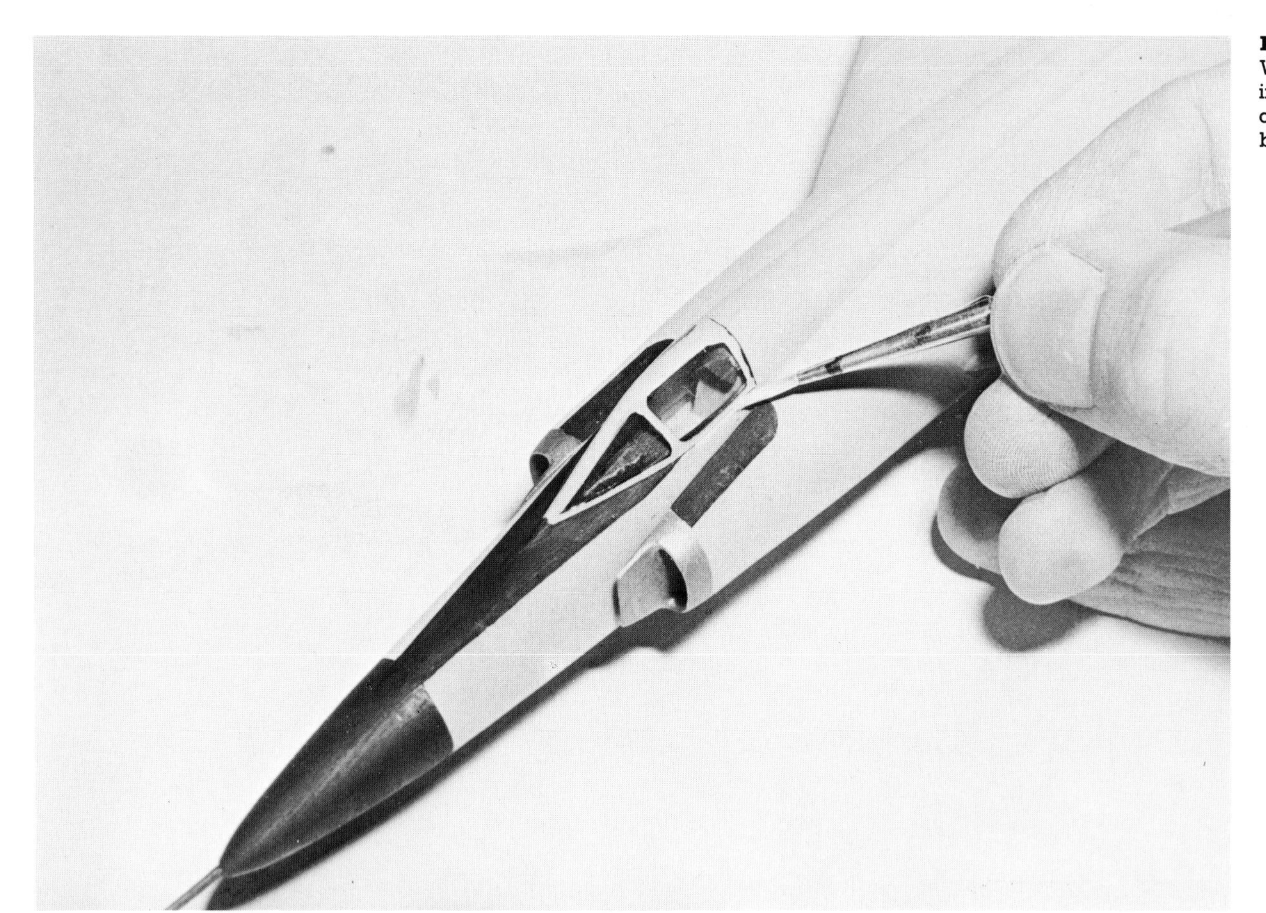

Left
When the canopy has been installed, any touching up can be done later with a fine brush as shown.

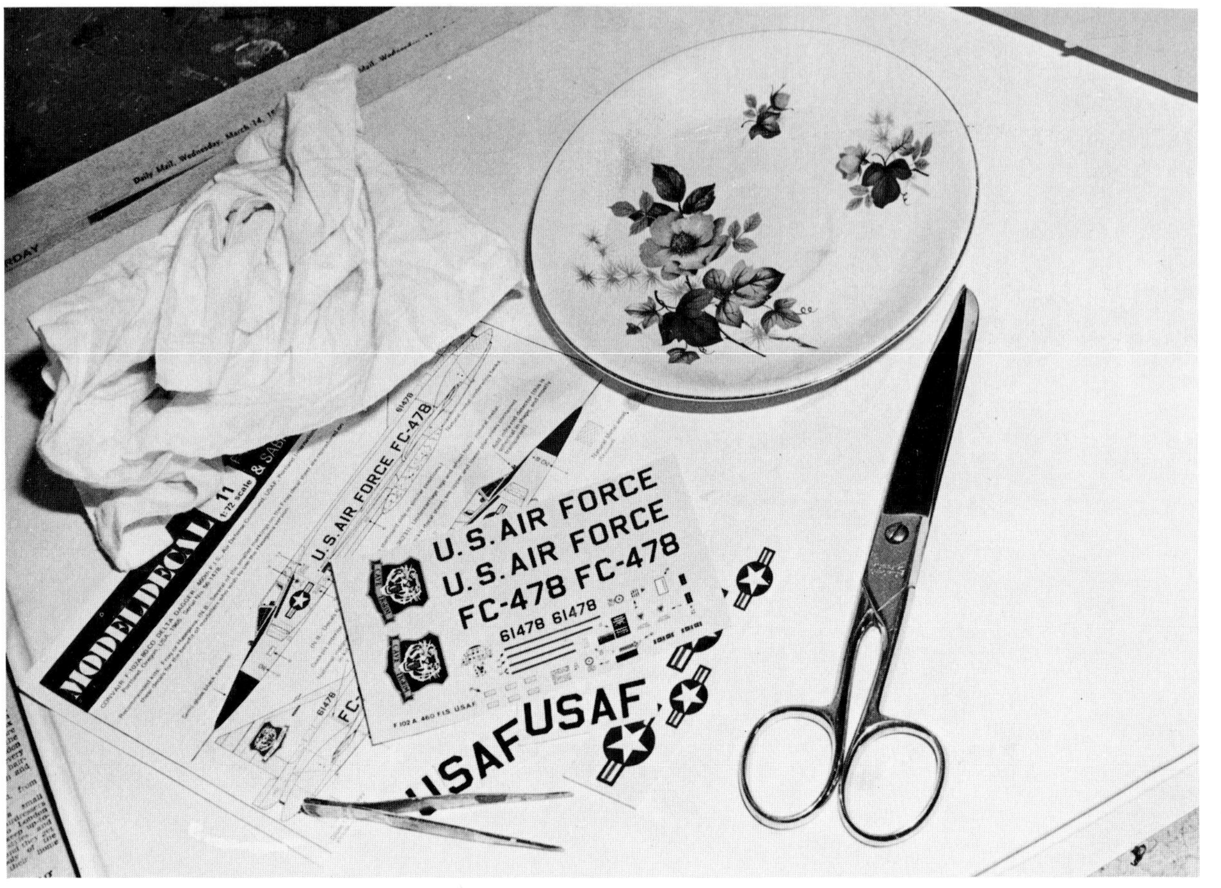

Left
All the basic 'equipment' for the application of decals: scissors, knife, tweezers, luke warm water and a lint-free cloth.

Above right and center right
Monogram's 1/48th Boeing B17G has recently been joined by Revell's B17E version and both exhibit impressive detail. This is the Monogram kit and remains one of their finest to date. Stains on upper wing were airbrushed by holding a paper mask in front of the vents and sweeping the airbrush away from the paper. Further weathering was achieved by buffing with lead graphite dust to represent scuffed metal.

Below right
Cockpit section of the Monogram B17 with a minimum of additional detail added. Careful painting and weathering is essential to create a more realistic impression. 'Maps' on the navigator's table are thin paper squares.

to which kit parts are attached can be used; again, heat the plastic and pull it to the required diameter.

Cockpit details which are not supplied with the kit can be constructed from plastic card (scribed where necessary), sprue, thin fuse wire and cotton. In making all additions it is important always to bear in mind the scale to which you are working. A good model can be spoiled by the inclusion of detail which is out of scale and this is particularly so with stringers made from sprue which has not been pulled thin enough. The question of scale is particularly important when making instrument panels, as it is all too easy to make dial faces of the wrong size. Close study of reference plans and photographs and care in scaling down will pay dividends here. If it is not possible to obtain a transfer sheet of the correct instrument panel which can be applied to painted plastic card, it will be necessary to make the whole panel yourself. If the scale is large enough to accommodate a fair amount of detail a good method is to use two pieces of plastic card cut

to the correct instrument panel shape. One card is painted black and used as a backing for the other, in which holes of the correct diameter for the scaled-down dials have been drilled. The matt black card can be painted with detail of the instrumentation before being cemented to the front of the panel. The effect of glass can be obtained by drops of clear varnish in the holes.

Where bulkheads are to be added it will be necessary to obtain an accurate profile of the internal fuselage shape at the point where the addition is to be made.

U.S. AIR FORCE
24428
FU-42
USAF

Above and below far left
The North American F86 Sabre was one of the earlier Hasegawa 1/32nd scale models and one of their best. Cockpit slides back to reveal complete interior detail, airbrake doors can be modelled open or shut and the whole rear fuselage can be detached to reveal a complete replica jet engine. Kit decals have been used here.

Top left
There are several Tomcat kits available in at least four different scales and this 1/72nd scale model by Airfix is probably one of the best. Finished in the old USN scheme of Gull Gray and White, Microscale decals have been applied and there is scope for further detail. Airfix provide a fully furnished cockpit and a full complement of weapons.

Above left
Like the Tomcat, F15 Eagle and F-16, the Mirage is highly popular with kit manufacturers. This Mirage III is a Revell 1/72nd scale kit and has been hand-painted and spray varnished with French Air Force decals from a commercial set by Modeldecal which include full stencil details. 'Remove before Flight' tag on nose probe is merely a red painted strip of paper.

Top right
The Airfix General Dynamics F-IIIE has recently been reintroduced with improvements over the earlier release. The complex three-color pattern was airbrushed using carefully cut paper masks, an extremely difficult procedure, over a complex shape and should be undertaken with care. The model is finished in temporary 1976 US Bicentennial markings – swing wings actually operate.

Above right
Another classic aircraft is the Convair F102 Delta Dagger and this Hasegawa model has been decorated with MicroScale decals. This would be an ideal subject for a beginner as the kit is easy to assemble and features a simple paint scheme of an overall single color.

This can be done by inserting a plug of Plasticine or modelling clay in the fuselage and molding it to the internal shape with the two fuselage halves held firmly together with elastic bands. Make sure that the Plasticine is pushed well into the curves. When the fuselage is separated you will have a plug which will provide a template for the shape of the bulkhead. Another method is to use solder wire inserted into the fuselage half and worked to the internal curvature. This half profile can be used to make the whole template by tracing around one side and then reversing it. Plasticine can also be used to determine the accurate shape of the fuselage over an area to be covered by a floor. The Plasticine is simply rolled soft and inserted in the bottom of the fuselage; place half at the point where the floor is to be positioned and press the second half on top to obtain an accurate impression, making sure that the top, at the floor level, is completely flat. As with the bulkhead, the resulting plug can be used as a template.

If the model is of that type of aircraft which has side consols, these can be made from plastic card built into boxes on the floor on either side of the cockpit, leaving sufficient space for the one or two seats to be inserted between them. Remember, too, that you may need to leave sufficient room for a central control pedestal as well and that if you are working to small scale – say, 1:72 – the amount of detail you can add without over-filling the cockpit is limited. On larger scales there is room to add further refinements such as hand levers for throttles, prop pitch, undercarriage selectors and control columns, consol switches and wiring looms. Levers can be made, depending on scale, from short clips of reasonably stout, single-strand wire, plastic rod or sprue – all suitably painted and with knobs made from small balls of putty or blobs of PVA adhesive. Switches can also be made from putty blobs, very small

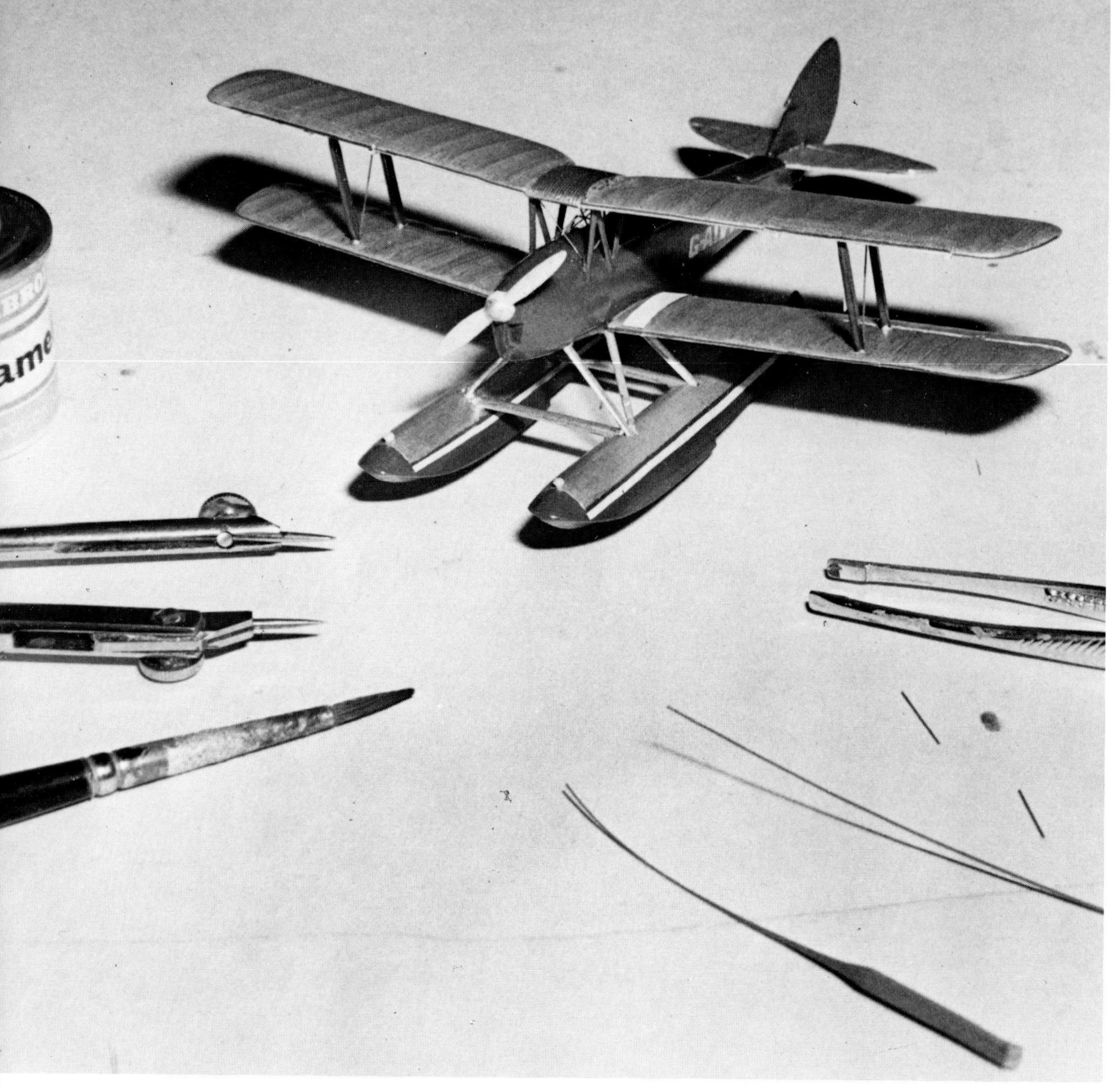

Above left and left
This Airfix Tiger Moth has been converted to floatplane configuration by using parts from a Japanese Cessna kit. The modification is simple enough yet the basic model can be even further improved by replacing the wings with those from a Frog Gypsy Moth. The model (left) is ready for rigging using stretched sprue attached by tweezers and using clear varnish as an adhesive.

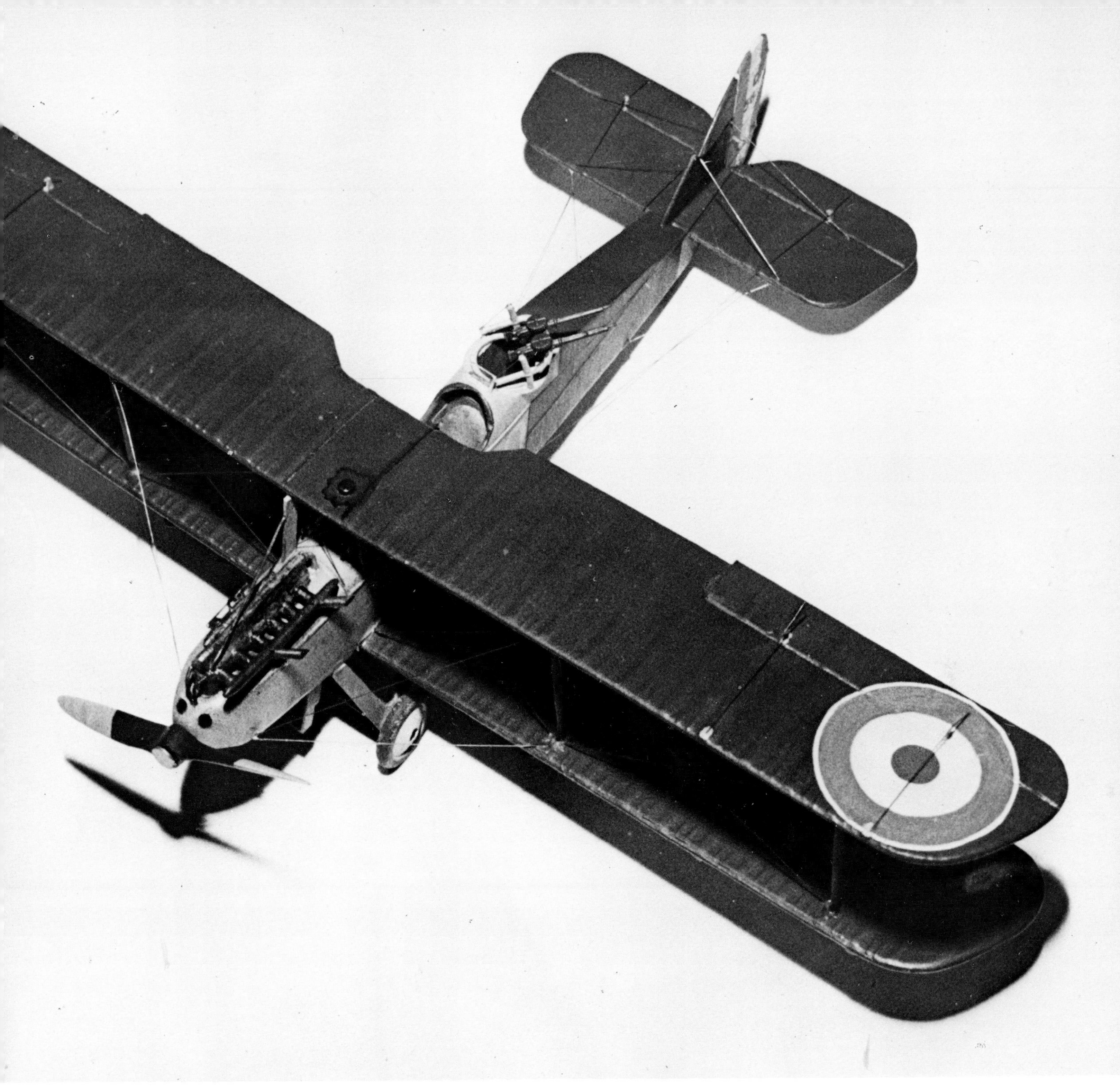

Conversion of the 1/72nd Airfix DH4 to DH9 configuration is effected by scratch-building a plastic card fuselage and grafting the remaining kit parts to it. Full engine and cockpit detailing has been applied and a new undercarriage fabricated from plastic sheet.

snippets of wire or sprue, or they can be scribed on to painted consol faces so that they show up as white lines. Again depending on scale, wiring can be from stretched sprue, cotton or cord ready-colored or painted the appropriate colors.

Before leaving the cockpit it is worth paying some attention to the pilot's seat. Though most kits now include more than just the basic 'bucket' and have added some detail, this is often shown as part of the molding or is inaccurate. Time spent on researching the correct type of seat and adding your own three dimensional detail is well worthwhile, particularly when you have taken the trouble to make the rest of the cockpit look realistic. Even though there is only a certain amount that can be done on 1:72 scale, the exercise is particularly worthwhile on large-scale models in which it is possible to include such refinements as linen safety harnesses with wire buckles, ejector seat firing handles, oxygen hoses, bomb sights, and navigator's instruments.

There is often quite a number of improvements which can be made to the external appearance of a kit model. It is not unusual to find that the trailing edges of wings or tailplanes are thicker than they should be. It is tempting to make the reduction on the outside edges of the two halves of these components, but this will almost certainly result in a wrong profile. Instead each half should be carefully reduced by sanding the inside surfaces on a flat surface. It is important to ensure that the sanding with wet and dry paper is carried out evenly across the surface and that each half is reduced by the same amount.

Wheel wells are areas which frequently call for attention. Wheel doors are very often supplied at almost twice their true-scale thickness, and these should be sanded down in a similar manner or can be replaced by new doors made from plastic card of the appropriate gauge. Another common failing is that the wheel wells are open to the inside of the aircraft and are not 'wells' at all. Strips of plastic card can be inserted around the edges of the well to form an enclosing wall and, if necessary, a recessed bulkhead. Fine detail of hydraulic systems, wiring, and so on can then be added.

A not uncommon error in some kits is for the intakes to be left hollow so that daylight can be seen through

Above and below
The Messerschmitt Me 363 six motor transport of World War II was undoubtedly a most impressive aircraft and so is this Revell/Italaerei replica to 1/72nd scale. Spanning nearly 3 feet, this is one of the largest plastic kits on the market, yet in no way is it the most expensive. The model was camouflaged by airbrushing and much added detail to the capacious interior. More ambitious modellers could take the opportunity of creating a diorama with additional figures and suitably scaled tanks or soft-skinned vehicles.

Above
Before the Me 323 came the Me 321, a huge transport glider that required a specially adapted twin fuselaged Heinkel bomber to tow it. Here the glider is disgorging a Panzer IV tank as officers look on. This is another Revell/Italaerei model which has had the entire fuselage interior detailed with fine plastic rod prior to assembly. Loading ramps are mainly scratch-built from strips of plastic sheet and the figures are based on those found in commercial ranges.

Left
A Revell Fokker DVII in the process of assembly with all sprue struts in place and awaiting installation of upper wing. As with most biplane models, full painting and application of decals are undertaken prior to final assembly. A tooth-pick in the propeller shaft hole makes for easy handling while completing final details.

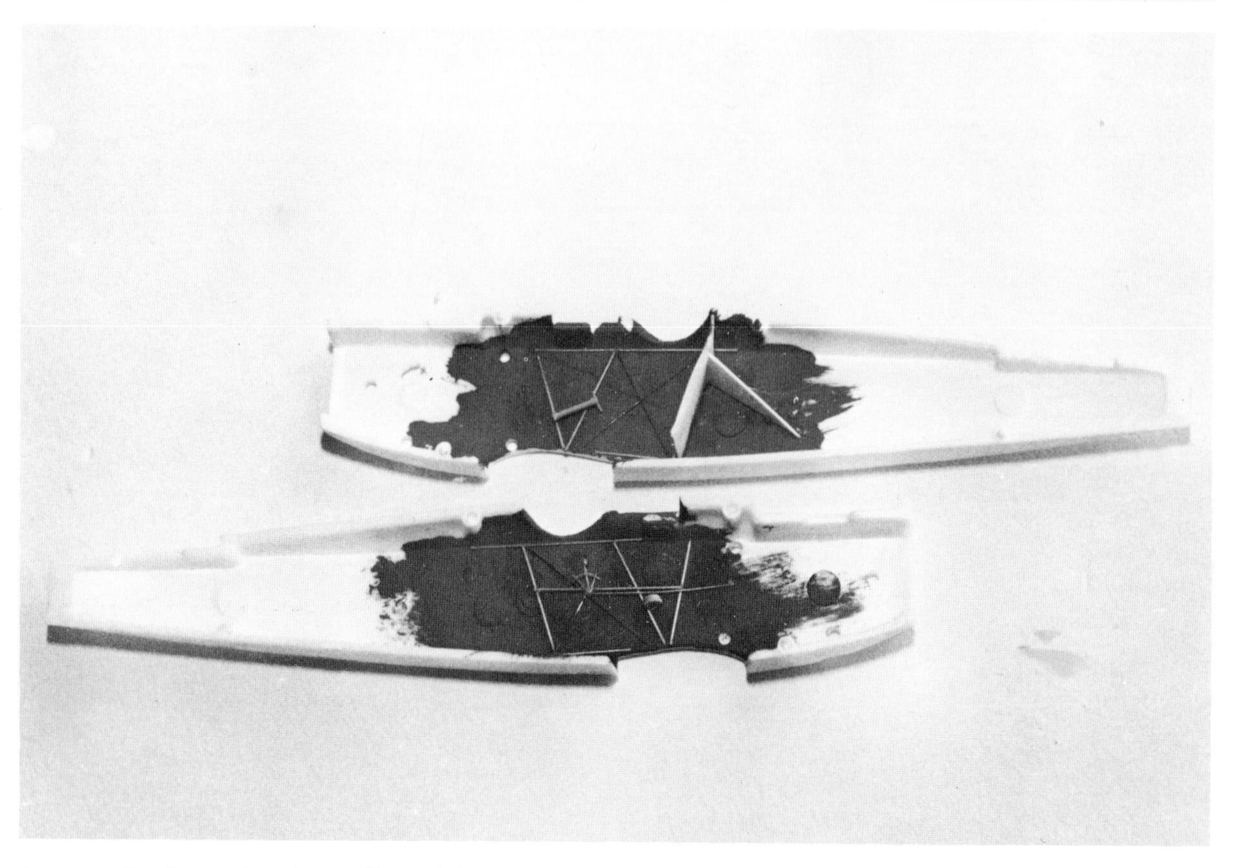

Left
This Revell 1/72nd scale Fokker DVII has had the fuselage sides fully detailed with stretched sprue 'structure' and wire rigging applied. Also added are the magneto, throttle quadrant, compass and pressure pumps all fabricated from scrap. Other instruments are added to the cockpit after the fuselage halves are assembled.

them, totally destroying the realism of the model. In such cases the offending parts should be blanked off with discs of plastic card or cardboard painted black and set far enough back in the intake or tail pipe not to be intrusive.

A small sin of omission but one which will be spotted immediately by the experienced modeller is to complete a model and fail to check whether the cockpit canopy looks right. In large aircraft and bombers entry was usually by hatches and the canopy itself was an integral part of the body, while in fighters it was of the lifting or sliding variety. In the latter case it is correct for the canopy to be fixed in its chosen position, with a distinct line between the glazing and the body structure. Where the canopy was 'built-in' that line should not be apparent. The gap should be filled with a little putty which is then gently dry sanded, finishing off with the finest wet and dry. Any abrasions on the canopy can be removed with a gentle abrasive paste such as jeweller's paste or tooth powder. This paste can, incidentally, also

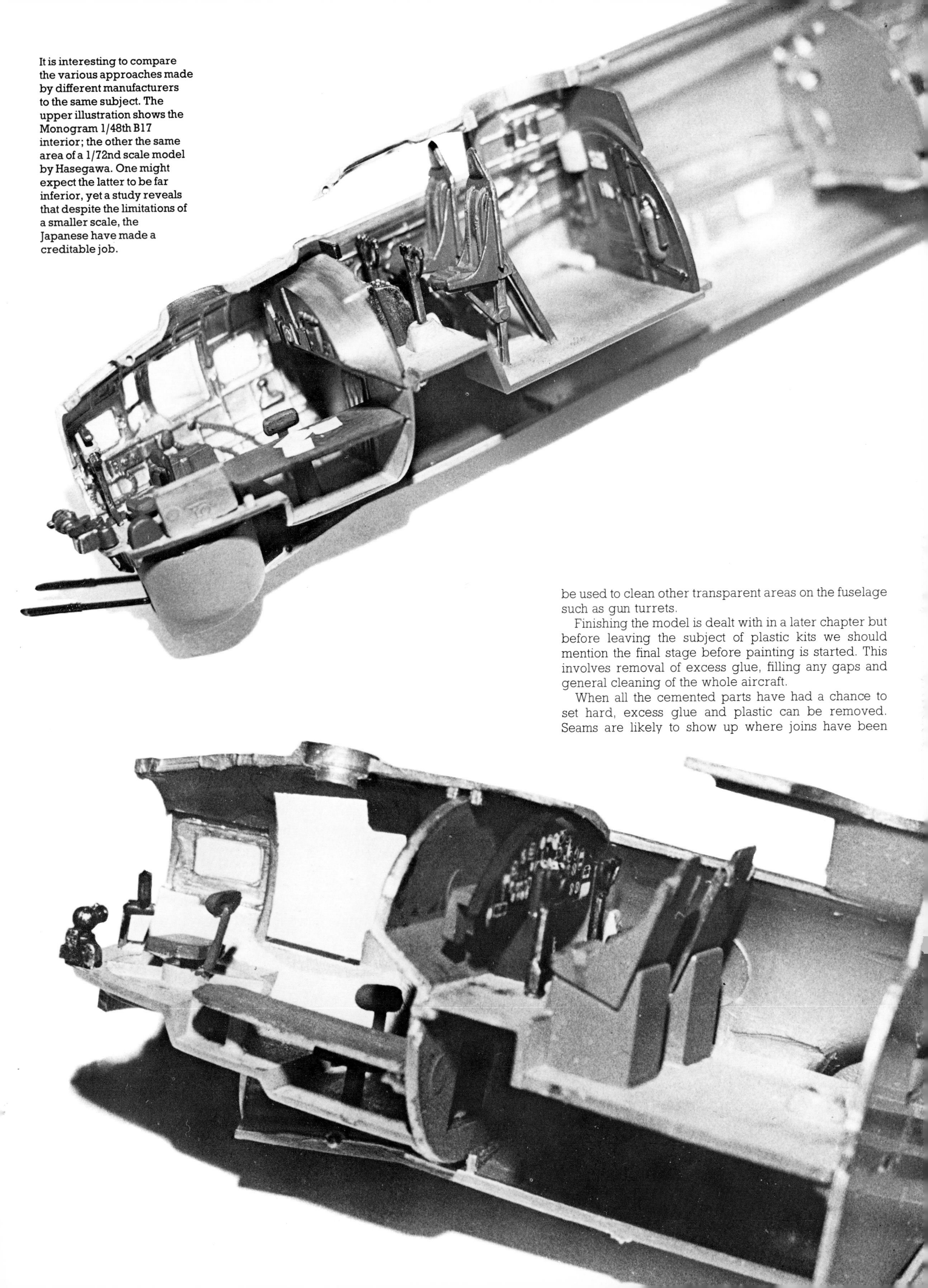

It is interesting to compare the various approaches made by different manufacturers to the same subject. The upper illustration shows the Monogram 1/48th B17 interior; the other the same area of a 1/72nd scale model by Hasegawa. One might expect the latter to be far inferior, yet a study reveals that despite the limitations of a smaller scale, the Japanese have made a creditable job.

be used to clean other transparent areas on the fuselage such as gun turrets.

Finishing the model is dealt with in a later chapter but before leaving the subject of plastic kits we should mention the final stage before painting is started. This involves removal of excess glue, filling any gaps and general cleaning of the whole aircraft.

When all the cemented parts have had a chance to set hard, excess glue and plastic can be removed. Seams are likely to show up where joins have been

Above left
Civil vintage 'airliners' are rare in kit ranges and the Airfix Ford Trimotor is almost unique in this field. Corrugated wing surfaces present special problems when applying decals, yet commercially available decal solvents are a great help on such surfaces. The model, to 1/72nd scale, has been airbrushed – control cables are from fine wire.

Above right
Airliners make popular modelling subjects, especially now that there are so many commercial livery decals available. This modified Airfix kit Boeing 707 is finished in the colors of Iraqi Airlines and required careful painting and masking to achieve the scheme as presented. Windows in the fuselage are formed by a special liquid which dries as a transparent 'pane.' The whole is then varnished in clear semi-gloss finish.

Below
The Airfix 1/144th Concorde is the best kitted version of the supersonic airliner and the careful reproduction of the undulating wing leading edges is most noteworthy. This would also be an ideal subject for the novice, with a simple white paint scheme and a minimal number of parts.

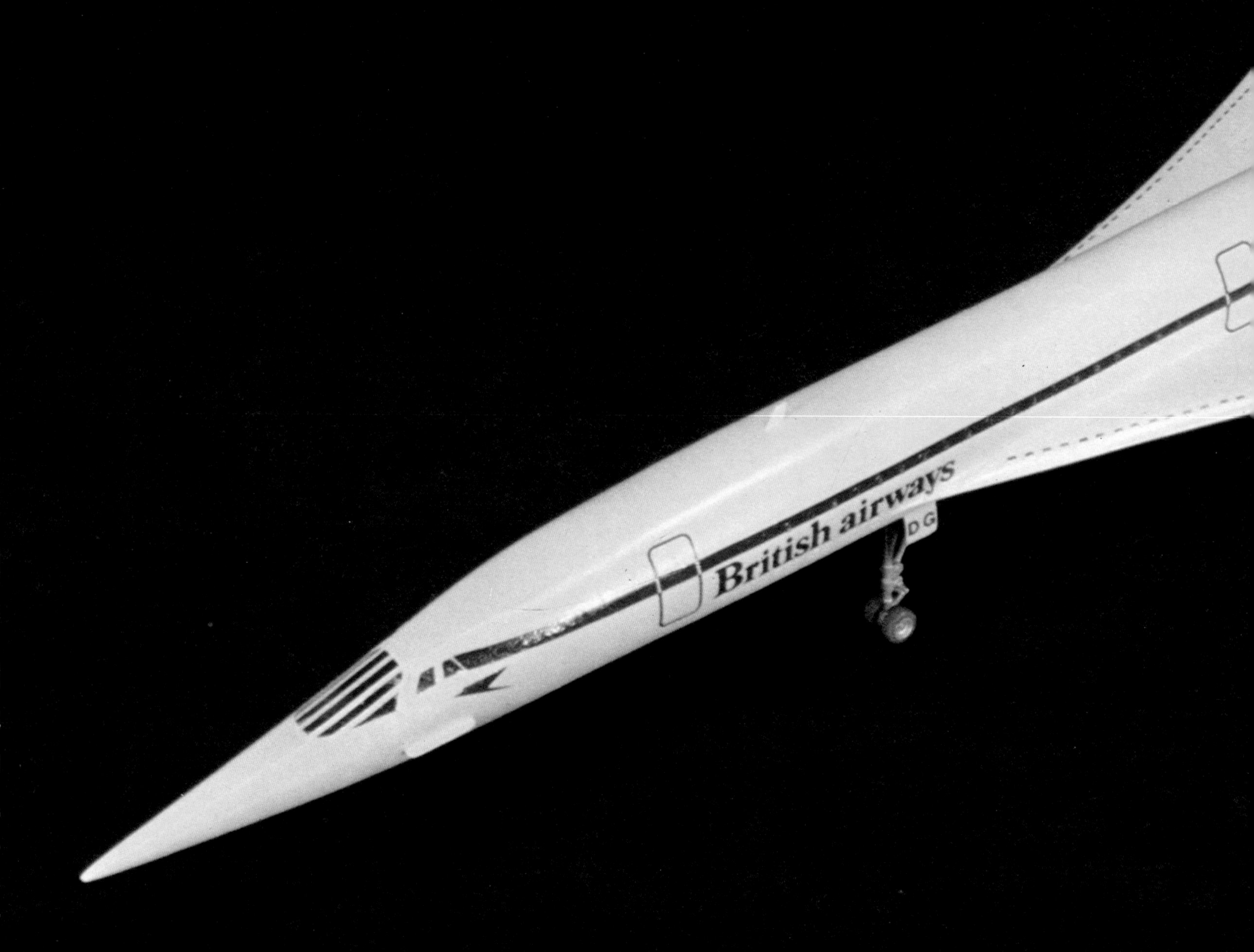

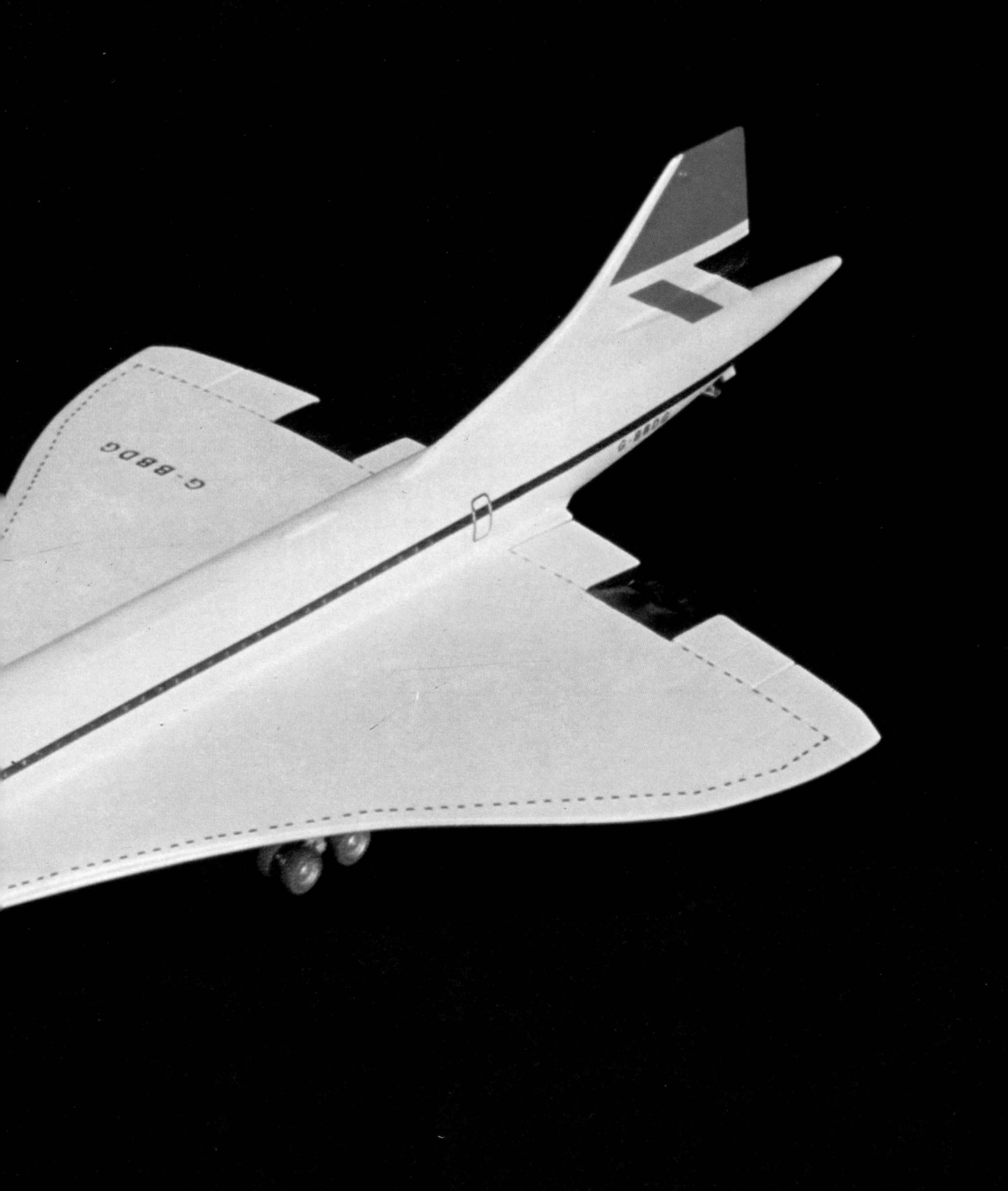
G-BBDG

Right and below
The Tamiya Lancaster contains a fair number of interior parts – yet even these can be improved upon. A new support has been made for the navigator's table, the pilot's seat has had a seat harness added and extra consoles, throttle arms, and reworked instrument panel. Such detail is rarely wasted on a large model and the modeller can cut away portions of the canopy (if molded in one piece) so that even more of the interior can be viewed on completion.

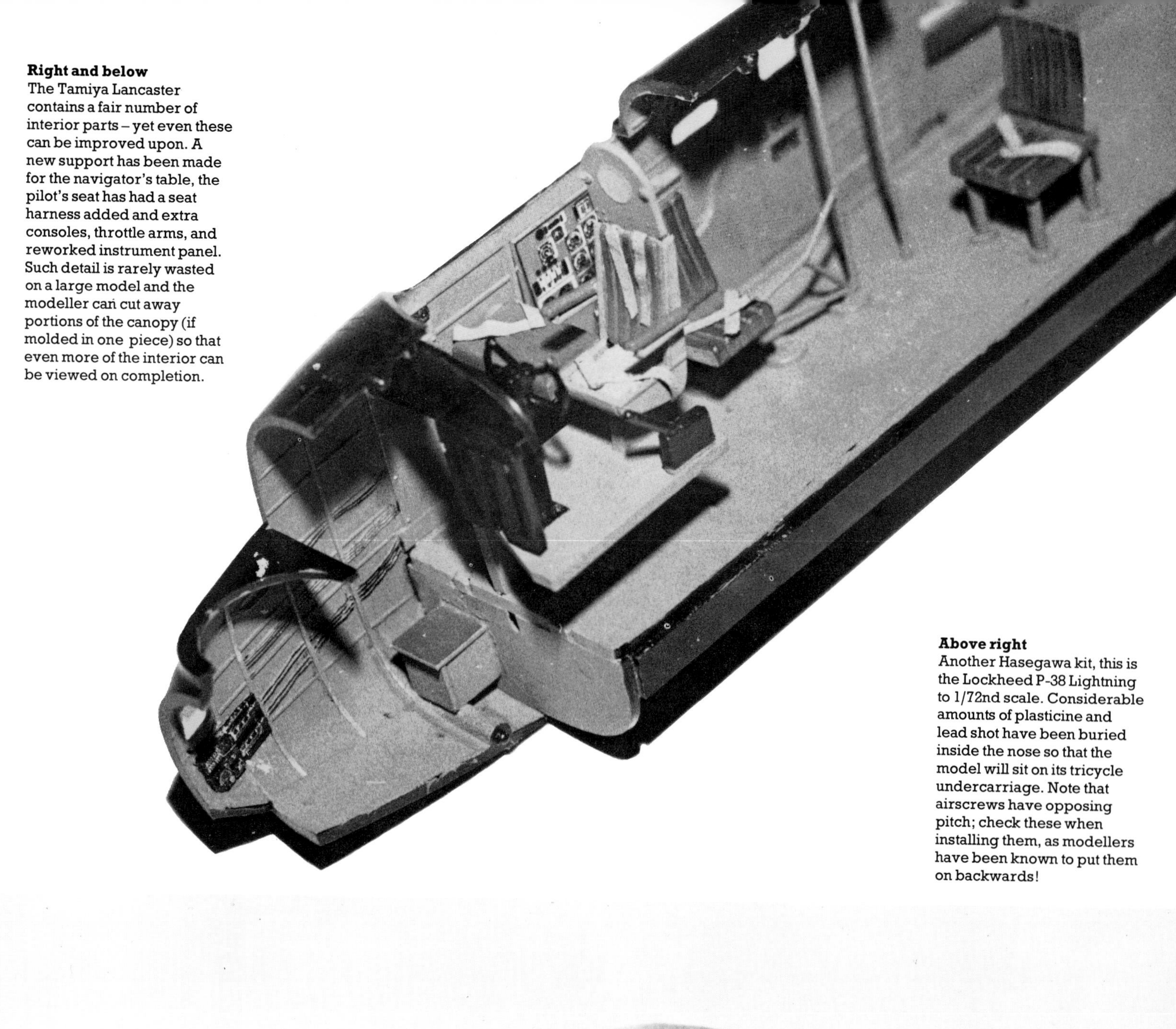

Above right
Another Hasegawa kit, this is the Lockheed P-38 Lightning to 1/72nd scale. Considerable amounts of plasticine and lead shot have been buried inside the nose so that the model will sit on its tricycle undercarriage. Note that airscrews have opposing pitch; check these when installing them, as modellers have been known to put them on backwards!

made because the cement melts the plastic surfaces before hardening. These can best be removed by scraping with a modelling knife which is quite blunt, making sure that it is not used as a cutter but only to shave the protruding lips of plastic. Once the seam has virtually disappeared, wet and dry paper of a fairly fine grade takes the place of the scraper to continue the work of smoothing. Finally a finer grade is used with plenty of water. A gentle buffing with metal polish will restore the treated part to its original finish.

Below
Revell Sopwith Triplane fitted with twin Vickers machine guns and representing the aircraft now in the RAF Museum at Hendon. The engine cowl has been covered in thin foil to represent highly polished metal and all rigging is from fine sprue.

It is likely that during this work some surface detail will have been removed, such as panel lines or rivets. In fact many models bear rivet impressions where flush riveting has been used on the original and are therefore inaccurate in this detail. The 'rivet heads' can be quite simply removed by knife blade or wet and dry paper, depending upon their size. Panel lines which have been inadvertently removed can be rescribed, but again there is a tendency to mark them in where no such line would appear on the full-size aircraft. This is mainly

Revell's 1/28th scale Fokker DR1 Triplane much modified with full interior detail represents Manfred von Richofen's 425/17 in which he was killed in April 1918. The model later formed part of a diorama of the crash site (above left). The markings are thought to present accurately the last color scheme change of this famous aircraft, and the red color was matched to existing fabric patches for absolute authenticity, being nearer vermillion than scarlet.

true in the case of models on which panel lines are shown as ridges. Since these lines are an indication of where panels meet flush, to represent them as raised edges is incorrect. Check, too, that where panel lines have been inscribed by the kit makers the indentations are not too thick for the scale. In either case – ridges or out-of-scale lines – remove the offending marks and replace with very fine scribed lines.

Where excess glue is present it should always be allowed to dry, when it can be removed with a sharp knife and the surface restored with wet and dry. *Never* try to wipe wet glue as this will spread the solvent liquid and cause damage to a wider area of the model.

Any gap between joints should be filled with body putty, using a strong wooden spatula or the tip of a small screwdriver to work the putty in and smooth off the surface. Continue by filling any dents or blemishes there may be on the body.

The last step before painting is to remove all grease from the model by washing it thoroughly in a luke warm mixture of water and liquid detergent, thereafter using a clean cloth or tissue if it is being handled.

Below
With the converted Jumbo Jet carrying the Orbiter Enterprise, the Space Shuttle is one of the most amazing sights in the aviation world. The subject has been seized upon by several kit manufacturers and the version shown here is by Revell.

Right
The Revell MiG 21PFS variant is to 1/32nd scale and built here by Alec Gee. The model is finished in Syrian scheme of dark olive green, sand and light blue and has been hand painted. Exceptionally detailed, the model features opened canopy, speed brake and full cockpit interior.

Plastic from Scratch

One of the most rewarding of all modelling pursuits is that of scratch-building an aircraft yourself, making all the parts through your own craftsmanship, and that certain degree of ingenuity which must accompany any modeller along the path to successful completion of his work.

Before dealing with the subject generally it may be as well to clear up a point or two about the term 'scratch-building.' It is true to say that the term is nowadays in common use and is applied to modellers who build their models from parts which they have made entirely themselves, augmented sometimes by 'spares' from kits but relying very much upon ingenuity and upon the use of plastic card.

It is equally true to say that those who are involved in plastic card modelling detest the use of the description 'scratch-building.' Harry Woodman, a prize-winning plastic card modeller and respected author on the subject, recently wrote to me saying, 'The term "scratch-built," apart from sounding rather unhygienic, was invented by the plastic kit modellers and seems to suggest that it was a by-product of kit assembling. In fact, most of the people who build in plastic card are people in middle age who built models long before the plastic kit epidemic started. They built in wood and card and merely adapted plastic (polystyrene) card when it appeared in the 1960s.'

He continued: 'The other reason why the correct term should be used is that it uses many techniques known for decades by card modellers (or paper modellers as they are sometimes called). In fact plastic card modelling owes almost everything to card modelling and nothing to kit-building. The fact is that if plastic kits were not available about 95 per cent of the kit modellers would be helpless. . . . Very many superb model builders are completely unknown to the general public because they build in their own way and do not, as a rule, contribute to modelling magazines, which have become largely plastic kit model magazines. . . .

'My definition of a modeller, plastic or otherwise, is someone who can sit down at a work bench with a handful of raw materials and basic tools and create a miniature of the original, using his skill and knowledge.'

That seems to me to be a fair statement of the case for plastic card modellers. However, in this chapter we shall be dealing with a somewhat wider field which, for

Below
Scratch-built 1/48th scale De Havilland DH2 with only the wheels and nacelle having their origin in kit components. The wings are made from plastic sheet scored and folded over balsa cores. Rigging and tail booms are from stretched sprue and all markings are hand painted. This model represents a machine of No 24 Squadron RFC.

many, will be entered only *after* initial experience and confidence has been gained from basic kit-building. Some of the techniques involved apply not only to static models but also to the making of parts for flying models. I can find no more convenient a description than scratch-building.

For each type there are two basic elements which are essential for success – patience and absolute accuracy; the latter will not be achieved without the former. A further requirement is an accurate set of plans plus an adequate back-up of suitable photographs of the aircraft chosen as your subject. These are not only useful for showing up any inaccuracies which may be incorporated in the plan but also are a useful key to the positioning of detail which will be added later and even of weathering stains which you may wish to include in finishing the model.

The choice of subject is of course a matter for the individual, but a beginner would be well advised to select an aircraft which has fairly simple lines, such as a Comper Swift, a MiG 15, a Mitsubishi Zero or a Fokker D V111. Plans for any of these are available or you may wish to prepare your own and choose the scale which best suits you.

For the modeller who is also something of a do-it-yourself man, scratch-building presents an opportunity to enter the field of vacuum-forming by constructing a homemade vac-form machine which is far cheaper than those which are available commercially. All that is required is a box made from quite thick ply (about 15mm) with four sides and a base. In one side cut an opening to accept the pipe or hose of your ordinary household vacuum cleaner as a tight fit. To make the inlet airtight it can be lined with rubber or the tube can be sealed in place with any of the strong sticky tape with a fabric base. The actual size of this box will depend upon the size of the model and also on the fact that the greater its area, the less efficient will be the suck of the vacuum cleaner. All the joints should be thoroughly sealed.

The top of the box is made from an outer rectangle of thick wood surrounding what will be the molding area of the machine, which must be made big enough to accept the largest part of the aircraft to be molded. This outer rectangle can be used to mark out the size of the removable frames required to hold the plastic sheet molding material in position. Three frames are required, two of ply, between which the plastic card will be sandwiched, and a bottom one cut from aluminum. The bottom ply frame is bonded to the aluminum with

Below
Two views of a 1/72nd scale BE2c which, apart from modified kit wings and various small items, is completely scratch-built from plastic sheet and scrap plastic. Fully rigged with 44 swg wire, the model has complete cockpit detail and represents one of the machines flown by Lt W L Robinson of 39 Squadron RFC.

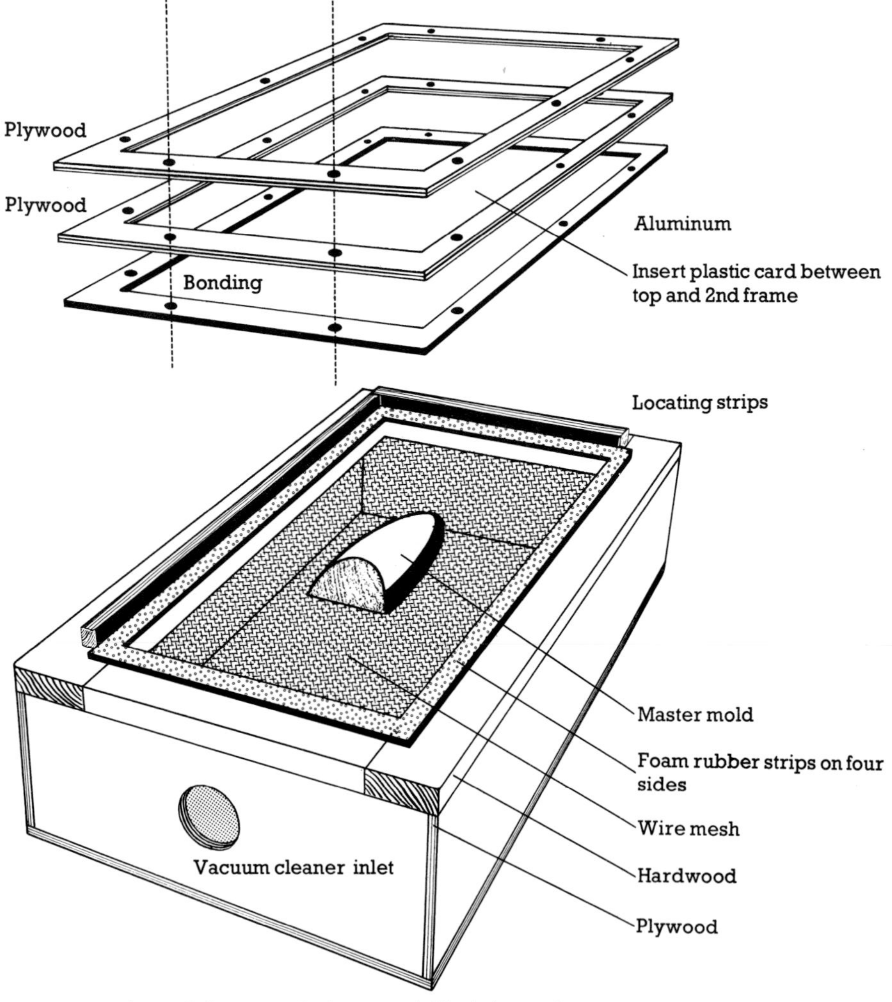

an epoxy resin and then two holes are drilled through each side of the three-decker sandwich. When the plastic card from which a shape is to be vacuum formed is placed between the top frame and the lower bonded pair, it is drilled with holes in the same locations and held in place by bolts, the heads of which are countersunk in the aluminum. Wing nuts secure the bolts and make for easy loading and unloading. The lid is completed by securely fixing a rectangle of strong wire mesh to the inside edges of the outer wood frame which is attached to the box. On this mesh will rest the master molds to be used for the aircraft parts. It is, therefore, important that the wood used to make the frame of the lid be deep enough to form a molding bed which will accept the widest cross section of any part to be formed within it.

Around the outer edge of the molding area stick strips of draft excluding foam upon which the removable molding frames will rest over the master mold. After positioning the molding frame over the molding area of the box satisfactorily in a 'dummy run' to check that there is no warp to break the vacuum, keep the frame in position while you fix two locating strips of wood along one long and one short side of the box lid using the quick-setting epoxy as an adhesive.

When the plastic card to be used to make a part has been secured in the movable frame, place the master mold on the wire mesh bed and switch on the vacuum cleaner. Then hold the frame in front of a reasonably hot heater, moving it slightly up and down and side to side to ensure even distribution of heat. Alternatively, if the frame is not too big, slip it under the cooker grill (broiler), having given the grill a chance to heat up first. In either case, protect your hands with oven gloves. As soon as the plastic shows signs of being sufficiently pliable all over remove the frame quickly from the heat source and place it, aluminum side down, over the molding area. The plastic will be sucked over the master mold to its exact shape. When the shape appears rigid, switch off the vacuum cleaner. The molded shape can be cut out of the plastic card once it has cooled and the edges trimmed and finished with modelling knife, scraper and sandpaper.

Above
Home-made vac-form machine
Right
A 1/24th scale LVG CV1 completely built from plastic sheet with markings and camouflage hand painted and the interior fully detailed. In fact, the fuselage formers are properly scaled-down versions of the originals, complete with fittings and reinforcing plates. Wheels are sprung with fine elastic representing the original bungee and full rigging is from fine gray thread.

This model of a Nieuport 24 bis used the fuselage of a Hawk kit as a base over which a new outside surface was skinned in thin plastic card. The remainder was built entirely from plastic card techniques.

N
1895

One of the advantages of the vac-forming process is that it does not require two molds, male and female, for each part. On the other hand it does require just as high a degree of accuracy in finishing the master mold as is needed in making male and female molds.

In the latter case if you are making a fuselage, for example, it is necessary to build an accurate, solid wood version of the fuselage from two blocks of balsa joined along what will either be the horizontal or vertical center line. Make sure the run of the grain in the two blocks matches. The shape of the fuselage is then transferred to the blocks by one of the methods described in an earlier chapter and the wood is cut to shape using modelling knife, razor plane set fine, and finished with glass paper and finest sandpaper after filling any blemishes. The shape should be checked constantly against the templates.

When this solid version of the fuselage is completed it is split at the center line and the two halves are used as the templates for the female molds. Add temporary handles of block balsa to the inside faces of each half. Lay the two halves over a sheet of balsa about $^1/_4$in thick and carefully draw around the outlines. Cut through these shapes very accurately so that the male molds will pass through, leaving a clearance equal to the thickness of the plastic card from which you are making the fuselage – about 30thou is usually sufficient. Since the male mold is going to be pushed through this shape with a covering of hot plastic it is a sensible thing to add four short legs of block balsa to each corner of the sheet in which the female mold has been cut to provide clearance above the work surface.

Now pin the plastic sheet to this frame or use four heavy-duty paper clamps for the purpose. Draw in the

Left
Winner of the 1969 Model Engineering Exhibition Championship Cup in its class: the Harry Woodman plastic card model of the Boulton Paul Overstrand. It was the first plastic card model to gain the class championship cup.

Bottom
Another Woodman plastic card model from his own drawing, the Blackburn 'Blackburd.'

Below
Harry Woodman's model of an Avia BH 33 in Polish colors built from his own drawings in plastic card.

outline of the fuselage half exactly over the cut-out shape in the balsa to indicate where the male mold must be pushed through. (This is best done by holding the frame up to strong light and tracing around the shape.)

As with the vac-form process, the plastic is heated until it is soft, first curling toward the heat source and then tending to sag and smoke. At this stage, remove it from the heat, place it on the work surface and press the male mold through the shaped section of the female mold to just below the top surface of the frame.

It is important to apply a firm, even pressure at right angles to the frame and to judge the pliable state of the plastic accurately. If it is too hot there is a likelihood that the male mold will pass straight through the card (which will also happen if the card is too thin), or the finished molding will be too thin; if the card is not hot enough, or if there is insufficient clearance between the two molds, the male will not pass through or, if it does it will cause stretch marks and pull the card too thin.

The male mold should be left in position while the plastic cools. It can then be removed and the card bearing the molded shape can be taken off the frame. The shape is cut from the card and brought to the correct dimensions using wet and dry paper. Repeat the process for the other half of the fuselage and then cut in any locating slots or holes when the plastic has cooled.

Another method of building a fuselage using plastic card is the box construction in which top, bottom and sides are cut to shape and butt jointed, with bulkheads added at suitable points such as fore and aft of the cockpit. There are few aircraft types which lend themselves to this method on its own and many benefit from a combination of molding and box building.

A fine model of a Supermarine Walrus on a Scott McTaggart catapult. The aircraft's builder, Harry Woodman, utilized old Merit kit hull and wings scraped down to hulks on which the model was built. The model won the 1978 Model Engineering Exhibition Championship Cup and was built mainly to show off the complicated catapult structure.

K
559

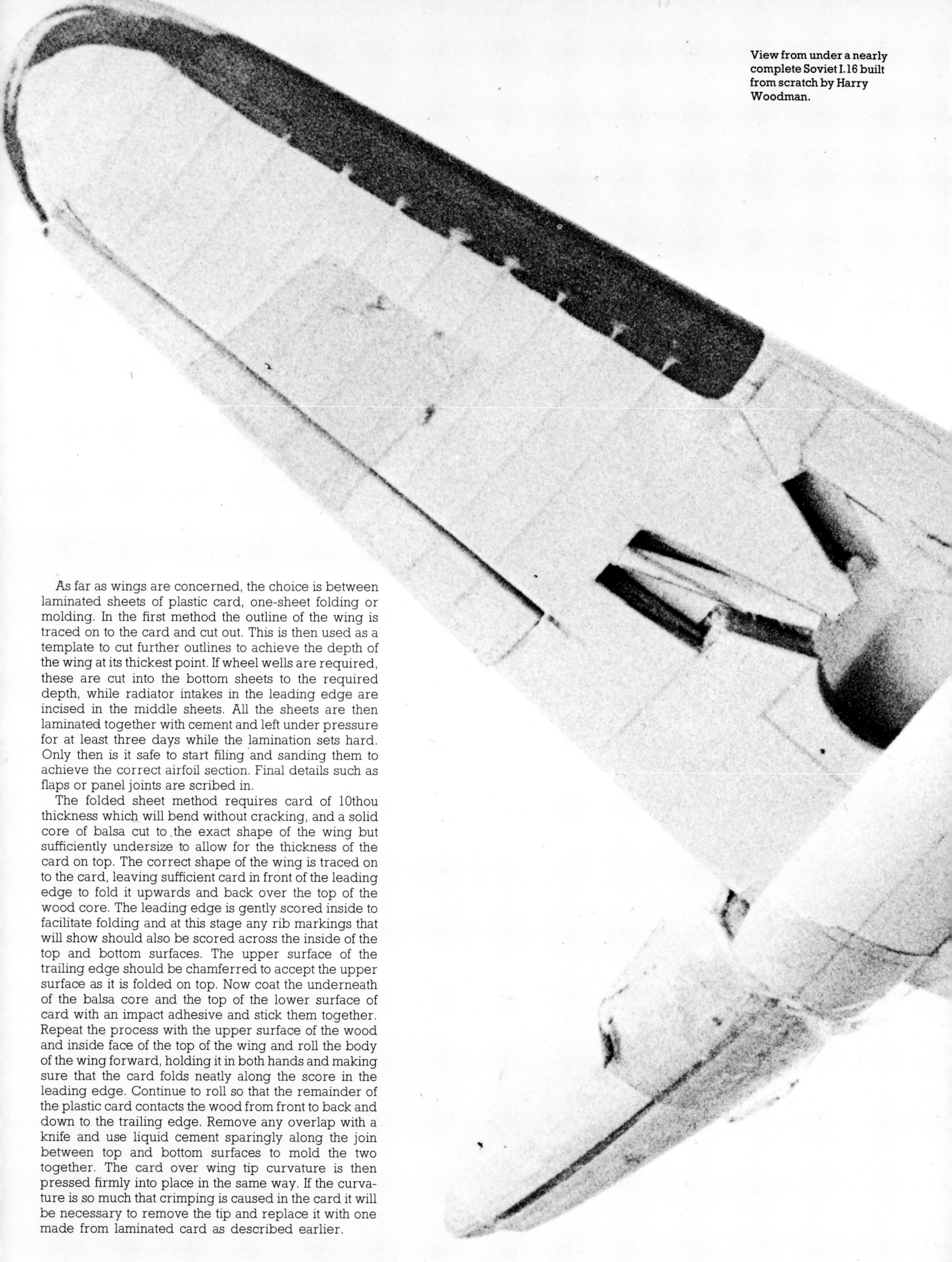

View from under a nearly complete Soviet I.16 built from scratch by Harry Woodman.

As far as wings are concerned, the choice is between laminated sheets of plastic card, one-sheet folding or molding. In the first method the outline of the wing is traced on to the card and cut out. This is then used as a template to cut further outlines to achieve the depth of the wing at its thickest point. If wheel wells are required, these are cut into the bottom sheets to the required depth, while radiator intakes in the leading edge are incised in the middle sheets. All the sheets are then laminated together with cement and left under pressure for at least three days while the lamination sets hard. Only then is it safe to start filing and sanding them to achieve the correct airfoil section. Final details such as flaps or panel joints are scribed in.

The folded sheet method requires card of 10thou thickness which will bend without cracking, and a solid core of balsa cut to the exact shape of the wing but sufficiently undersize to allow for the thickness of the card on top. The correct shape of the wing is traced on to the card, leaving sufficient card in front of the leading edge to fold it upwards and back over the top of the wood core. The leading edge is gently scored inside to facilitate folding and at this stage any rib markings that will show should also be scored across the inside of the top and bottom surfaces. The upper surface of the trailing edge should be chamferred to accept the upper surface as it is folded on top. Now coat the underneath of the balsa core and the top of the lower surface of card with an impact adhesive and stick them together. Repeat the process with the upper surface of the wood and inside face of the top of the wing and roll the body of the wing forward, holding it in both hands and making sure that the card folds neatly along the score in the leading edge. Continue to roll so that the remainder of the plastic card contacts the wood from front to back and down to the trailing edge. Remove any overlap with a knife and use liquid cement sparingly along the join between top and bottom surfaces to mold the two together. The card over wing tip curvature is then pressed firmly into place in the same way. If the curvature is so much that crimping is caused in the card it will be necessary to remove the tip and replace it with one made from laminated card as described earlier.

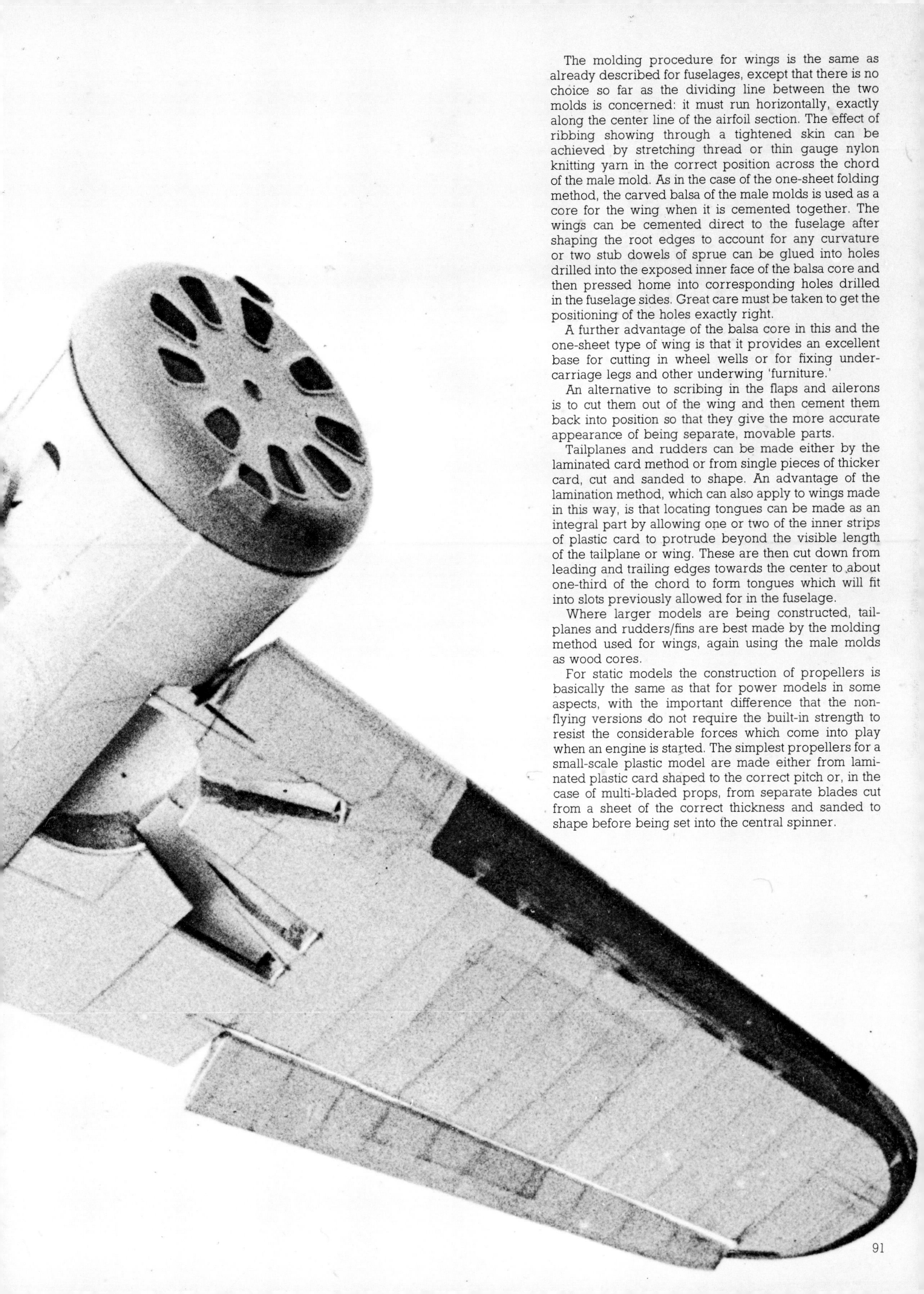

The molding procedure for wings is the same as already described for fuselages, except that there is no choice so far as the dividing line between the two molds is concerned: it must run horizontally, exactly along the center line of the airfoil section. The effect of ribbing showing through a tightened skin can be achieved by stretching thread or thin gauge nylon knitting yarn in the correct position across the chord of the male mold. As in the case of the one-sheet folding method, the carved balsa of the male molds is used as a core for the wing when it is cemented together. The wings can be cemented direct to the fuselage after shaping the root edges to account for any curvature or two stub dowels of sprue can be glued into holes drilled into the exposed inner face of the balsa core and then pressed home into corresponding holes drilled in the fuselage sides. Great care must be taken to get the positioning of the holes exactly right.

A further advantage of the balsa core in this and the one-sheet type of wing is that it provides an excellent base for cutting in wheel wells or for fixing undercarriage legs and other underwing 'furniture.'

An alternative to scribing in the flaps and ailerons is to cut them out of the wing and then cement them back into position so that they give the more accurate appearance of being separate, movable parts.

Tailplanes and rudders can be made either by the laminated card method or from single pieces of thicker card, cut and sanded to shape. An advantage of the lamination method, which can also apply to wings made in this way, is that locating tongues can be made as an integral part by allowing one or two of the inner strips of plastic card to protrude beyond the visible length of the tailplane or wing. These are then cut down from leading and trailing edges towards the center to about one-third of the chord to form tongues which will fit into slots previously allowed for in the fuselage.

Where larger models are being constructed, tailplanes and rudders/fins are best made by the molding method used for wings, again using the male molds as wood cores.

For static models the construction of propellers is basically the same as that for power models in some aspects, with the important difference that the non-flying versions do not require the built-in strength to resist the considerable forces which come into play when an engine is started. The simplest propellers for a small-scale plastic model are made either from laminated plastic card shaped to the correct pitch or, in the case of multi-bladed props, from separate blades cut from a sheet of the correct thickness and sanded to shape before being set into the central spinner.

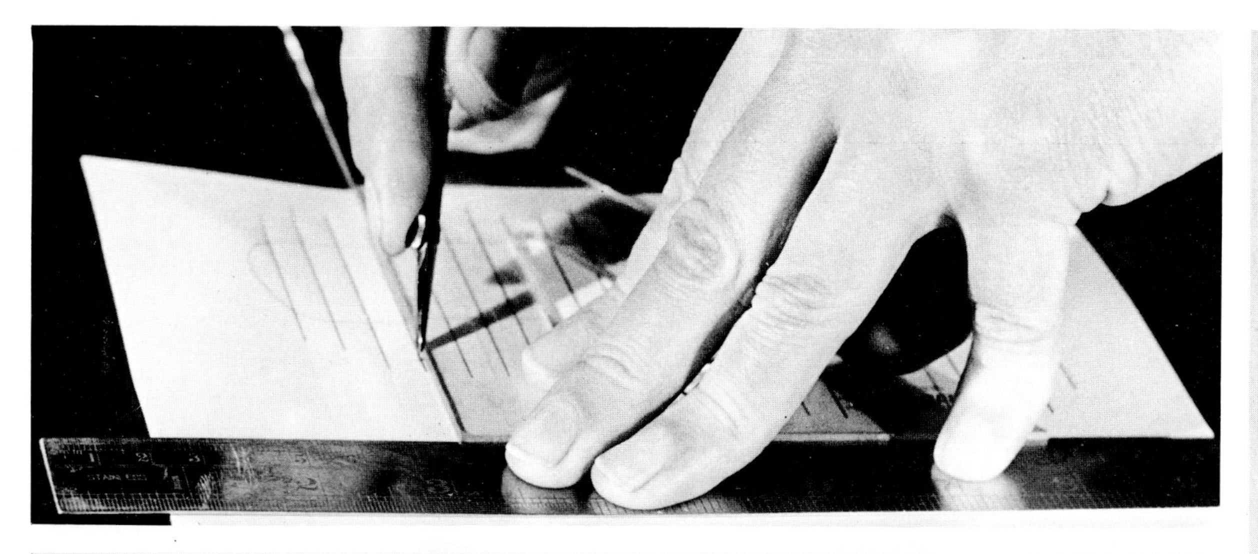

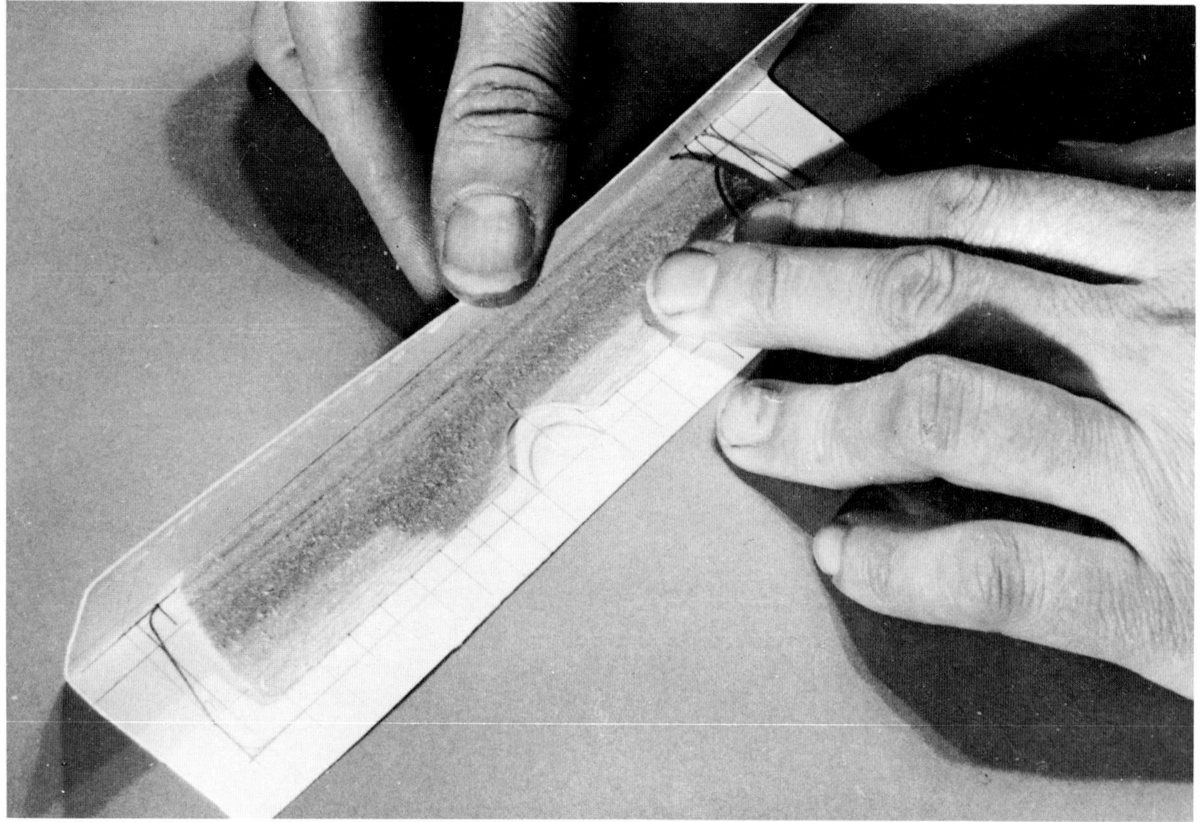

Vintage aircraft can be provided with beautiful propellers by using wood veneers of two different colors. Strips of the veneers are cut to be slightly over-width and a little longer than the diameter required in the finished propeller and are glued together with a good wood glue, alternating the veneer colors and building up the lamination to the required thickness. The center point is marked at exactly right angles when the glue has thoroughly set. The shape of the prop is marked out on the front of the block, which is then carved to shape. A sensible precaution against damaging the central boss during the carving and of ensuring that it is perfectly round is to protect it by fixing metal washers, discs or coins of the required diameter to the front and back of the center. Having carved the front elevation, which is a simple enough operation, the more complicated task of carving the propeller to the correct airfoil section is then undertaken. Here experience and constant checking are the only real answer – plus a predetermination of exactly what profile you want in the propeller. After removing the metal washers, finish off by sanding, applying a coat of clear varnish, a further smoothing with finest grade sandpaper and one or two final coats of varnish.

The additions of wing struts and undercarriage legs, wing rigging and undercarriage braces are a comparatively simple matter. Legs and struts can be made from plastic card of the appropriate thickness – probably 60thou for 1:72 – or from raw sprue from the left over racks of kit models. This will require sanding down to the right diameter, which needs care to obtain an even finish, but has the advantage of providing very strong struts. An alternative is to make the struts or legs from balsa which is then covered with 10thou plastic card rolled round it, the edges being carefully melded together with liquid cement applied sparingly to disguise the seams. Rigging wires can be represented by thread, or, better still, nylon fishing line, by stretched sprue, by stretched card or by real wire depending upon the size of the model.

In the case of fishing nylon it is necessary to drill holes in the lower and upper wings. The nylon is drawn through the lower hole and fixed in epoxy resin applied from below very sparingly in the hole. Allow this to set and then thread the nylon through the upper hole and hold it taut while the epoxy is dropped in to the locating point from above and allowed to set. The line is then trimmed off and both holes are finished with body putty or well-mixed Polyfilla and sanded. This method, though more complicated is better than the untidy practice of tying threads to struts or fixing it in blobs of glue – which is inclined to cause some sagging.

Top left
Making scratch-built wings from plastic card. The inside of the card is scored, the scorings appearing as wing ribs on the outside when the card is folded.

Above left
The plastic card is folded over the balsa wing core, the front fold being the leading edge of the wing.

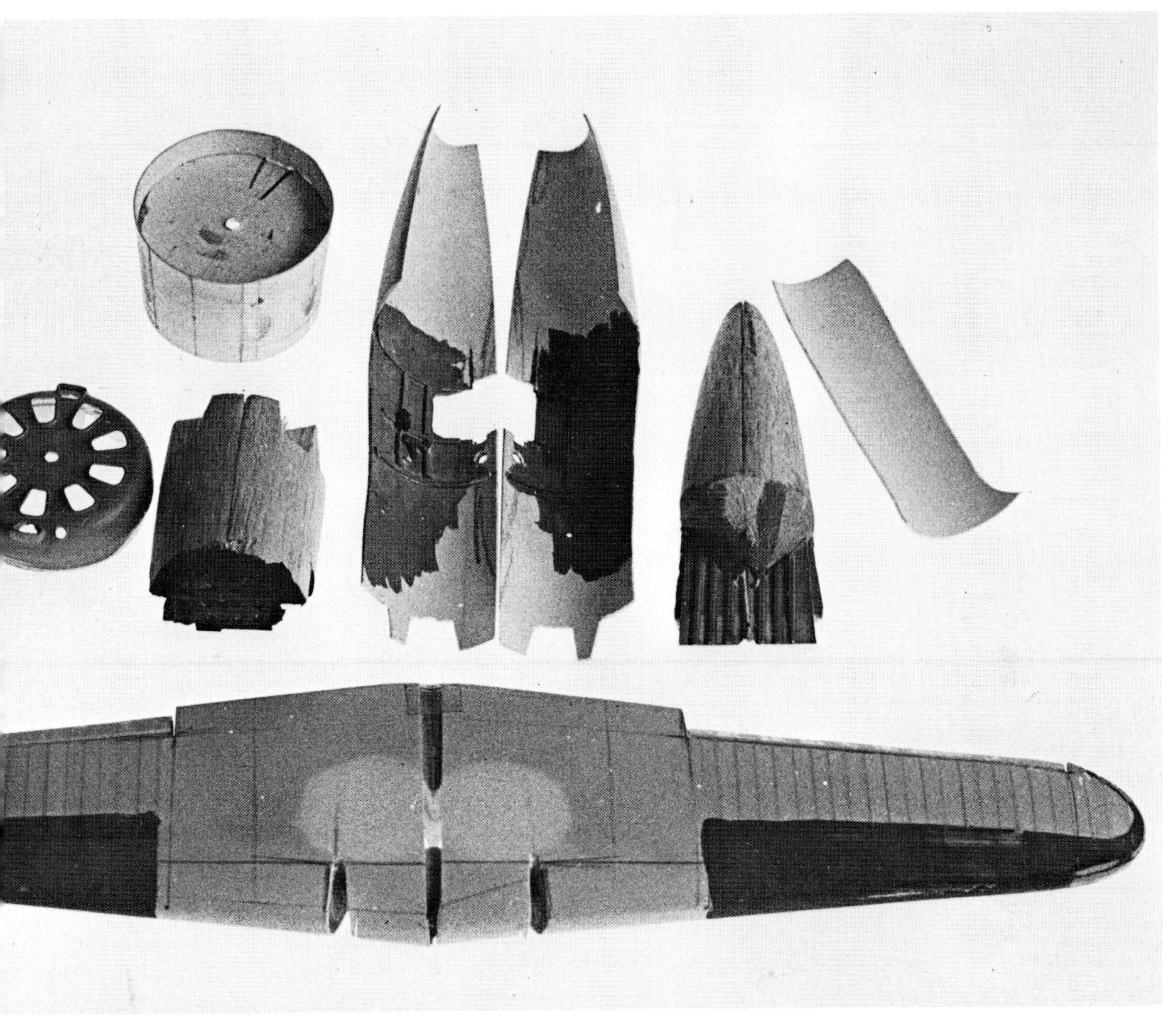

Above
Components used in the construction of a Soviet I.16.

One of the great problems of scratch-building can be in providing the models with the correct wheels. For example, almost without exception pre-1918 aircraft had spoked wheels, which, though the job can be done, are extremely difficult to make in small scale. Perhaps the simplest answer is to compromise by adapting a conical-shaped modern wheel from the commercial kit and painting on the spokes or painting a fabric cover such as was commonly used, laced to the spokes, to prevent the wheels mudding-up. Plastic curtain rings can be used as vintage tyres and press studs are effective as wheel hubs. A more ambitious way of producing larger wheels from scratch is to make a Plasticine master mold of half the wheel shape. This is then covered in plaster of paris, the Plasticine wheel being held in the molding box by a pin or panel pin through its center. The resulting plaster cast is then used as the mold into which paste-soaked paper discs are pressed firmly to make a papier maché wheel. When the two halves have been made they are trimmed of excess papier maché, glued together and painted after any join marks have been smoothed off. The center hole, which will need reopening, is plugged with brass tube or the hard plastic outer covering from electric wire (with the wire removed) to provide a sleeve in which the axle can move freely.

The difficult part of this method is in preparing the initial Plasticine mold and ensuring that the half wheel made at this stage has an accurate profile. One method devised by Rupert Moore and here quoted from R G Moulton's *Flying Scale Models* is to make a template of a quarter section of the wheel in tin or stiff card. This is pivoted in the center of a disc of Plasticine. By rotating the wheel section an impression is carved out for one half wheel. When the second half has been made in the same way the two papier maché sections are made from the mold prepared in plaster of Paris as before. The wheel halves are then joined together over a brass tubing hub.

A refinement which can be added successfully for larger models is a telescopic undercarriage. This is most effectively achieved with a tripod arrangement in which the two inner struts move freely from their attachment points on the fuselage and the third is telescopic. The 'telescope' is made from a metal tube of the right scale diameter sliding over stiff wire which lies against a small spring at the fuselage end of the tube. Since the model will not be flying and landing, the refinement is, strictly speaking, unnecessary, but it is an added detail which will give certain satisfaction to the modeller. Other seemingly unimportant embellishments also increase the model's appeal to the casual observer.

There are many other details which can be added, depending largely upon the ingenuity of the individual. It is a matter of looking about and deciding what every-day items can be converted to the needs of your model. Therein lies much of the fascination of scratch-building.

Two views showing the final appearance of the completed Soviet I.16 built by Harry Woodman.

Power Sources

Although the internal combustion engine is undoubtedly the most widely used source of power among aeromodellers, there must be very few who have not at some time made use of the simplest and cheapest means of propelling an aircraft – rubber power.

The model which Alphonse Pénaud flew in 1871 and which made history as the first aircraft to fly by power from a twisted rubber band was little more than a pair of wings with a stick which had the sole purpose of holding apart the two ends of the rubber. Since then, though the basic principle has remained unchanged, the design of rubber-driven aircraft has become increasingly sophisticated, to the extent that models driven by this method can be equipped with gears, cranks, flexible drives, they can be twin-boomed, triplanes, single-engine or multi-engine, or even rotary engine and they can be beautiful scale reproductions of the full-size or delightful flights of the maker's fancy.

Assuming that the aircraft into which the rubber motor is to be fitted has been so designed and built that it is flight-worthy, the final, all-important factor in lifting the model into the air is the quality of the rubber itself. In buying rubber, which is measured in pounds and ounces or kilograms, it is not unusual to find that the properties of it vary from one end to the other and it is a lucky man who can purchase a hank in which the quality is constant throughout its length. It is therefore wise to examine the rubber carefully for any obvious defects.

Having made the purchase of a hank, work thoroughly along its length and remove any large splinters of wood which, inevitably, will be present. Then wash it off thoroughly in natural soap – not detergent. The most efficient transfer of power from the stretched and wound rubber to the propeller is gained if the strands have been lubricated so that they unwind smoothly. There are a number of rubber lubricants on the market and there are many more which are made up by flyers themselves. Usually, whether proprietary or private, the mixtures are based on glycerine and soft soap diluted with water. Straight medicinal castor oil is also acceptable as it is light and not cloying. Whatever the choice, it is best to wash the lubricant off before storing rubber for more than a day or two, the strands being lightly dusted with talcum powder after drying. The strands should be coiled at rest – with no stretch in them – and can be kept in jars or in polythene bags.

Below
D Woolstenholm released this famous 1940 Wakefield designed by the legendary Bob Copland which typified the streamlined approach of model designers of that era.

Right
Martin Dilly hangs on while Paul Masterman stretches out the rubber motor and piles on the turns on his Wakefield model. Binoculars help to follow the model during flight to spot it down, often up to a mile away.

Usually a simple rubber motor will consist of one long loop of rubber which is turned into anything from six to 24 strands. One end of the resulting skein is connected by hook to the tail end of the fuselage and the other to the propeller. The amount of power which the rubber band can generate depends upon its torque or twisting force, and this is related to the cross section of the individual strands. Most commonly the strips of rubber are available in widths of $^3/_{16}$ in, $^1/_4$in, and 6mm, by $^1/_{30}$ in, $^1/_{20}$ in or 1mm.

Apart from the quality of the rubber itself, the lifespan of a rubber motor will depend a great deal upon the way it is treated, particularly in its early stages. No one would expect to get into a new car and drive it without running it in; nor should a rubber motor be wound to the full on its first winding. Like the auto engine, it requires running in. The number of turns which a motor of a particular rubber band cross section can, theoretically, be given is shown in the following table:

Strands	Turns to inch			
	$^3/_{16}$ x $^1/_{30}$	$^3/_{16}$ x $^1/_{24}$	$^1/_4$x$^1/_{30}$	$^1/_4$x$^1/_{24}$
6	44	42	40	37
8	38	36	34	31
10	34	32	30	26
12	31	30	28	24
14	30	27	26	22
16	28	26	25	20
18	27	24	24	—
20	26	23	—	—
24	24	—	—	—

A brand new motor should first be wound to about two-thirds of the theoretical maximum and then be allowed to unwind, either while the aircraft is held or by letting it take a test flight. For the next winding the motor is taken to about three-quarters of capacity and the unwinding procedure repeated. The motor should then be ready to accept its full winding.

There are various methods of winding for flying, depending upon the construction of the model concerned. For external winding it is necessary to have two people and both the nose block and the tail unit detachable. The tail is removed and the rubber attached to a hook on the winding rod which must be both strong and a hand's width longer than the fuselage. The rubber is passed through the fuselage to the nose and then stretched forward by the operator while the rod is held firm at the tail end by the helper, with the hook protruding from the nose. On the completion of winding from the nose end the body of the aircraft is slipped over the rubber and the back end engaged with the anchorage point. The tail is relocated, the nose and propeller fitted and all is ready for flight. An advantage of this method is that if the rubber breaks during winding it will not damage the fuselage as it flails about.

However, a quicker method is that of tube winding. Here the rod is slipped through a tube, the diameter of which will fit inside the fuselage, from the nose end and the winder is engaged with the end of the rod. The rubber is then placed on the hook end of the rod. As winding proceeds the tube is slid toward the tail and comes to rest against the rubber anchor point in the fuselage. With the tube now fully inside the fuselage and the rubber stretching forward from the nose, winding is continued to the recommended capacity, the stretching being gradually relaxed until the motor is fully wound inside the tube. Now the tube is slid forward over the rod and the noseblock and propeller are attached to the wound rubber as it is slipped off the rod hook.

The important thing in winding is to prevent bunching of the rubber which can stop the motor unwinding smoothly and also increases the likelihood of a break by accelerating fraying. An aid to the prevention of bunching is the commercially sold bobbin which will comfortably accept the looped ends of rubber around the smoothly rounded surface.

Internal Combustion

The improved technologies which made it possible to produce perfect internal combustion engines in miniature brought about as much of a revolution in aeromodelling as they did in other forms of modelling. Not only did it mean that model aircraft could look more like the real thing, it also provided a vastly more efficient means of powering the craft so that its performance was more closely related to that of the full-size version.

Use of internal combustion engines in aircraft was given a considerable boost in the early 1930s after William Brown of the Junior Motor Corporation of Philadelphia, Pennsylvania, introduced his 9.8cc 'Brown Junior' single-cylinder two-stroke at the US National championships. It ran on a mixture of petrol and motor oil, using spark ignition for firing and had an adjustable contact breaker fitted around the crank shaft for timing. The engine weighed only 7½oz (212g) and could lift models with a span of 8ft (2.4m). Indeed in 1936 it was said that one such model, made by Maxwell Bassett, had flown 70 miles (112km) from Camden, New Jersey, to Middletown, Delaware, at a maximum altitude of 8000ft in two and a half hours.

Though spark ignition remained extremely popular up to the outbreak of World War II it presented problems in weight because of the need to provide a coil, condenser and dry battery and associated parts. However, this form of model aero power is still used by enthusiasts who have an exhaustive knowledge of the idiosyncracies of what, in effect, is a miniature auto engine.

Meanwhile, after the outbreak of war, research continued to reduce the weight of engines. The answer came in 1946 with the glowplug, a coil of platinum wire which is heated by a detachable battery to a temperature at which the fuel will ignite. Once the engine has fired, the heat of combustion is sufficient to keep the wire glowing and the battery can be disconnected. The fuel is based on methyl alcohol and castor oil with various additives such as nitro methane.

To start it a glowplug will need to be connected to a battery of 1.5 or 2 volts to heat the wire coil. First, the needle valve controlling the flow of fuel is unscrewed so that it is in the 'open' position, to allow fuel to enter

Right
A 1.5cc Webra glow engine (minus plug) fitted with silencer.

Left, above and below
Diesel and glow versions of the same basic engine.

Below right
A very modern German glow engine.

Below center
The largest model glow engine, a 15cc German Webra 91.

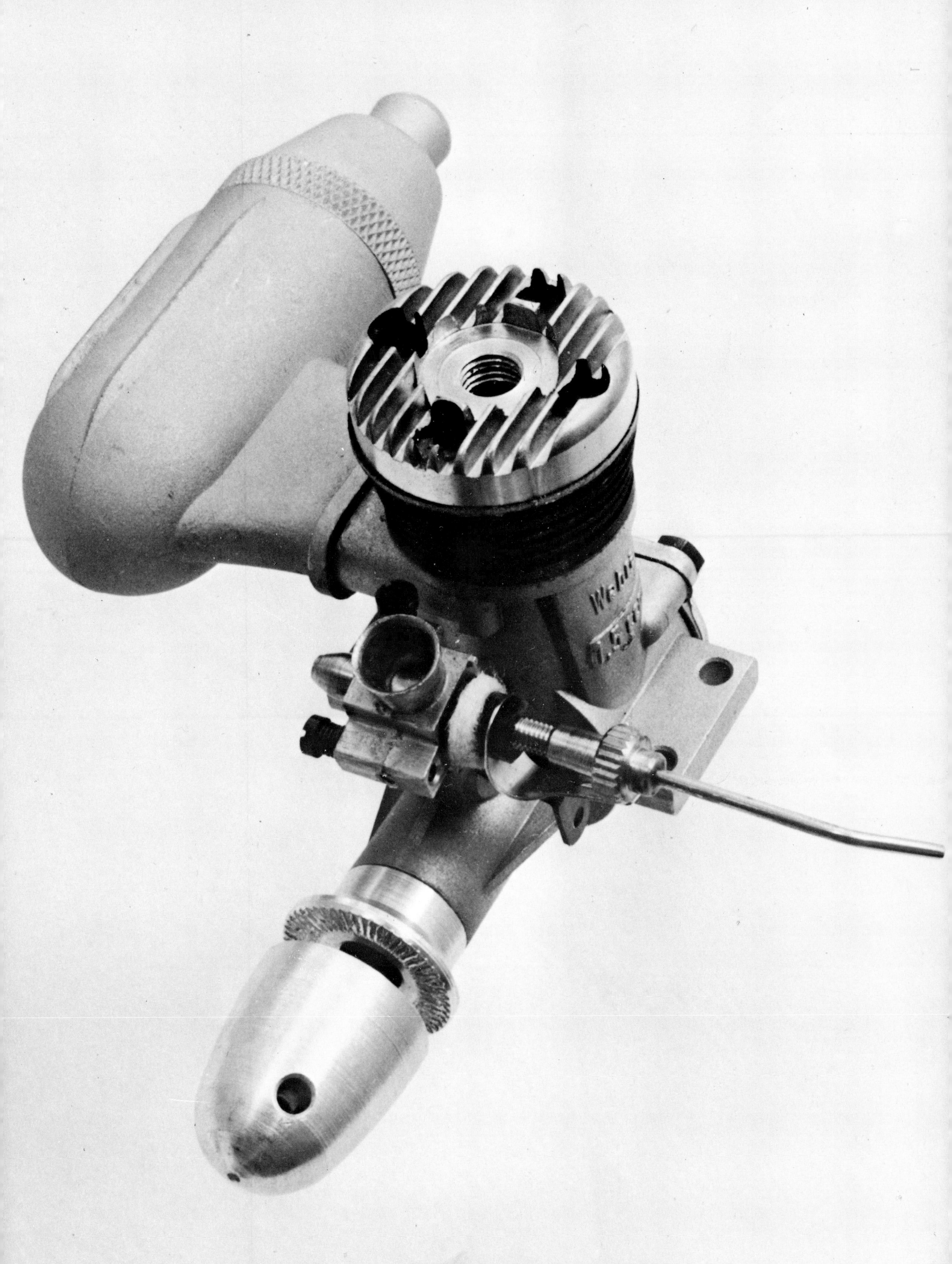

HEATH

when the carburetor intake is sealed by a finger tip and the propeller is revolved. A few drops of fuel are injected into the exhaust port to prime the engine, which is then turned over several times by flicking the propeller in a counterclockwise direction. Now the battery connection can be made. The engine should fire, and continue to do so, after a few more flicks but if a fizzing sound can be heard it is likely that there is too much fuel present or that the battery has not delivered enough power to heat the wire sufficiently. Once the engine has fired successfully the needle value is reset to give ideal smooth running without emitting exhaust smoke.

At about the same time that research was leading to the commercial introduction of the glowplug, other work was being carried out – principally in Italy and Switzerland – on the compression ignition engine, now more commonly known as the diesel. Quite simply, the firing of this type of engine depends upon a highly volatile fuel being increased in temperature to the point at which it explodes. This is done by mixing it with air under compression – and therefore hot. The orthodox diesel incorporates an injector which pumps a carefully measured amount of fuel into the cylinder as the piston is coming up to maximum compression, at which point the air in the chamber is already hot from the pressure. The resulting combustion produces the power to drive the piston down. The compression involved in a diesel is considerably higher than that for glowplug engines: in a diesel it is about 18:1 to 22:1; in a glowplug the range is more like 9:1 to 12:1.

Compression ratio in a diesel is variable by means of a screw-adjustable contra-piston in the piston head and this enables alterations to be made to suit different fuels or weather conditions. The fuel used is usually a mixture of paraffin or diesel oil plus a lubricant and ether. Although the latter is by itself a poor fuel, it has a very low ignition temperature and helps to ignite the rest of the mixture at a lower compression than would otherwise be necessary.

Starting the diesel involves injecting the right amount of fuel into the upper cylinder under the right compression ratio to obtain combustion, whereupon the piston action will continue to suck in fuel. This will usually involve an alteration to the setting of the contra-piston to reduce compression slightly and, once firing is achieved, resetting it for continuous smooth running at higher compression. Diesel engines are invariably chosen for team racing events because they are more easily started than glowplugs and also not vulnerable to burning out. However, the wrong fuel mixture can result in seizing up through insufficient lubrication or overheating.

Left
A close-up of the beautiful Heath Baby Bullet, a highly detailed F/F (free-flight) Scale CO_2 powered model of the original – even the engine turned metal cowling has been faithfully reproduced. The small tail area makes it a tricky model to fly.

Above
Standard (above) and high performance (top) versions of a 10cc glow engine.

Ducted Fans

The ducted fan model was an American invention developed in the early 1950s by Thomas H Purcell Jr of Morton, Pennsylvania, following experiments which began in the mid-1940s. It provides an excellent means of using a conventional internal combustion engine to simulate jet propulsion. The basis of ducted fan design is that both the engine and the 'propellers' are buried inside the fuselage of the model so that, as with a real jet aircraft, air is forced rapidly through the ducts to provide forward impulsion.

In place of the propeller this type of model has a multi-bladed fan or impeller which is used to draw in and blow out air through the duct, which is streamlined and converge towards the tail to improve the thrust. There is usually a downfall of between 15 and 20 percent in the work efficiency of an impeller compared to a conventional propeller fitted to an engine of the same size but much depends upon the design not only of the engine, fan and duct but also of the aircraft itself. For greatest efficiency the model must fly fast and because the fan is heavier than the propeller it is necessary to reduce the size of the aircraft so that it is smaller than it would have been with the same engine powering a propeller.

It is generally accepted that the most efficient performance as well as the best appearance are achieved by setting the fan in a horizontal rather than a vertical plane, but this is by no means an inflexible rule. The choice between horizontal or vertical depends very much on the type of aircraft being modelled, particularly if a scale version of a full-size is planned. The number of blades on the fan will depend upon the diameter of the fan itself.

A choice must also be made on the positioning of the engine in relation to the fan. For the horizontal rotating it may be above or below and for the vertical it can be fore or aft of the fan. There is a good case to be made for placing it in front so that the air drawn in by the fan is not impeded by the engine on its path down the cone and out. There is the added advantage that an engine in front of the fan will tend to diffuse the air drawn in through a small intake and 'spread' it over the full face of the fan.

There are several ways of making the fan. They include individual fiber blades set at 30–40 degrees in a solid dural boss and securely screwed in place at their root by screws inserted from the back face of the boss – a method favored for fans to be powered by engines of

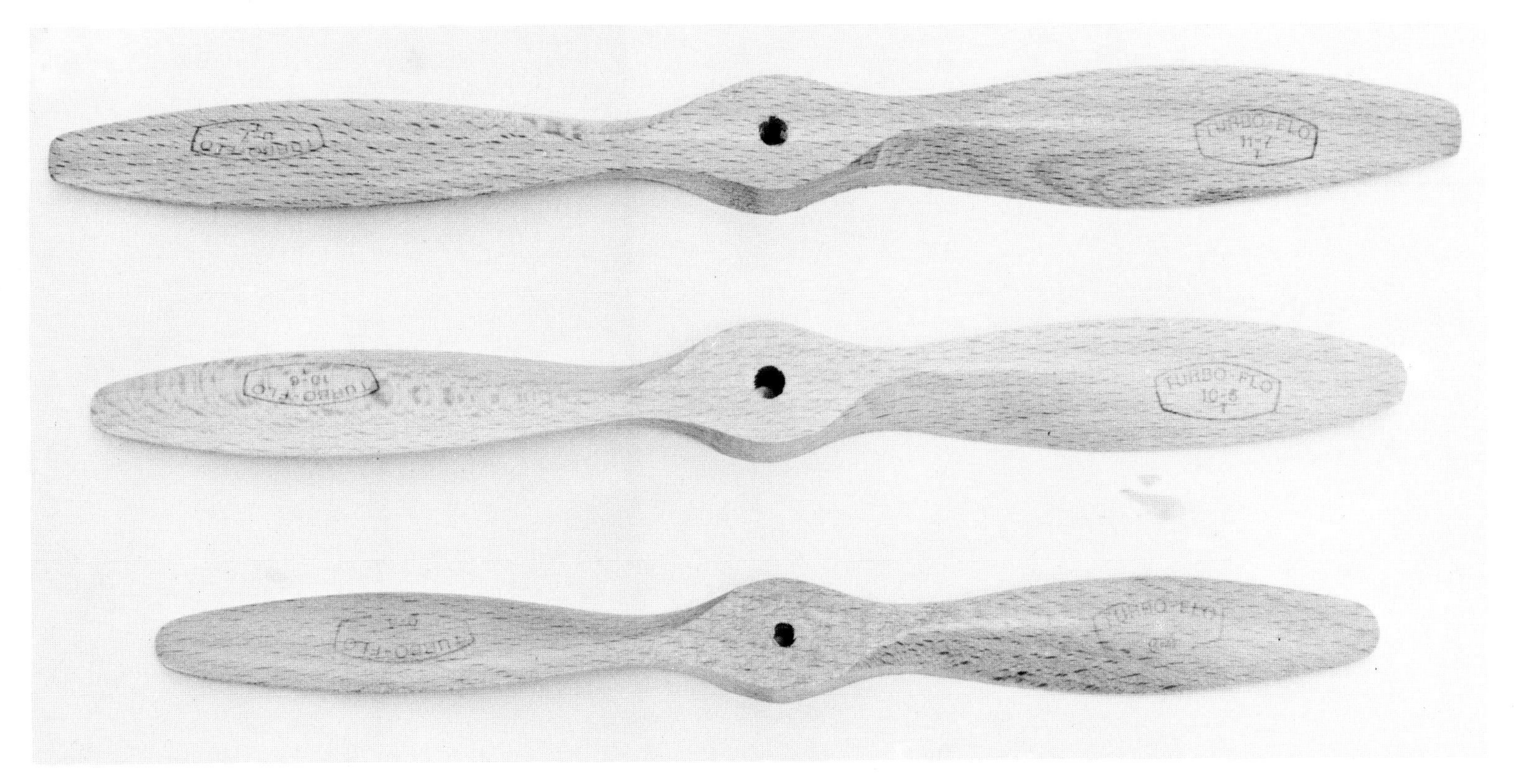

Left
A close-up illustrates the amazing detail of Terry Manley's Blackburn Swift, complete with dummy torpedo and spoked wheels.

Above
Typical wooden propellers by Punctilio, in three common sizes, 9 x 5 inches, 10 x 6 inches and 11 x 7 inches (eg 9-inch diameter x 5-inch pitch).

more than 1cc. For lesser engine sizes aluminium sheet discs can be used, the blades being cut in and twisted from about 45 degrees at their roots to 30 degrees at their tips. Alternatively the same individual blading method can be used, employing alloy in place of fiber. In either case it should be remembered that stresses at the blade root will be considerable – probably in the region of 1500lb per sq in – and that the possibility of a blade being thrown at something like 16,000rpm cannot be overlooked.

However, a refinement which is added to the fan assembly to increase efficiency will also act as a useful guard against accidents and possible injury. It is the plywood ring or can which is fitted around the blades with a small clearance between it and them. Its purpose is to minimize spillage of the air thrust from the blades and utilize the maximum amount of air in an efficient rearward flow. Its effect is also to act as a guard if a blade is thrown and the out-of-balance engine runs wild.

Since the ducted fan system relies upon an enclosed engine it follows that some method of starting the engine from outside has to be devised and this can be by the cord-and-pulley system such as is commonly seen on outboard motors. This, in turn, makes it even more important that the engine should be firmly seated. The engine and fan must be reached for tuning and maintenance and for the latter to be turned as the cord is wound on for starting. Whether access is by hatch or lifting cockpit cover, the fitting must be made as tight as possible, particularly if access is behind the fan and therefore at a point where thrust could be lost through an ill-fitting hatch.

A further point to consider is that because the engine is enclosed exhaust waste will not disperse and will gradually accumulate on the inside of the duct. A sensible precaution is to ensure that the duct is well varnished so that not only can deposits be easily cleaned off but airflow can be improved.

Jetex

While ducted fan engines are a good means of powering a simulated jet propelled aircraft, they do present problems in terms of design and scale. A means of propulsion which is much closer to the real thing is the Jetex motor, which was pioneered in Britain and originally marketed in 1948 by the firm of Wilmot, Mansour. Government regulations on the use of explosives have meant the disappearance of Jetex from the British scene, but they are still popular in other countries.

Essentially, these motors are more like rockets than jet engines. They consist of a light alloy, cylindrical case with a spring-loaded cap at one end containing a small orifice to allow the emission under great pressure of the gases created by burning solid fuel pellets inside the case. The pellets are ignited by a wire-cored fuse or wick and will burn for up to twenty seconds with a maximum thrust ranging from 0.5oz (14g) up to 6oz depending upon the size of the unit. The thrust can be increased by the use of special augmenter tubes. The units themselves have the advantage of being light – the smallest weigh only 0.25oz (7g) and will power a model weighing 1.5oz (42g).

Gauze washers are used to keep the fuel pellets pressed against the wicks and these have to be kept clean, as does the orifice, which should not be enlarged, on any account, as this will drastically reduce the thrust.

A Jetex cylinder can be mounted on an aircraft externally, preferably in a trough under the fuselage, using a clip fastener and a light asbestos sheet to protect the bodywork. Alternatively it can be installed inside the fuselage, using a hatch to provide access to the fuse and also making sure that the exhaust has a free exit passage.

By using an augmenter the model comes even closer to the real jet aircraft since the Jetex (and tube) can be fully enclosed in the fuselage and the fuse ignited through the tube without the need for a hatch.

There are a number of points to watch when installing and using a Jetex. The engine should be fitted so that its position can be altered to gain the most efficient directional thrust and balance. It should also be possible to reach the cylinder easily so that it can be cleared, recharged and replaced. It is important to remember that considerable heat is generated and that not only is it advisable to provide a cooling space around the cylinder but also that the cylinder will remain hot for a time after burning out.

One of the major advantages of the Jetex is that once the pellets have finished their work and burned out there are no problems of inertia or torque reaction to overcome as with a 'feathered' propeller or a 'dying' fan. However, points to watch are that the model is launched gently – like a 'chuck' glider – only after the Jetex has had two or three seconds to build up; a low-

A range of glow engines produced by just one Japanese manufacturer, from 1.5 to 10cc. Each model has different characteristics according to the type of model intended to use it (Enya range).

mounted Jetex will give the model a tendency to loop but this can be removed by setting it forward of the center of gravity.

An American, Sergeant Bill Tenney of Minneapolis, was the first person to develop a commercial jet unit for model aircraft – the Dynajet which went on the US market in 1947. His idea came from studying one of the captured German V1 'Flying Bombs' or 'Doodlebugs,' the pilotless gyro-stabilized rockets launched against Britain towards the end of World War II. Tenney saw a V1 on display at the US Air Force test center at Wright Field near Dayton, Ohio, and went away to design his own version of the rocket unit which was mounted high above the bomb.

His first effort was a massive 6ft (1.8m) unit weighing 35lb (15.8kg), but subsequent refinements brought the Dynajet down to a weight of one pound (.45kg) and a length of 22in (56cm). The appeal of the unit is its simplicity. Working on the pulse jet principle, it consists of a narrow pipe of thin steel expanded at one end into a combustion chamber. High pressure air is fed to the front of the engine by means of a bicycle or car foot pump or compressed air cylinder. As the air enters it sucks in a small amount of pure petrol, delivered as a spray. This atomized fuel mixture passes through a metal petal-valve into the combustion chamber, where it is fired by a small spark plug connected to a vibrator coil on the ground. The resulting combustion closes the valve so that the force of the explosion is directed down the narrow tube to create thrust. Emission of the pressure wave from the tube in turn results in suction on the valve, which reopens to allow the next spray of fuel to enter the chamber. When the cycle has repeated several times it becomes self-perpetuating, the tail of the flame from the previous explosion being sufficient to ignite the succeeding charges of fuel so that the coil and pump can be disconnected.

The Dynajet burns with an ear-shattering roar which turns to a continuous boom as the tailpipe heats up and glows dark red. Because of the noise and also the considerable power of such units, they are not flown in competition in Britain and there are very strict safety rules for international competitions, including a weight limitation of 1.1lb (500g).

Electric Power

In recent years there has been a considerable growth of interest in electric power for model aircraft. It was spurred by the improved technology which enabled manufacturers to produce high-powered batteries at low weight.

Previously, certainly until the early 1950s, the great problem in electric flight was that of the power-weight ratio; it seemed impossible to build an electric motor large enough to develop sufficient power without it being too heavy and the batteries themselves were also too weighty to be carried by a reasonably sized model.

Adherents to this kind of power source had to content themselves with tethered flying, using control lines to carry the current from batteries on the ground to the model. However in 1957 Colonel H J Taplin made a successful free flight with a converted prototype kit from the British firm of ED (Electronic Developments Ltd). It was powered by an ex-government Emerson 24-volt electric motor which weighed 28oz (794g). Loaded with twenty expensive silver-zinc accumulators which needed to give eight amps for takeoff, the model weighed 8lb (3.6kg).

Since then great strides have been made in combining successful miniaturization of electric motors with improved efficiency. The advances in this direction were helped by the development in the late 1950s by the German Graupner Company of a motor far smaller than that used by Colonel Taplin. Fred Militky, a design engineer with the company, made use of a miniature electric motor originally designed to power camera shutter servos. Weighing only 0.9oz (25.5g), it incorporated a gearbox which gave 14,000rpm at its most efficient speed and had a reduction to the output shaft of 15:1. The motor was extremely efficient and with two tiny lead-acid accumulators weighed only 2.5oz (70g).

Top to bottom
(1) One home-built device (top), 'Venetian Blind' valves, 5½-pound thrust, 2½-pound weight. (2) 'Decojet' from Warneford kit. (3) Juggernaut, British Dynajet copy. (4) Dynajet. (5) o.s. 'Scaled Down' Dynajet, same design.

Militky achieved a power run of two minutes using the motor in a model weighing 4.5oz (127.5g).

The Graupner Company put the engine on the market with the name 'Mikromax' and one of them was used by Chris Soenkson, an American, in an indoor radio-controlled model powered by salt-water power cells. With motor, cells and radio equipment the model weighed 5oz (142g). The company, presently one of the largest model specialist companies in the world, has continued to refine the motor, now known as the 'Micromax,' and keep pace with progress being made in this field of aero power.

Two of the most effective power sources for electric motors are the nickel cadmium, or nicad, cells and silver chloride water activated batteries. The former have the advantages of being quickly rechargeable and lightweight as well as being dry cells. The latter are excellent for short, high output runs and both are suitable for larger models. The range of electric motors has increased considerably, as has the number of model kits for electric power. It is now possible for the enthusiast to buy a kit consisting of all the necessary parts, plus motor, gearbox and batteries, or for him to indulge in scratch-building the whole thing.

Free as the Wind

For the aeromodeller there can be few thrills of the sport to equal that of seeing his own model take to the air and complete a flight successfully for the first time. It means that all those hours of work have been worthwhile nonetheless, and it is a moment in which he can experience a justifiable sense of pride and achievement.

Once, in the far-off days of the earliest models, it was a matter of just getting a machine off the ground, defying gravity and emulating the birds by flying free. Today the achievements are different – to climb higher, fly faster or keep going longer before descending gently.

So far as free-flight models are concerned there are three types of model which fall into the category – gliders, rubber-powered and engine-powered aircraft. Whether the flyer is an entrant in a competition or a 'weekender' (a term which in this context is not meant to derogate), the aim should be to achieve a flight of the longest possible duration. In competition the matter is usually decided by several flights but in flying purely for the sport it is merely one for self-congratulation.

Right
Isaenko, one of the top Russian glider flyers, prepares to reel his tow line out for another flight at the World Championships in Bulgaria in 1975.

Below
Elton Drew, member of Bristol and West Model Aero Club, with his A-1 class glider Little Lady, a small version of his famous Lively Lady with which he became World Champion in 1969.

A
CCCP
AL-25
CCCP
AL25

Left
Brian Dowling holds fellow Leicester-clubmate John Abbey's A1 class glider ready for launch. This, the smallest class of tow line glider, will perform two-minute flights from the 50-meter tow line. The pattern is color tissue doped on.

Left
Typical scene at any F/F glider contest (1978 British National Championships at RAF Cranwell) as competitors line up to tow their models and hopefully locate those thermals that will increase the model's duration and chances of winning. Poles carry thin mylar streamers to show wind direction for launch.

Above right
Phil Ball with his 20-inch span hand launched glider. Such models are made from solid sheet balsa ¼-inch wings, 1/16-inch tail and fin and are thrown like a cricket ball to 80 to 100 feet, from which height they will glide for up to a minute, or longer if in a thermal.

Whichever may be your particular choice of free-flying model, success or failure will depend upon the successful building-in of stability in flight. Although gliders are the simplest of flying models, they require just as much attention to this detail and others as do the rubber-driven and engine-powered types. This is particularly so if a scale glider is being constructed; many full-size gliders have remarkably small tail areas, whereas the model requires as large a tail area as possible, compatible with balance and weight considerations. For beginners, high-wing scale models are the best as they offer the greatest stability.

There are various methods of curing any signs of instability in a glider. If the model shows a tendency to dive into the ground it may be a simple matter of reducing the nose ballast or moving the wing forward; if it tends to stall, more nose weight or movement of the wings back are indicated. However, the answer may not be as simple as that and may involve alterations to the settings of the wing and tail angles.

For example, the model should glide evenly to earth from a gentle hand launch in a test flight. If it shows that it wants to soar up, then 'hangs back' before the nose drops and it dives, the chances are that there is too great a difference between the angles of the wing and tail surfaces. The leading edge of the tail will need to be raised slightly – but not enough to make the angle the same as that for the wing, the leading edge of which will already have been set at about five degrees.

A nose-dive symptom already mentioned may be due to a wing warp which effectively reduces the angle of incidence between wing and tail so that the tail angle actually becomes positive relative to the wings. The remedy in this case is to lift the leading edge of the wing.

Chuck glider is the name of the event and that is what it is all about as demonstrated here by Oxford's Andy Crisp who heaves his 'Mister Jazz' skyward after a long run-up. Models use drop-off noseweights to prevent loss in long thermal flights.

Above
Structural details of APS Rolling Stone A/2 glider designed by Dave White. Wings consist of airfoil shaped ribs and square stripwood spars, while the fuselage is a hollow balsa box.

This need to alter wing or tail settings is the reason why these units should not be fixed in place or their locating points finalized until the flyer is entirely satisfied that the model is perfectly trimmed.

The simplest glider and one which is ideal for youngsters is the hand-launched or 'chuck' glider. The next step up is to the tow-line variety which is launched from a self-releasing line either pulled by a willing accomplice or by a winch. In this case a hook is fitted under the fuselage, forward of the center of gravity, and a ring attached to the end of the tow-line slips over the hook. When the glider appears to want to fly on its own, the operator releases the tension by slowing down his run or by stopping the winch and the ring drops off the hook. A pennant attached to the line just below the ring facilitates the release by creating drag.

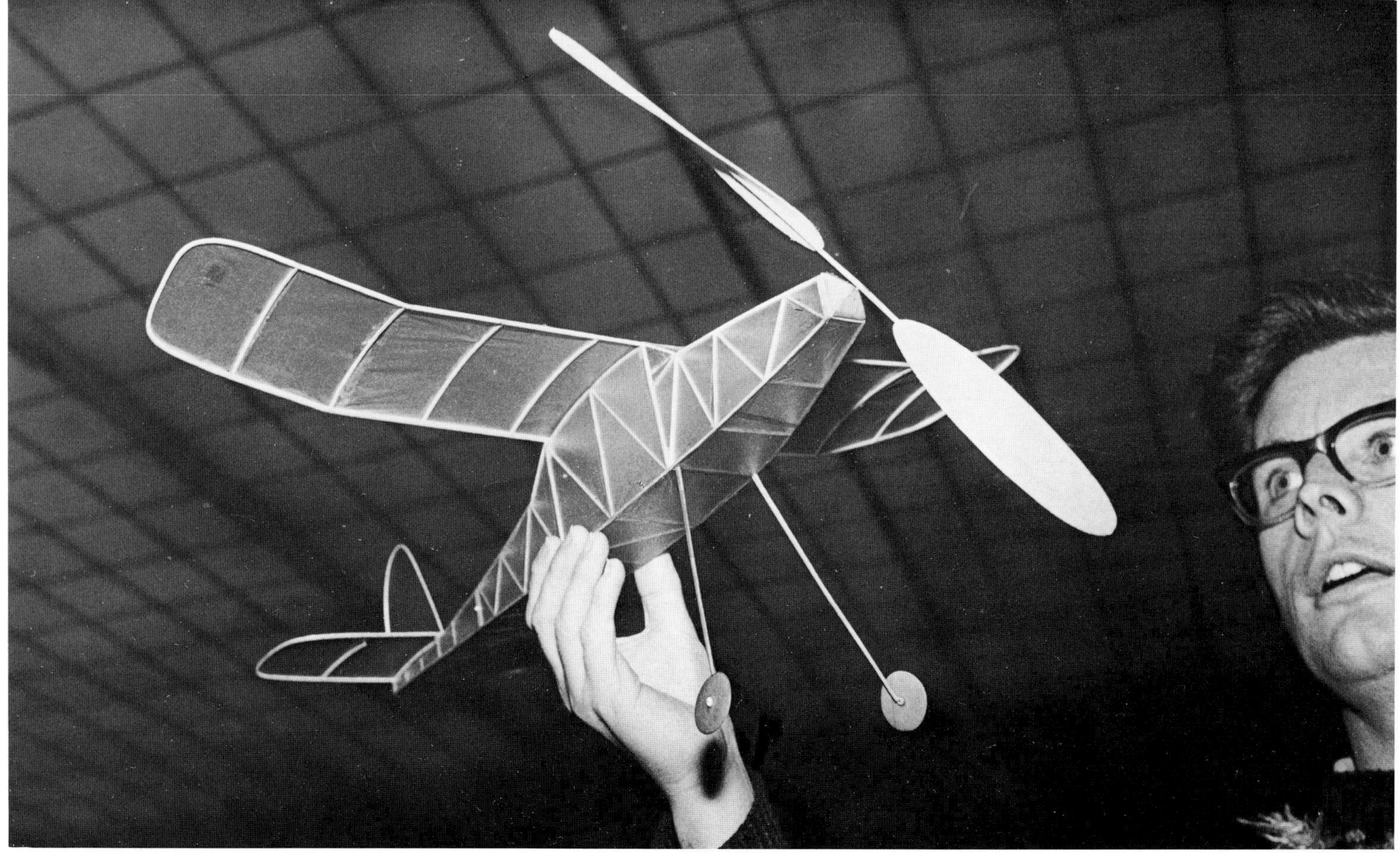

Above left
Bernard Aslett releases his rubber powered Indoor EZB Class model. These simple models weigh only a fraction of an ounce. Flights up to 10 minutes are possible though the world record stands at over 20 minutes.

Below left
Bob Bailey shows off his Manhattan Class indoor model, another lightweight class in which the rules call for more realism in appearance, with under-carriage, cockpit, fuselage etc. Flights up to 10 minutes are possible but the average is five to six minutes.

Below right
American Dave winds the rubber motor on his 'Two Cents Plain' model designed to the US Penny Plain indoor rules requiring simple models with 18-inch span weighing not less than a penny.

Right
Flying characteristics which will need correction

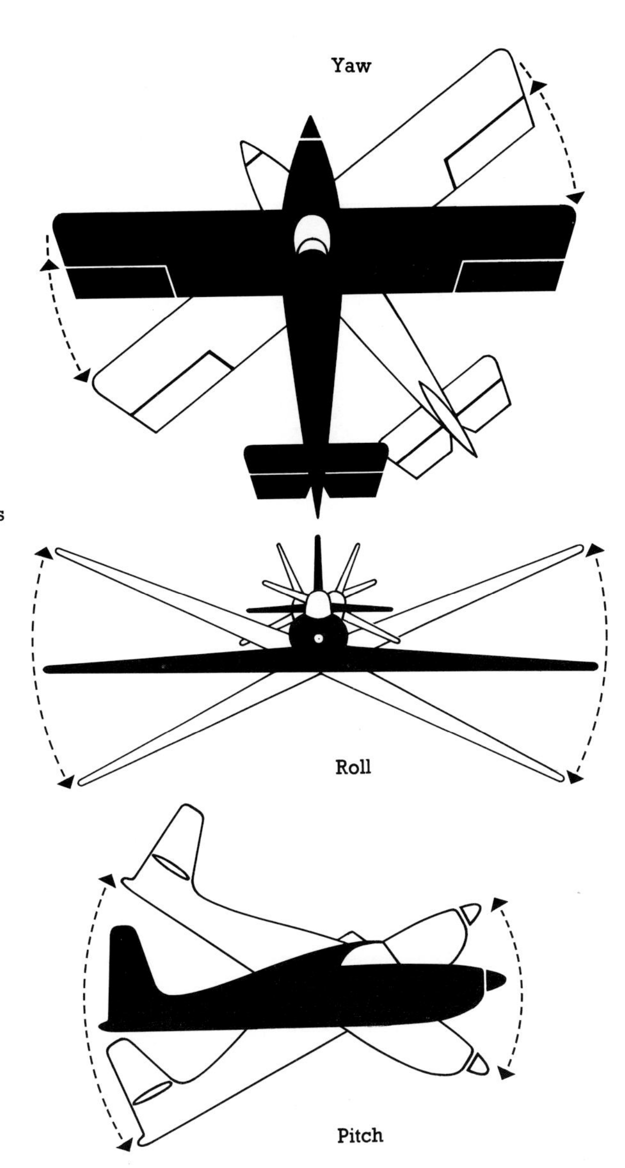

An offset rudder is ideal to keep the glider circling in thermals – assuming ideal gliding conditions! – but it is a positive hazard during a launch and will cause the model to veer off the straight path which is essential for a good takeoff. The answer lies in the auto-rudder, a device which holds the rudder in line while the glider is under tow and allows it to take up an offset position on release.

The auto-rudder is an extremely simple yet effective device which works from a pivoted arm, the free end of which is engaged by the towing ring at the tow hook. A cord is attached from the arm to a bar fixed to the rudder so that when the arm is under tension the rudder is pulled straight. As soon as tension from the tow line is released as the ring drops away a rubber band on the other end of the rudder bar pulls it to the offset position.

The use of thermals – rising air columns – is an essential of all successful free flight. For gliders they provide the only means of sustained flight available once the tow line has been released, while for powered models they are the means by which a flight can be prolonged once the engine has cut out or run down. Detection of good thermal currents therefore becomes of great importance, particularly to competitive flyers.

Various methods of 'thermal hunting' can be used but success will depend upon knowing what it is you are looking for – and where it is more likely to be found. It must be fairly obvious that there is no such thing as still air; there is *always* some movement, even if the air appears and feels totally still. As the sun rises, even on a day when the sky is completely overcast, there will be changes in temperature which cause movement, there will be evaporation or condensation which will result in high and low pressure areas. As the day warms up certain ground surfaces will reflect the warmth better than others, creating stronger up-currents. These are what the flyer is seeking – and the wider the column of upward moving air the better. Large areas of concrete or tarmac (such as airport runways), sandy areas, cornfields, closely packed rooftops – these are all likely sources of reflected heat and therefore of thermals.

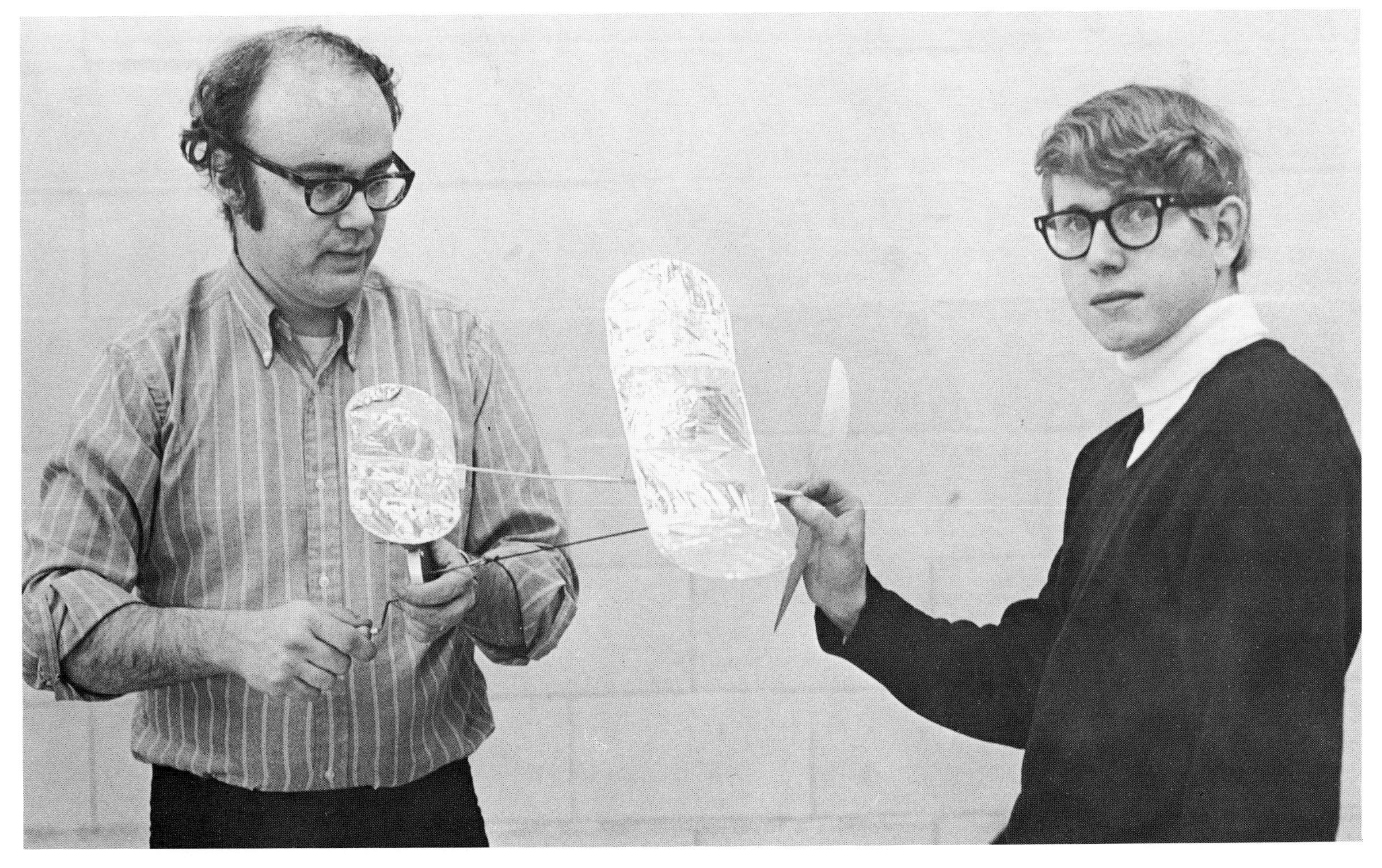

Above
The reigning World Glider Champion Kostadin Abadjiev of Bulgaria won his title at the F/F Championships at Roskilde in Denmark. The contest was flown from 3am to avoid thermals making the event too easy. The model has wings covered in 1/16-inch balsa sheet covered in red silk.

Right
North Korea is currently the world's leading nation in Wakefield model flying. Here the 1975 World Champion Baik Chang San carefully winds his motor; an aluminum disc protects propellers from damage if the rubber breaks. He is also a member of the winning North Korean team in 1977.

Far right
Austria's Herbet Chmelik, winner of the 1974 International Pierre Trebod Free Flight event at Marigny le Grande in France with his Wakefield class model. The fuselage is hollow rolled balsa tube and the propellers hinge flat alongside fuselage for a streamlined glide.

Left
Brian Downham from North London winds the rubber motor in his ABC Robin built from APS plans while his lad holds the model steady.

Far left
Britain's Joe Barnes combined his summer holiday with the Pierre Trebod International F/F contest at Marigny le Grande. The model held by his son David uses aluminum tube to house rubber motor – good protection in case the rubber bursts!

Left
Jan Zetterdal from Sweden almost completed winding his Wakefield class model, powered by 16 strands of ¼-inch rubber. The motor is wound using a geared hand drill with the propeller being refitted later. The photograph is taken at 1974 Pierre Trebod International.

Trevor Grey with his tailless rubber-powered model. Ailerons at the tips prevent unwanted stalls, propellers fold flat at the nose after the rubber has run down for a long glide, and the flaps at the back spring out to disturb the flight path and bring the model back to earth.

Peter Carter displays his Coupe d'Hiver class model which is only allowed a mere 10 grams of rubber, yet flights of up to two minutes are possible. This was originally a French class but is now universally flown.

Probably the simplest – though not the most reliable – means of detecting a thermal is by tossing a dandelion-fluff ball into the air. Aids of nature can also be employed by watching the behavior of small winged insects or of gliding birds and whirlwinds of dust. However, there are other methods which are more practical. One is simply to watch the behavior of other models already airborne and see whether they are taking advantage of a thermal. If they are, move downwind of them, since the thermal will then be travelling towards you. The art now is to judge exactly the right moment to take advantage of the thermal. With a glider you will need to launch into the wind and release the model into the thermal. With a powered model it is more a matter of flying the aircraft so that it is in the right position to use the thermal when the engine cuts.

Far left
A brightly colored Veron Cardinal takes to the air on yet another breathless sunny day at Old Warden Airfield, England.

Left
The moment of launch for this Keil Kraft Ladybird, finished very realistically in US invasion camouflage markings.

Left
America's Jack Headley is one of the all-time fun sport flyers. His designs combine simplicity and speed of construction with a pleasing model enjoyable to fly.

To add to the complications, there will be an opposing downdraft around the thermal. The thermal itself will almost certainly be a bent column because the air nearest the ground meets more resistance than that above, and the thermal column will widen because the air expands as it rises.

A popular and accurate way of detecting thermals is by using soap bubbles. These can either be made by the child's method of a wire loop dipped into a soap solution or, if you wish to save your breath and to have your hands free, by a bubble generator which is a simple enough instrument, usually powered by a battery which drives an air blower directed on to the soaped-up loop. Ideally these are set above ground level. Another aid is a ribbon of mylar – the thin, light-weight insulation material – some 20ft (6m) long attached at one end to a pole. The ribbon will trail in the wind but will lift as its tail detects a thermal.

John Brooke with his version of Emmanuel Fillan's 1937 Wakefield Winner. Large box fuselages were a prerequisite of the rules, and a solid balsa propeller would free the wheel during the glide.

Right
Gary Dowsett releases this Coupe d'Hiver model designed by Canada's Stuart Savage for a near vertical rise-off ground launch while an anxious looking Roy Miller of Croydon Club records the flight score on a stop watch.

The bronze medalist at Roskilde World Free Flight Championships was Russia's Eugene Verbitsky. The model, which features wings covered in .03mm thick duralmin for stiffness, was actually flown by Igor Ziljberg (shown here) after Eugene was bitten by a snake while out flying.

Thomas Koster tunes the Rossi 15 which powers his Hot Stoned Tuna. The model uses wing flaps, lifted for a fast climb which then drop to give an undercambered wing section for slow glide. Here he is seen at 1974 Pierre Trebod International in France.

Once the glider is airborne, and assuming that the flyer has found a very good thermal, there can be another problem – getting the model down again. This is particularly important in competition flying when entrants must glide for a specific time. It is just as relevant to the hobby flyer, who is not likely to want to stand helplessly by while his model glides off into the unknown. The answer lies in the dethermalizer system which ensures that a model is made to land at the end of a specific period.

There are two popular forms of dethermalizer: the timed fuse and the timeswitch. The first relies upon a slow-burning fuse to burn through a rubber band which is used to hold the tail down at its correct flight incidence. When the band is released the trailing edge of the tail is pulled up so that lift is destroyed and the model descends. The degree of lift to the trailing edge (or leading edge in the case of an under-fuselage tailplane) is fairly critical because, if it is too much, the model will dive vertically into the ground, quite possibly damaging itself. The time fuses come in lengths which can be cut to give a burning time of three minutes, which is the usual length of time allowed in a competition flight for model aircraft.

The timeswitch is simply a more sophisticated version of the timed fuse and depends upon a clock mechanism weighing little more than ½oz (14g) and compactly made. The disc on the timer rotates slowly until it opens a slot in which the restraining crank is fitted. As the crank is released it drops the rubber band holding the tail in position.

Both these dethermalizing systems can be used on gliders or powered models. However, in the case of gliders in competition, the flight is timed from the moment the model is released from the towline and it is necessary to use a clockwork timer which is activated when a pin on the tow-line drops out to allow the mechanism to start rotating.

There are other forms of dethermalizer, including the simple parachute released from the tail by the timer to cause drag and the highly sophisticated versions of the clockwork mechanism which operate automatic rudders, elevators and engine cut-outs.

Timeswitches are also used to make automatic flight adjustments to wing or tail incidences as the rubber motor unwinds and the torque reduces. Similar adjustments can be made by a system that detects the reduction in torque and compensates by changing the angles of 'attack' on tail and wings.

It was to rubber-powered models that the honor of the first international competition for model aircraft went in 1927, when Sir Charles Wakefield donated a trophy, the Wakefield Cup. The first winner in this open-to-all contest of duration flying was a Mr T H Newell whose plane achieved a flight of 52.6 seconds. The competition is held every other year and attracts entrants from all over the world under the control of the Fédération Aéronautique Internationale, the body which organizes all official international competitions. The FAI lays down strict regulations for the Wakefield Cup – and all world championship events – which govern the weight and surface area of models and maximum weight of rubber used in motors. Essentially the successful competitor – and, indeed, the successful hobby flyer – will be the one who has the motor which, while conforming to the regulations, is sufficiently powerful to allow the model to climb high enough to achieve a long glide once the power output has stopped. Once again, therefore, the use of thermals is essential. In addition there are other means of achieving the duration of flight. The propeller, for example, will be set on a shaft running on the smoothest bearings and its pitch will be carefully selected to make the maximum use of the power in the longest time possible; if the pitch is too low there will be excellent immediate acceleration but the motor will run down quickly; on the other hand, if it is too high there will be too little acceleration to achieve the powerful climb required.

Bob Wells, Anglia MFC, releases his Keil Kraft Gypsy which has already lifted off into a long sweeping climb. The model is packed with rubber, and often half of the model's 8 ounces all-up weight consists of rubber.

Above
Sopwith Schneider Trophy float plane built from APS plans powered by a Mills .75 diesel.

Top left
Ray Hall from Leeds visited the Shettleworth Museum airdrome of Old Warden to fly this Mills .75cc-powered Tiger Moth built from the Mercury kit.

Top center
A nice group of peanut-scale rubber-powered models clustered around a most unusual 20-inch span model of a Bleriot Canard by John Blagg of the St Albans club. Light weight is the secret to success and the model is completed with miniature spoked wheels.

Top right
Mick Oakey's CO_2-powered scale model built to 1/18 scale DH6, whose color markings are still incomplete. A rubber-powered Curtiss Jenny is on the right.

One of the problems of a rubber motor is that the power from it is not constant and reduces as the rubber unwinds. Thus there is a variation in the torque from high to low. To cater for this, variable pitch propellers have been developed so that at maximum torque the blades are sharply angled, and as the torque reduces the blades automatically adjust to a shallower angle.

Once the rubber motor has unwound the propeller can present problems by upsetting the trim of the model as it windmills or stops dead. The best method of avoiding this is to use a folding propeller, the blades of which fold back to streamline along the fuselage, allowing the model to glide with greater ease. Another way of overcoming the resistance which can be created by a propeller attached to a 'dead' motor is to fit a freewheeling device. The propeller is engaged to a clutch on the shaft and as the rubber unwinds the propeller disengages and is allowed to spin freely.

World and European Champion, Thomas Koster, with his Zooki Zooki 2.5cc-power model. Flying surfaces are skinned with 1/16-inch balsa and covered in 0.6-ounce glass cloth for rigidity during a fast seven-second power burst before continuing the flight on glide for three minutes plus.

A most unusual model, this rubber powered twin Lockheed Lightning is ideally suited to containing twisted rubber motors in its long twin tail booms. Richard Falconer, the model's builder, winds while John Blagg holds on.

Tom Stark's Loening M8 is a very detailed F/F scale model powered rather uncharacteristically with a fast Cox glowplug engine.

Internal combustion engines present a model with entirely different characteristics and with a constant power output as opposed to the declining output of the rubber motor. The duration of power runs by diesel and glowplug engines are usually limited to ten or twelve seconds in competition. Thereafter they must cut out and the model must glide successfully for the rest of its flight. As with the rubber-driven model, it is therefore vital for the diesel or glowplug motors to provide the right amount of power to achieve a good rate of climb and sufficient height before the power cuts out. Again, timers such as those we have mentioned for rubber power are used to cut the engine on time and, in the case of multi-function timers, to adjust the control surfaces of the model at precisely the right moment.

Clearly a model with a fixed wing designed with a high degree of camber to achieve a steep climb will be useless once the power has cut off. If the model is to be able to perform successfully in its dual role of powered aircraft and glider it must have control surfaces which suit each of those roles. Not only does it want to climb steeply on high-cambered wings, it must also glide gently on the thermal which, hopefully, the flyer will have found, descend gently *and* not soar into the distance.

BABY BULLET
X6784

Left
Pete Sutherland with this beautiful Heath Baby Bullet, a highly detailed F/F Scale CO_2-powered model of the original. (A close-up of this model appears on page 100.)

Right
Bill Dennis's superb LVG CV1, a highly detailed APS plan designed for .75-1cc free flight. The color scheme is the authentic original lozenge camouflage used by Germany. The fuselage is stained plywood and the laminated propeller adds the final touch of realism.

To obtain this amount of control of an aircraft flying without a pilot aboard obviously requires a certain amount of built-in instrumentation which can be relied upon to perform accurately. However, there is still plenty to be done on the ground before even the model makes its first powered flight.

Test glides need to be made with the engine fitted but not running to check the glide pattern of the model and make the necessary adjustments to movable control surfaces to ensure that when the model switches from power to glide they set in the desired position. For example, when the model goes into the glide you will want it to circle in the thermal. The rudder will therefore need to move to drop the right wing. This can be brought about simply enough using an auto-rudder device operated by a multi-function timer so that the rudder adjusts from neutral to offset as the power dies. Before takeoff the correct offset position must be determined.

The multi-function timer can also be used to cut off the fuel supply so that the engine has stopped at the end of the timed power-run and to alter the airfoil section of the wing to the under-wing curvature required for a good glide. Again, the adjustment of the angle must be set before the model is put to flight.

Below
This is a delightful little CO_2-powered F/F scale Farman Moustique by America's Bill Hannan. Only the rear right-hand cylinder is the CO_2 motor; the others are dummies of the original.

Despite every sophistication that can be added to a free-flight model it is inevitable that at some stage the aircraft will take it into its head to wander off on its own. It is then that the importance of making the model as distinctive as possible becomes paramount. (For competition flying, of course, the model also needs to be easily seen by timekeepers.) Bright coloring is obviously an aid to keep the machine in sight for as long as possible. The addition of bands of fluorescent paint or of reflective strips of plastic or very thin foil are also useful not only to keep the model in view but also to help in spotting it when it has landed.

It is, after all, both expensive and disheartening to waste all your efforts on a model which is so well camouflaged as to be indistinguishable when it decides to roam free.

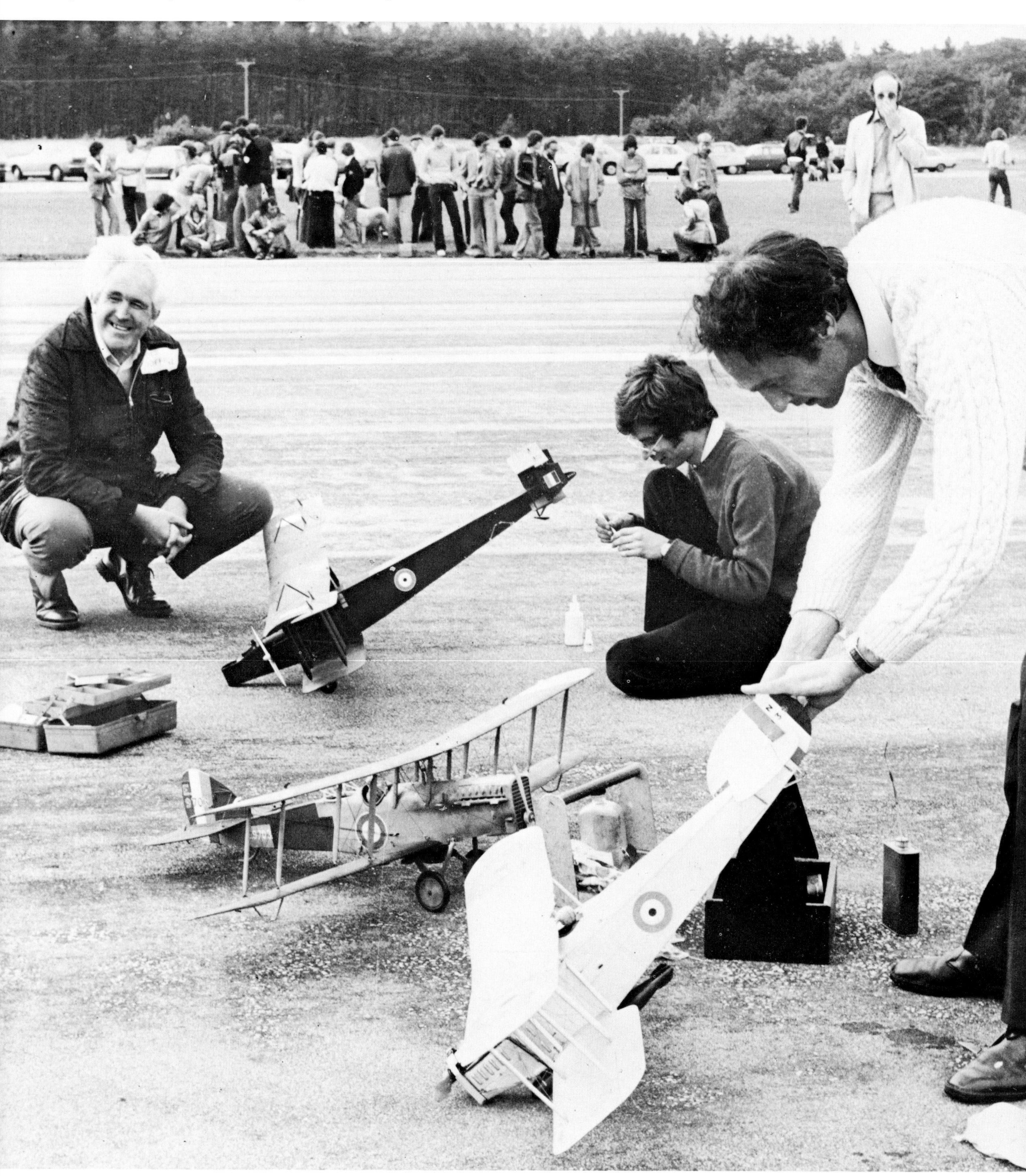

Above
This close-up illustrates the amazing detail of Terry Manley's Blackburn Swift, complete with dummy torpedo and spoked wheels.

Left
Nigel Druce with a scale model of the NC4 which completed the Atlantic crossing in 1919. The model was built by his brother and was originally rubber powered with motors extending back behind the propellers, although there are now plans to convert the model to CO_2 power.

Far left
Here is a fine line-up of F/F Scale models: Bill Dennis works on his Handley Page 0/400-powered by twin Mills .75s at the rear, Eric Coates with his de Havilland 9A sits in the middle and Terry Manley's Blackburn Swift is in foreground.

America's Al Rabe, himself an airline pilot, relaxes flying precision control-line aerobatics. His semi-scale Mustang looks most impressive especially when flown inverted just a few feet above the asphalt. The motor is based on a Super Tigre 61, and the rudder is linked to the controls for extra line tension during extra flight maneuvers.

Power on the Line

There can be few people who have not heard at some time the high-pitched buzz of a miniature motor and, tracking its source, have not watched in delight or awe as a 'tethered' model aircraft was put through its paces. To see a beautifully built model flying at the end of a control line which is in the hands of an expert is to watch a form of artistry and to appreciate why this category of flying has achieved such popularity.

Apart from the purely aesthetic attractions of control-line flying there were more practical reasons which gave rise to its growth into a 'boom industry.' There was the purely geographical point that, in Great Britain at least, there are not a great many places where model aircraft can have the space to fly free in ideal conditions. In addition there was and is the point that pursuing an errant free-flight model can be a tiring, time-consuming and sometimes fruitless occupation. Third, there was the desire among flyers to have a greater degree of control over their models and to be able to make them perform maneuvers, impossible in free flight.

As we have seen in the first chapter of this book, 'tethered flying' has been with us since the earliest days of aviation when experimental models and full-size machines were tied down – often without need – to prevent them from escaping. Later, when models were achieving some degree of sophistication, they were allowed to fly around poles to which they were attached by cord. Rubber models in particular could fly for some distance indoors, circling on short lines. However, at this stage no one had devised a means of controlling the models by transmitting 'instructions' along the lines.

A step in the right direction was made by a Texan, Victor Stanzel, in 1940 when he began advertising 'G-line Flying' for 'gas-powered super speed planes.' It transpired that the line was actually a simple rod with which the operator could alter the height or flying attitude of Stanzel's 'Shark' models assembled from kits. There were no movable controls which could be adjusted by the flyer.

The next step followed quickly when Nevilles E – 'Jim' – Walker invented the 'U-Control' system, which the American Junior Aircraft Company of Portland, Oregon, advertised in the United States in September 1940. The system was incorporated with Walker's Fireball model, which came in semi-finished kit form including a two-line control system. In the aircraft was a bellcrank, pivoted at its center and with one line running from the base corners out to the operator. The lines ran either in the wing, above or below it, depending upon the particular design of the model. From the top of the bellcrank a push rod can back to the elevator horn. The ends of the two lines were attached to the top and bottom of a U-shaped handle. By simply tilting this up or down the bellcrank was moved either to lift or lower the elevator, making the model dive or climb as it circled.

Walker toured the country with his models and, flying three at a time (one tethered to a helmet on his head), attracted enormous interest. He added refinements to the system, including a third control line to adjust the engine speed and even an extra pair of insulated lines which carried current to an electric relay which altered the ignition timing.

Such was the success of his model and the American Junior Aircraft Company's advertising that control-line flying caught on and other enthusiasts began developing their own versions of Walker's system. By 1945 aerobatics had become such a popular feature of model flying that the Aeromodellers Association of Northern California had drawn up a schedule of maneuvers to be used in aerobatics competitions. From takeoff the models were required, among other things, to perform five consecutive loops, climb, dive, execute a figure of eight and fly inverted. Control-line flying was becoming an art.

Multi-engine models are rare and always draw a crowd as witnessed by this superb Vickers Viscount finished in Aer Lingus colors, green and white, when it was flown at Old Warden All-Scale Day, England, June 1978.

NGK
BP
AER LINGUS

ATLANTIS

Far left
Marco Beschizza's fabulous Atlantis, a huge stunter powered by a Super Tigre 60 with a truly amazing airbrushed spray-paint color scheme. The model is fitted with flaps and elevators to enable tight corners.

Left and below
Peter Tindal, designer of the APS Chipmonk, with a Control-Line aerobatic model styled on the full-size Chipmunk. Detail of cockpit is shown at the left. Tindal was often on the British Team and twice the winner of the Gold Trophy at the British National Championships.

One refinement which came in 1950 was the single-line control or monoline, which has the advantage of offering less drag than the two-line method. Here the aircraft is controlled by twisting the wire with a slider moving along an archimedean screw to turn the bell-crank in the fuselage through a worm attachment. The monoline requires two hands to operate it, one holding the handle and the other moving the slider.

In the 'U-Control' system the two lines must be kept taut all the time to retain control of the model, but with the monoline it is possible to maintain control even while the wire is quite slack. On twin control-line models the bellcrank pivot is usually set so that the center of gravity is forward of it and the engine is offset outboard of the control lines. In this way the lines are kept taut more easily. Whatever type of control-line flying is undertaken, such as aerobatics, team, speed or combat, the model requires wings which will give good lift but which are trimmed so that it will respond quickly when required to climb. For aerobatics airfoils can be completely symmetrical, while for straightforward sport flying the Clark Y airfoil with a straight undersurface is ideal.

Initiation into the art of control-line flying can be a breathtaking as well as a dizzy-making experience and the novice will be very tempted to overcontrol the model, using accentuated and jerky wrist movements. The ideal is to start with a rigid arm, grasping the handle so that the top of it will control up movement and the bottom down. When the engine has been started it should be allowed to gather and settle to a steady running speed while a helper holds the model. The operator then calls for it to be released and as the model moves forward he keeps his arm pointing at it. After about 5 or 6yd (4.5 to 5.5m) the model should be wanting to take off and the operator should be encouraging it by lifting his arm (taking care that he does not try to drag the machine into the air). The tendency, as the machine leaves the ground, is for the pilot to try to help it up by moving the top control wire or to react in entirely the opposite way and dive it into the ground. In fact, so long as he follows the model round with his arm, no movement of the controls should be necessary if the pilot or his instructor have ensured before takeoff that when the model is at slightly above shoulder height the elevators are in a neutral position.

Once he has the model airborne, the novice should allow it to circle, 'straight and level' (it will probably be rather wavy, in fact) until he begins to get the feel of the machine. A few more flights and he will begin to get used to turning in circles, will not feel giddy and should gain the confidence to try a few tentative maneuvers up and down. Ideally he will have chosen to gain his experience on a training model which has controls that are not too sensitive and flies at a reasonable speed. To attempt to learn on a full-blown, lively aerobatics or speed model is to court disaster.

For aerobatics models, which fly at around 50mph (80.4kph), extra controls are usually added: in addition to the elevators there are coupled wing flaps which work simultaneously with the elevators but in the opposite direction, thus making a maneuver more abrupt and immediate. Use of the extra controls, the additional speed and the fact that the aerobatics model is likely to be a good deal bigger than the training version mean that there is a world of difference between operating the two. The 'stunt' type calls for a high degree of concentration and a great feel for the aircraft's abilities to perform particular maneuvers at split-second command. Because there is often no control over the speed of the engine during maneuvers the model must be fitted with a fine pitch propeller which makes the most efficient use of the power from the engine.

In competition stunt flying the model will be required to do a good deal of inverted flying. This calls for the incorporation of special features at the design stage, including a fuel system which will continue to give a constant flow to the engine while the aircraft is upside down.

When you consider that the model will be flying at speed in a circle, performing loops, wingovers, hourglasses, stalls and other maneuvers, it can be appreciated that the fuel is going to be thrown about in its tank. Baffles inside the tank will help to stop the fuel from slopping about too much. The centrifugal force generated by the model flying in circles throws the fuel to the outer edge of the tank and some tanks are designed as a wedge shape to take advantage of this. The fuel is thrown into the point of the wedge and fed to the engine from there.

To avoid a vacuum being formed as the engine sucks fuel from the tank, air vents are placed at the bottom as well as the top of the tank. Valves ensure that fuel

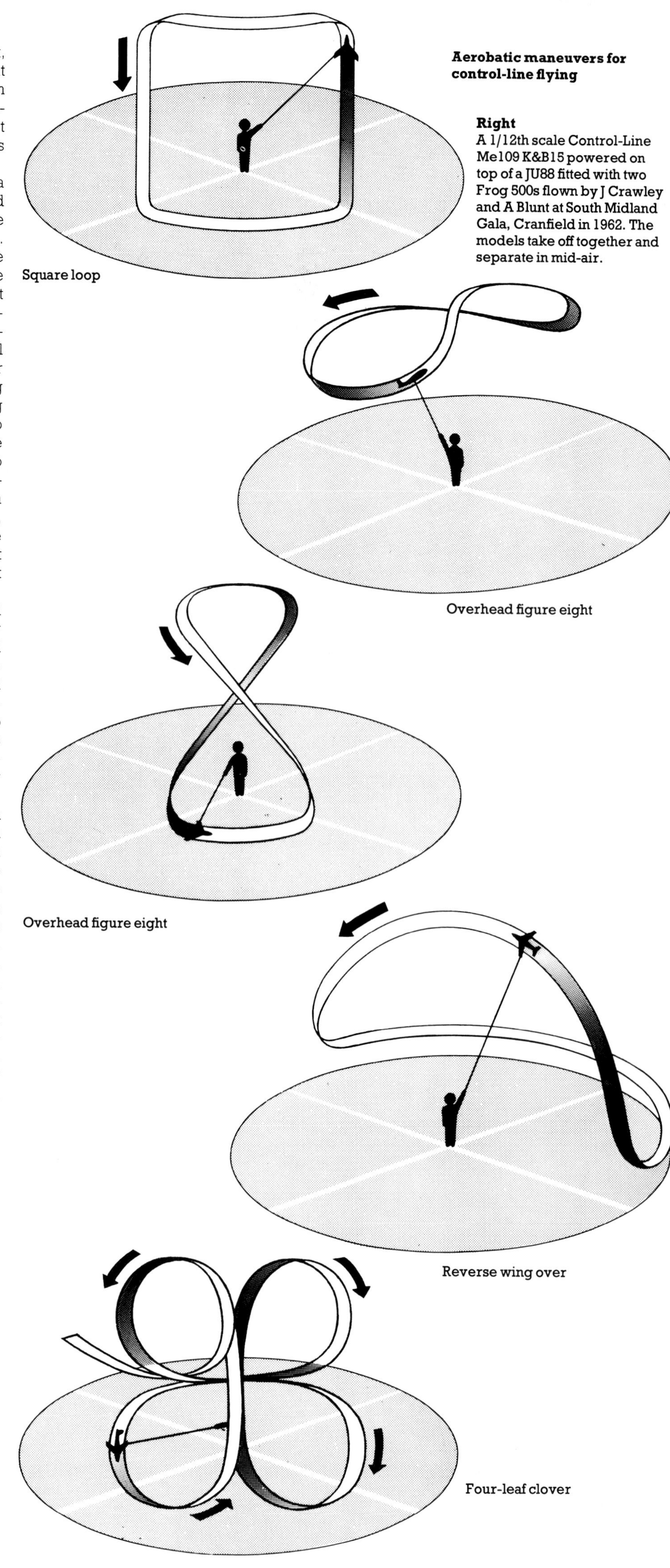

Aerobatic maneuvers for control-line flying

Right
A 1/12th scale Control-Line Me109 K&B15 powered on top of a JU88 fitted with two Frog 500s flown by J Crawley and A Blunt at South Midland Gala, Cranfield in 1962. The models take off together and separate in mid-air.

cannot escape through the venting tubes. A pressurized fuel system will also ensure constant flow. This can be worked from the pressure generated by exhaust gases; by a deflating bladder which is inflated by the fuel as it is fed in and forces fuel out as it returns to its natural shape; by coil tanks or by 'clank' tanks which have a rotating feed pipe to collect fuel.

Aids to keeping a stunt model under tight control include a weighted outboard wing tip, the offset rudder and engine, and a larger wing area on the inner wing to give it greater lift. In fact, the outer wing will be flying faster on its circular flight than the inner one and will therefore have more lift, so that the increased area of the inner wing is merely a countermeasure.

Though it may not seem so at the time, the best maneuver to attempt after graduating to aerobatics flying is the wingover. Imagine the normal flight path of a control line model as a visible ribbon floating horizontally in a perfect circle 6 to 8ft (1.8 to 2.4m) above the ground. The wingover is a matter of tilting one half of the circle up so that the aircraft performs an arc almost above the pilot. The maneuver involves turning the model from low level flight into a sharp climb to the top of the arc – making sure that the line

Left
In the middle Oliver Mittler (Belgium) and Cliff Gibson (Canada) battle it out during their Combat bout. Pilots have to be careful not to get their lines tangled during such exchanges.

Top
Mid-air action as Tourne of Belgium closes in on the streamer of Tomelleri of Italy. The idea is to cut your opponent's streamer with your own propeller; the most cuts win and pilots perform all manner of maneuvers to shake the opponent off their tail.

Above
Two flyers from the Northampton Club, Marc Harrison and Robert Roy, with their ½A size Banshee Combat models based on Derek Dowdeswell's famous Pink Panther. The motors used are PAW 149s and this form of Combat is rapidly catching on as it is much cheaper than the larger FAI class.

remains taut – and then bringing it down to the same low level again. In keeping your eye on the model – as you always must – you will almost certainly lose sight of the ground line and the beginner may well feel totally disoriented for a moment. It is at this second that there is the greatest likelihood of loss of control, for you must be concentrating on bringing the plane up, over and down to low flight again – but where is the ground! It is still there and so long as you do not over-react and remember to keep your arm rigid but tracing the pattern of the maneuver smoothly in the air, you will not go wrong.

Below
Mike Ennis with his monster sized Pfaldz DIII powered by a Veco 61 and fitted with a third-line throttle control.

Right
Wal Cordwell's fabulous Avro Tutor Control Line scale model, equipped with extra third-line control to operate throttle and allow touch-and-go landings.

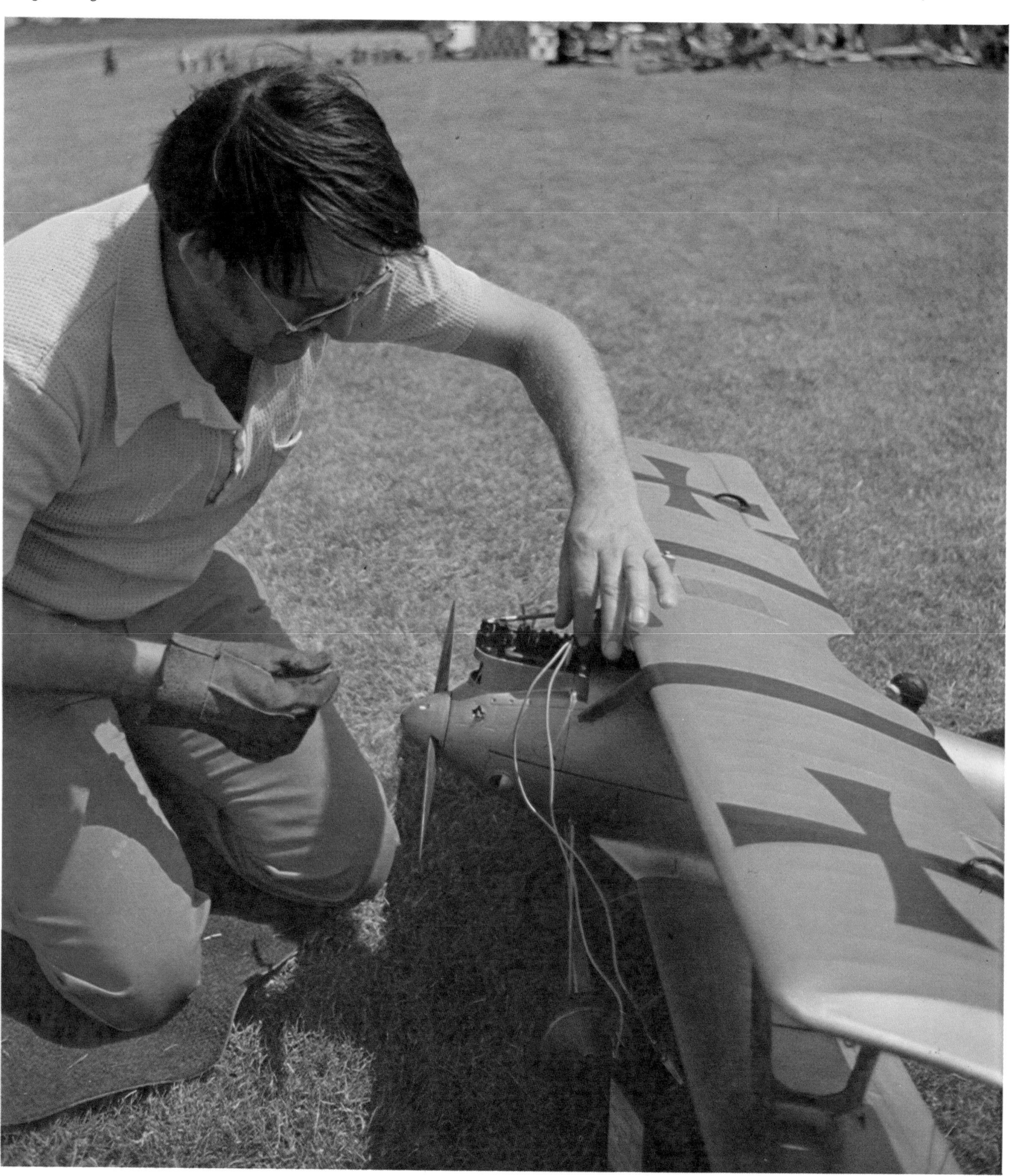

The smooth swing of the arm becomes even more important in performing a loop. Here the arm must describe a smooth, *round* circle on edge (if we continue to think of that solid ribbon) and the speed of the model must be maintained so that it does not stall. The slightest jerk in the arm movement will ruin the maneuver and action of the wrist, often performed in a moment of near panic, will tend to make matters worse. Repeated practice is the only way to achieve the fluency of performance which will not only satisfy you but also – if you enter competitions – gain points from the judges.

In control-line aerobatics competitions models are expected to fly a series of compulsory maneuvers during which they and the pilots are judged on their performance. In particular the judges will be watching for instability in flight, wobbly or wandering patterns in maneuvers, a tight control line, clean takeoffs and landings and an overall smoothness of flow both during and between maneuvers.

Each performance is timed from the moment that the pilot starts (or attempts to start) the engine until the model lands again. Between times the pilot will be called upon to put the aircraft through a consecutive series of maneuvers including inside and outside loops, wingovers, inside and outside square loops, triangular loops, horizontal, vertical and overhead figure eights, square horizontal eights and an hourglass figure. The experienced flyer will know exactly where to position himself in relation to the judges and to the wind.

In fact the wind will play an important part in the performance and failure to take account of it could ruin an entire routine. Whereas the free-flight model flies with the wind, in effect, and, once the engine has cut, glides with it, the control-line aircraft is captive and must fly a circular path into, across and with the wind. The model is, therefore, going to be speeded up, slowed down and side-slipped and must have both the engine power and the necessary amount of manipulative control to cope with the quickly changing conditions.

From the outset of a flight the wind should be con-

Bottom right
These Mexican-built models are unusual by European standards as they use all-moving tails mounted way back on mono or twin booms. The covering is transparent Mylar film.

Right
Belgium's Oliver Mittler competed at the Woodvale World Championships Combat event. His models typify modern construction, and are made from expanded polystyrene in the spruce spars. The holes are to improve lightness. Engines are Super Tigre 2.5cc glow motors fed from pacifier pressurized tanks.

Below
The moment of launch for Ireland's Stoo Holland. Combat models do without the luxury of fuselages as this only adds extra weight. Instead they are designed for strength and maneuverability, highly desirable qualities needed to overcome the opponent.

sidered as a 'part' of the model rather than as something against which the flyer has to compete. Thus, it can be used as an ally to assist in maneuvers. The takeoff run should start on a crosswind section of the arc so that the model has lifted off and is exerting almost its fullest

Below
Ireland's Stoo Holland about to start another Combat bout. His pit crew start the motors and keep a spare model on standby.

'pull' on the control line as it reaches the downwind segment. At that stage the wind will give the model a further boost before it flies into the wind. Usually it is best to fly aerobatics maneuvers with the wind, that is, downwind, so that it is exerting some pressure on the model, thereby helping to keep the line taut and maintain speed in the build up to the 'stunt.'

One of the most exciting forms of control-line performance is combat flying in which models 'attack' each other and the pilots can give full vent to their aggressions. The flight involves two models each flying in the same circle and each intent on slicing off the paper streamer trailed by the other. However, points are awarded for cuts made into the streamer by the opponent's propeller and it is therefore pointless – almost literally – to cut off an opponent's trail in one fell swoop. The art is to nibble away at the streamer before delivering the *coup de grace*.

Because of the speed and aggression of the combat, crashes are frequent but reserve models are allowed to fly into the aerial arena. This form of control-line flying is so sophisticated that the aircraft have been refined down to flying wings which are highly maneuverable despite the extra drag imposed by the streamers. While the pilot flies the 'fighter' a mechanic can stand by with the reserve machine fueled, warmed-up and ready for immediate takeoff when required. As soon as the first model lands the art is to save valuable time and points by whipping off the streamer, attaching it to the standby aircraft, starting the engine and getting the reserve into the air as quickly as possible.

Instant reactions are vital to success and the winner of the dog fight is likely to be the pilot who has the ability to perform the unexpected maneuver at the crucial moment – as the enemy closes in to attack. There is an art, too, in the ability to maneuver one's own model 'blind' while watching what the other pilot is doing.

A line-up of Control-Line Stunters at Northern Heights gala at RAF Halton, England. The models are powered by .35 cubic-inch motors and are fitted with flaps and elevators to enable tight maneuvers to be performed, such as squares and triangles. A wide-track undercarriage gives ground stability for takeoffs from grass.

Mike Birch, later to become British National Champion in Radio Controlled Aerobatics, is seen in his earlier days at the Northern Heights gala with his 35-size stunter finished in semi-scale German markings.

Speed flying may seem by contrast a more sedentary affair but it, too, is an art demanding intense concentration, very quick ground work and excellent tuning of the engine to bring it to peak performance and keep it there. The design of the speed model will incorporate every possible streamlining technique so that the aircraft becomes almost a flying bullet.

The object of speed flying is to fly the fastest recorded speed over a measured course covered in a set number of laps. However, competition regulations are extremely strict and some are such that the fastest speed recorded is not likely to be the top speed that a model could attain if it were flown unrestricted. International competition rules impose restrictions on type of fuel, wing area, weight, thickness of control lines and, of course, engine capacities. Either two-line or monoline control can be used, the latter having the advantage that a single wire will produce less drag than two wires. Considerable importance is attached to the design of the propeller, which must be highly efficient, with clean and sharp leading edges and built-in flexibility to allow for alteration of pitch.

To assist flyers and also to ensure that the model is not given an unfair boost by being dragged or whipped along by the pilot, a 'pylon' is set up at the center of the circle. The elbow of the flyer is rested on the pylon and the method of control becomes completely different. Instead of the rigid arm pointing at the model, the pilot has to use wrist movement to effect control surface changes.

Yet another exciting form of control-line flying is team racing. Though the rules vary in different countries, the basic objective remains common ground: to set your model against two or three others flying in the same circle over a set distance at top speed. The regulations for competitions are so devised that all models are of the same specification and are limited in their full capacity so that pit stops for refuelling are necessary.

This limitation of fuel capacity has a considerable bearing not only on the way the race is flown but also on the type of engine and fuel used. Essentially it becomes a matter of working out an equation involving engine capacity, speed capability and range. Too powerful an engine will give good speed but will eat up fuel, entailing frequent pit stops for refuelling and, hence, lost time. Too lean a fuel mix will not give the power required and will result in overheating. Similarly, if the mixture is too strong, there is also a danger of overheating and therefore of engine damage. Standard fuel is mandatory for the uninitiated until sufficient tests can ensure the exact mix necessary.

Below
Gordon Isles, Dave Smith and Pete Halman, three of Britain's top Speed flyers. Asymetric layout models are now common; an outboard wing could only add more drag while the longer inboard wing streamlines control wires increasing speed. The wings are hollow alloy sheet. Speeds for these 2.5cc models is now reaching over 150mph!

Left
Vince Hawtree's model flashes through the picture during a Mini Goodyear race against Simon Coppock and David Wicks. The Mini Goodyear is for Profile racers powered by 1.5cc motors flown over grass and is very popular with junior control-line flyers.

Below
Strangely, this conventional layout model is unusual by Speed model standards. Sam Burke of Canada modelled it on the full-size racing plane of the 40s, a full length tuned pipe exhaust to the Rossi 15 motor exits at the rear of the fuselage.

Below
Two Aerobatic models from the USSR competed at the 1966 World Championships at Swindersby, England. Viatcheslav Simonov's model is in the foreground and Kari Plotsin's behind.

Right
Danny Jones of the USA visited the UK World Championships in 1966 to fly this Oliver Tiger 2.5cc-powered Splinter. All moving elevator pivots are on twin plywood booms.

749
SPLINTER

Below
The excitement of the Team Race where pairs of flyers, pitman and pilot, race with others over a 100-lap course. Bert Mekemeijer, Holland (left) takes off and runs forward to join Britain's Derek Heaton already in the middle, while Hans Getschwendtner's model slows down for a landing to be refuelled. An electronic scoreboard behind keeps a record of the laps.

Right
Goodyear racing is very popular because models are realistic yet simple, having been made from all-sheet balsa with profile outlines ⅛-scale of the original full-size American facing planes. Any engine up to 3.5cc capacity is allowed, and the one in the picture is a Super Tigre 15. The gadget behind the motor is a fuel cut-out activated by the down line and the fuel tank is fitted with a quick-fill rubber valve.

Far right
This is a neat model of America's Albrittan/Joy team ready for a first flick start of their Nelson 15 diesel. Speeds of 90mph are common for these racers. The can on the arm contains pressurized fuel for quick refuelling.

The mechanic's role in refuelling is vital to the success of team flying. The moment the aircraft touches down he must run to meet it as it rolls along – taking care that he does not interfere with the control lines of other models in the race – fill the tank, restart the engine and set it off again. To save valuable seconds, refuelling is invariably by a pressure system, the most popular being by the use of a medicinal syringe already primed. The engine must be very finely tuned so that it restarts with one flick of the propeller and gathers power for re-takeoff without 'stuttering.'

Rules for team racing stipulate that the models must at least look like real aircraft. That is to say, they cannot be merely flying wings or super-streamlined bullets but must be a semi-scale reproduction of an actual airplane.

Because the models are working at high speed and landing fast for refuelling, and since their 'under-carts' are subjected to some hefty bangs, they need to be built to withstand high shock loads. The undercarriage has to be both strong and well-sprung and the engine should be securely bedded to reduce vibration. The difficulty is to match the strength of the model with the need for it to be as light as possible so that, once the engine cuts, inertia will fall away quickly, allowing the operator to land the aircraft quickly.

To watch team racing is to see a breathtaking display of finely-tuned flying and of co-ordinated effort between the pilot and mechanic.

Waves of the Air

The biggest step in making model aircraft not only look but also perform like their full-size counterparts came with the introduction of radio control. Now it became possible to retain a hold on the flying model through the invisible 'control line' of the radio waves, yet have all the advantages – and more – of free flight.

It was as long ago as the early 1930s that first experiments began in piloting full-size aircraft by remote control, principally for the military purpose of providing gunnery targets which did not have to be towed. Details of a control system and radio circuits were published in radio 'ham' magazines and in 1936 the first issue of *Model Aviation* in America announced a new contest for radio-controlled models to be included in the American National Contests that year.

However, it was not to be: no entries were received and the first ever competition for radio-controlled model aircraft did not get off the ground until the Nationals of the following year. Six entries were received. Of those, only three actually flew and the judges decided that only one was genuinely *controlled* by radio. That was the model flown by Chester Lanzo of Cleveland, Ohio, which had a 9ft (2.7m) wing span and weighing 6lb (2.7kg).

Lanzo launched his machine by hand and the judges were satisfied that, although it flew almost straight, every time he operated the control the plane deviated a little from its course and wobbled. It was therefore 'controlled.' The rudder control was activated by signals to a receiver weighing just under 2lb (0.9kg). Lanzo used a system operating on the eight-meter band – reserved for radio amateurs – and found that at times it picked up signals from transmitters hundreds of miles away.

Left
Scale World War II fighters, shown here, are popular subjects for radio control models.

In 1938 the second American Nationals competition for radio-controlled models was held on a very windy day and the conditions brought disaster to the only aircraft to achieve takeoff. It climbed, stalled and dived into the ground.

The model which gained greater success, as well as second place, was one which did not leave the ground! Clinton Desoto, a member of the American Radio Relay League and a keen researcher, developed along with other League members a single-valve receiver to replace the two- and three-valve system. Using this he built a massive 14ft (4.2m) model powered by a twin-cylinder engine and weighing 28lb (12.7kg). The machine carried four separate receivers which were used to operate the elevators up and down and the rudder left and right. The judges were so impressed with the ingenuity of Desoto's electronics that he was awarded second place without the model taking to the air. He later manufactured radio-control equipment commercially.

It was inevitable in those days that the radio-controlled models had to be large since the equipment itself was bulky, with valves and tubes which then had not been miniaturized. The advent of the transistor

Above
The detail inside Mike Reeve's Fournier RF4 is clearly shown: the radio headset works, the altimeter works and ignition lights flash on the dashboard when the engine is started. He was deservedly the winner of the World Radio-Controlled Scale Championships in 1978.

system transformed radio-controlled model flying and headed it toward today's high degree of sophistication. However, it took years of research – principally of a military nature – and another war to give radio control its biggest push. During World War II remote control aircraft were used for spy missions (to bring back aerial photographs from behind enemy lines), for gunnery practice and as 'flying bombs' packed with explosives and directed by radio to the chosen targets.

Today radio control is used in a whole range of applications: in industry, medicine, transport and aerospace research as well as in all manner of toys and models. A subject which requires the highest degree of technological research and back-up has been made to appear simple in its application to everyday objects. Even so, it would be an unwise modeller who is deceived into thinking it is simple to make or assemble a radio-controlled model or to get it to perform well. There is nothing so deceptive as to go out on the local heath and simply watch the radio control enthusiasts flying their models with apparent ease. It all looks so simple and, apart from the occasional pile-up, so graceful – those miniature aircraft flying above you, climbing, diving and stunting are just like 'the real thing.'

It can be great, but only if you approach the subject with much thought, a good deal of preliminary study and a lot of advice from others. Do not just stand and watch those models; go and talk to their pilots. The advice you receive may well be conflicting at first but it will soon become clear that one thing is essential: the need to join a club or group.

The second piece of advice is not to overstep the mark and become too ambitious in the choice of your first model. Of course, it would be wonderful to have a superb, multi-function model at the command of your fingertips but that is neither likely (unless you are a genius) nor practicable. The way to success is through a simple first model, designed specifically for radio control, plus equipment which is made with the beginner in mind. The majority of systems include a 'buddy box' which enables an instructor to take over the controls if the novice gets into difficulties.

Top right
Two 61-horsepower Hawker Hurricanes constructed from a Mick Reeves Kit. They have a wing span of 84 inches.

Below
A CAP Thunderbolt at Old Warden Scale Day, England. The builder is unknown.

Below right
Brian Taylor, a member of the winning UK Team at the 1978 World Championships, starts up his Northrop Black Widow.

Bottom right
Jim Davis's Messerschmidt-Rowena. It was constructed entirely of wood and has a chain saw engine.

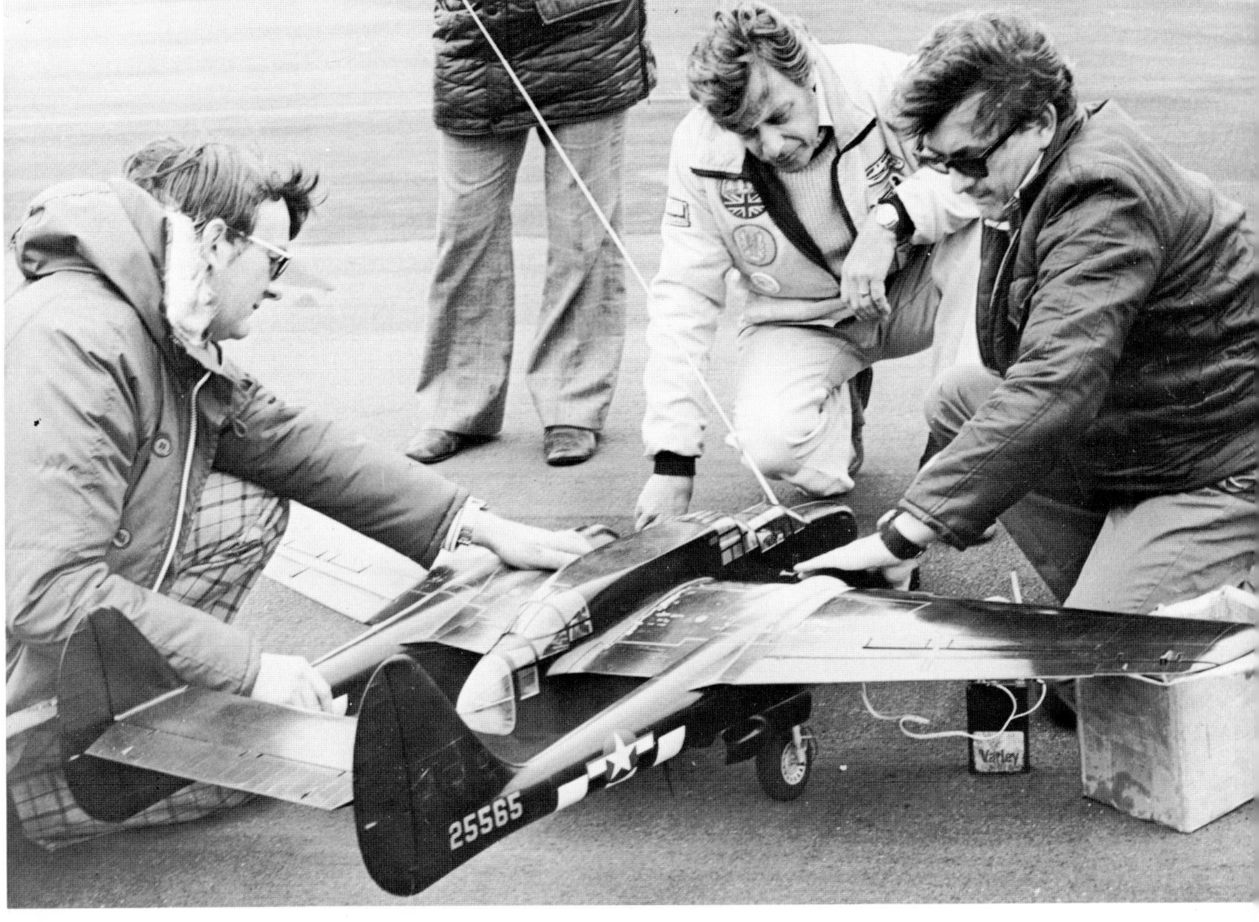

Jim Davis's Lancaster model, an all-wood construction with two free-wheeling propellers and powered by two Rowena chain saw engines.

The ideal model for a pupil pilot is likely to be of high wing design and with a strong tricycle undercarriage – high wing because these are more stable in flight; strong because there will inevitably be a good number of heavy landings to begin with; tricycle because take-off and landing are easier and can be better controlled. A further advantage of the high wing design is that the wings can be easily detached, fastened by rubber bands which will come free if the aircraft crashes and thus lessening the risk of expensive damage.

When it comes to choosing the radio equipment an initial decision must be made on whether to select a simple single-channel control or a multi-channel system, the most intricate of which can perform a considerable number of functions. The single-channel type of receiver has just one function on one relay – used to operate the rudder – and is therefore the cheapest. However, if cheapness is not the only consideration it is worth looking to a multi-channel receiver with perhaps six functions since the novice will, hopefully, soon outgrow the simpler equipment and will look for something which enables him to make his model perform as realistically as possible.

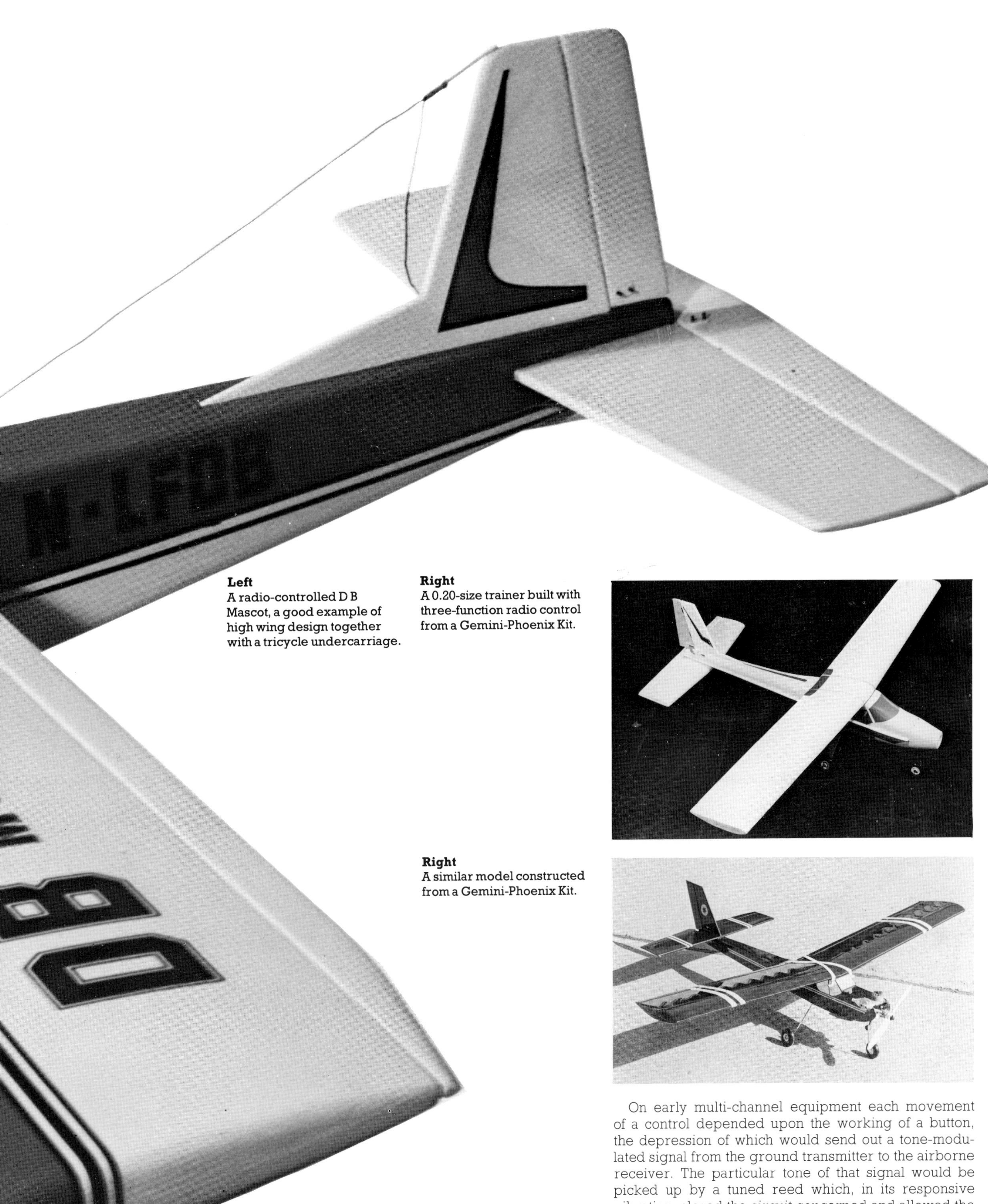

Left
A radio-controlled D B Mascot, a good example of high wing design together with a tricycle undercarriage.

Right
A 0.20-size trainer built with three-function radio control from a Gemini-Phoenix Kit.

Right
A similar model constructed from a Gemini-Phoenix Kit.

On early multi-channel equipment each movement of a control depended upon the working of a button, the depression of which would send out a tone-modulated signal from the ground transmitter to the airborne receiver. The particular tone of that signal would be picked up by a tuned reed which, in its responsive vibration, closed the circuit concerned and allowed the controls for just that one control surface to operate through a servo. Fine adjustment could be a problem and become a matter of experience: the control surface continued to move to its limit so long as the button was depressed and selection of an intermediate position depended on careful judgment and a series of depress-release-depress touches on the button.

Below
A half-size display model of a Cassat Goodyear type racer with a Rowena chain saw engine.

Not only was the equipment bulky, the reeds were not always reliable on pitch and the tonal signal itself could wander sufficiently for the receiver not to pick it up. The result was that the servo would not be set to work. In some models a safety device was built in so that all controls returned to neutral in the absence of a signal. The idea was to avoid the situation in which the model went out of control and dived to the ground. However, there was the problem that the receiver could pick up a signal from another transmitter in the absence of its own 'master signal' or if it flew close enough to the rival transmitter for its own signal to be swamped. This could cause total confusion.

The coming of the transistor and the technology which made miniaturization of moving parts as well as of electronic equipment possible has seen in a new breed of radio-controlled model. Basically the equipment remains much the same; that is to say that there must still be a suitable model aircraft, a ground transmitter sending out signals, a receiver to pick up the signal and a mechanism to convert the signals into actions. The difference comes in the refinement of modern equipment and in the widespread availability of components so that the experienced builder can make his own, highly sophisticated model from scratch. In addition the control surfaces can be moved to very fine limits, the undercarriage raised and lowered, the speed of the engine controlled instantly and accurately and the choke setting altered.

Today in Britain radio-control systems must be tuned to transmit on one of a number of exact spot frequencies which range through the officially allocated waveband from 26.96MHz to 27.28MHz. Each 'spot' is identified by a color code and this should be displayed on your transmitter aerial. The purpose of the color identification system is to avoid pilots using the same frequencies within range of each other or when one can see that another on his 'spot' is already flying.

The color code system is as follows:

Grey/brown	26.975MHz;	brown	26.995MHz
Brown/red	27.025MHz;	red	27.045MHz
Red/orange	27.075MHz;	orange	27.095MHz
Orange/yellow	27.125MHz;	yellow	27.145MHz
Yellow/green	27.175MHz;	green	27.195MHz
Green/blue	27.225MHz;	blue	27.245MHz

Before the days of ultra-sophistication to which we have referred, models commonly weighed between 20lb and 30lb (9 to 13kg) and some even more. Today it is unusual for even a high-speed, multi-function aerobatic model to weigh more than about 10lb or 12lb (4.5 to 5.4kg) complete. Aircraft commonly – and comfortably – exceed 120mph (193kph) and at this sort of speed the forces exerted on their structures – the 'G' forces – are far higher than would be expected in a full-size aircraft. For this reason as well as for the comparative lightness of the material, fiberglass is popular as a building medium. Parts can be bought ready-molded or, as we have seen elsewhere, can be scratch-built. A fuselage of fiberglass is strong enough not to require a great deal of inner strengthening by means of bulkheads, longerons and the like and therefore offers the additional advantage of providing plenty of space in which to install the radio equipment. Should the fiberglass be damaged it is a relatively simple matter to carry out a quite rapid 'running repair' using a glasscloth 'dressing' and one of the quick-drying resins to which we have also referred earlier.

The choice of engine and its best bedding to avoid vibration which could drastically affect operation of the radio equipment is important. Its size and capability will – or should – depend on the experience of the user and the novice pilot would be well advised not to be overambitious in his choice of power source. For single-channel flying with a trainer of around 48 to 50in (122 to 127cm) wing span an engine of around

Below
A DL5 lightweight model, an unusual prototype for 19 to 25 horsepower.

Bottom
A HB61-power Graupner Piper Cherokee semi-scale built by Jack Barnard.

0.8cc is perfectly adequate while an introduction to multi-channel flying could well be through the 57in (145cm) 'Tauri' with a 3.5cc engine. This model will happily take up to 6.5cc and is high winged, with a tricycle undercarriage.

A thought worth bearing in mind is that with the sustained flights which are possible under radio control, fuel costs will be considerably higher. Indeed, a fast flying aerobatics model powered by a 10cc engine and competing or just sport-flying regularly, will burn up a startling amount of fuel and flyers can find themselves buying or making up nearly a gallon a month.

Whatever the capacity of the engine, it is essential to good performance that it is kept well lubricated, is well run-in when new and is well maintained. These three points will take you several steps towards good, uninterrupted flying. Other considerations should be in the make up of the fuel itself, its purity, the provision of a filter in the fuel system and the correct adjustment of the engine to give smooth running at high rpm without overheating.

The selection of the equipment is very much a matter of individual choice, depth of pocket and experience, but the manner of its installation is of supreme importance to the eventual performance of the aircraft. After all, there has to be packed into the fuselage a surprising amount of additional equipment which, even with miniaturization, will add something like 10 or 12oz (283 to 340g) to the all-up weight of the model. That extra weight will obviously affect the trim of the aircraft and must be distributed as advantageously as possible. If the job is done with thought the equipment modules – usually a receiver plus aerial, servos, switchgear and battery – can be turned to a positive advantage so long as constant checks are made as each piece goes in that it is well positioned and held firmly in place.

The heaviest piece of equipment in the aircraft is likely to be the battery. Nowadays the most popular type of battery for radio-controlled flight is the nickel-cadmium cell or nicad, which gives a steady voltage rather than the dropping output of a dry cell battery. An additional advantage to nicads is that they can be recharged repeatedly and have a long overall life as well as good short-term endurance between charges, giving flights of five to ten minutes between recharges depending upon their age.

Because of the weight of the battery it is important to consider its placing not only in relation to the general weight distribution but also with the receiver in mind. If the battery is positioned *behind* the receiver and breaks free in the event of a crash there is a chance that the radio equipment will be damaged.

However, a sensible precaution is to allow, at the planning stage, for space to be allowed between the parts for protective packing such as polystyrene, plastic or rubber foam to be inserted once final positioning has been decided.

Before installing any radio-control equipment the balancing point of the model should be determined. This is simple enough and can be done either by balancing the model on a fulcrum point on the work-bench or, more satisfactorily, by suspending the aircraft from a line attached to the point at which you require the center of balance to be and trimming to it.

Below
An AEXI electric power aerobatic model with a 63-inch wing span designed by Gerald Johnson.

Bottom
A Micro-Mold Centerfire Sport aerobatic model with a 0.40 cubic inch motor. It has a vac-formed plastic fuselage with foam core veneered wings.

Above
Hub Dekkers of the Netherlands with the 'Flying Dutchman' at the 1977 World Championships in the USA.

Left
Jack Barnard with his pylon mounted engine sports model. It has all foam wings with a vac-formed fuselage and is slow flying for a 0.8cc engine.

Below
Don Beaumont releases Neville Holmes' 0.40 power Bobcat at the FAI races.

Thereafter it is a matter of installing the equipment using the layout plan you have decided upon, checking the balance and also that you are not placing a part in such a position that it will interfere with the servo movements or push rods to the control surfaces.

When carrying out a 'dry-run' – installing the equipment without fastening it – always remember to check that there is sufficient space left for whatever type of fastening you may have selected. There is a whole range of ready-made clips into which parts can be slipped and held fast. Alternatively the modules can be stuck in place with double-sided tape – if balsa forms the main structure it should first be doped to receive the tape – or can be screwed down to wood rails (a bit too permanent for some people's liking) or fitted into servo trays.

Once all the radio-control equipment has been fitted the servos can be connected up to the control surface systems, which will be push-pull rods, close looped cables or tube cables. The push rods are normally made from wood, nylon or stiff wire or a combination of wire-wood-wire. Wire on its own presents a problem if it is to run over more than a few inches as it will tend to flex, making movement of the control surfaces sloppy and reducing the range of movement.

Above
A model of the Flair Dara Club 20 pylon racer with a .20 cubic inch motor and two-function radio control, built by Dudley Pattison.

Right
Bill Frankham with his Cotswold FAI pylon racer. The model, which has a 0.40 cubic inch OPS engine with a tune pipe exhaust system, can reach speeds of 140mph.

The close-looped cable is best in a nylon-coated form which contains seven filament strands and is very lightweight. As with all control systems, care should be taken to avoid too many or too sharp changes of direction. Where there are obstructions, the cables can be routed in curves made as gentle as possible through guide tubes. The aerial should be installed unkinked and as far as possible from metal parts likely to cause interference.

Flying a radio-controlled model in competition is possibly the most exciting form of model aircraft flying, and requires a degree of concentration, an instinctive feel for the aircraft and for those against which it is competing that comes only from experience. A split second's loss of concentration or a fractionally wrong movement of the control stick can lose a competition or bring disaster.

One of the essentials of successful aerobatics flying is for the pilot on the ground to be able to imagine himself into the position he would occupy if he was actually flying in his model. If he can feel himself to be sitting

Above left
Tony Baker with his winning 1/3 scale five-meter DG-100. A superb performer, this model is constructed of an epoxy glass fuselage, glass-skinned wings and is complete with airbrakes.

Above
Max Tripp with his modified Veron Cobra which was recently featured in a Slope Special. Max suffered from an attack of competition shakes during the flight, but during the after hours flying around, the model and Max both performed superbly!

in the cockpit experiencing each maneuver he is more likely to retain the perfect control necessary to win competitions and he will carry out movements with greater precision. Beginners in particular will know all too well how easy it is to 'lose touch' with the model in the air and momentarily find that one is not sure which way the control stick should be moved. This is most noticeable with inverted flight when the pilot finds that he has become disoriented and cannot, for the life of him, remember whether he needs the port wing to lift or drop – and if he does, should he be transmitting an 'up' or a 'down' signal?

The superior performing and endurance capabilities of an aerobatics radio-controlled model mean that entrants in aerobatics competitions are called upon to put their aircraft through far more complicated maneuvers than those required in control-line contests. Each part of a maneuver in internationally recognized competitions is very precisely defined by the Fédération Aéronautique Internationale, the governing body for such events. The slightest deviation from the laid-

Above
Barry Jackson with his Seychelle (Acme Plan) model, a slope aerobatic/pylon racer.

down pattern will result in a downgrading in the pilot's points total.

Pylon races were introduced in the United States to bring back the spirit of the great air races of the past and they have proved as popular with crowds as they have with contestants. They became part of the British National Championships in 1972. In this form of racing four models are set against each other to fly a triangular course defined by three pylons so placed that a single lap comprises 400m, assuming absolutely straight-line flight was possible round the outside of the pylons. Speeds of over 150mph (240kph) have been achieved and control of models flying this fast is a matter of supreme accuracy and concentration. Reaction to the maneuvers of the other aircraft in the circuit and to changes in conditions must be so fast that it is instinctive.

Imagine the forces exerted on a model flying at this speed into a turn of about 330 degrees and it can be appreciated that the aircraft must be constructed with a considerable amount of built-in strength. However, competition rules lay down not only maximum engine capacity but also minimum wing thickness, wingspan and the fuselage diameter. There are also regulations governing the type of propeller and the type of fuel. All these rules have a bearing on safety and are intended to standardize competing models, which have to resemble full-sized aircraft.

So far we have dealt with only the most popular form of radio-controlled model, the engine-powered. However, there is another form of radio control which requires no internal combustion: that of the glider. The most popular method of gliding under radio control is 'slope soaring,' which is a more dependable form than the less popular 'thermal soaring.' The first makes use of the rising air current which will be found on the windward face of any prominence; the more prominent the slope the better, so long as it *is* a slope and not a sheer cliff face. The 'thermal soarer' must search out the upward thermal currents over flat ground and, having launched into a column of uprising air, makes use of the radio controls to sustain flight and perform aerobatic feats not possible in a free-flying glider.

Right
'Wildfleckers,' a 120-inch F3B and open-class soarer built from a Radio Sailplanes kit.

Below
Pat Teakle with his immaculate Swallow, a smooth performer of all-balsa construction.

Above far right
A Sirius lightweight open-class soarer featuring all built-up construction and a plastic film covering.

Below far right
F3B class (FAI Multi-Task) soarer photographed at the 1977 World Championships in South Africa.

The ideal launch point for a slope-soaring glider is some 30ft (9m) below the crest of the chosen hill, where the model will fly out from the hillside and soar upwards as it catches the up-current. Use of the radio controls will keep the glider nosed into the current and away from the slope.

Beginners will quickly discover, if they have not been previously warned, that launching nose up into anything more than the merest breath of air will have spectacular results. If you are lucky, the glider may loop; if not it will stall. The ideal is to stand on the slope facing outward and search for a clear stretch, free of boulders, trees or bushes which will cause early turbulence. Having found such a stretch, the model is launched into the wind, nose slightly down, and radio control takes over as it is lifted by the thermal. Initially it is best to trim for level flight and use only the thermal for lift as you get the feel of things.

Guide the model gently in a zigzag across the wind and always turn into the wind. With practice – quite a lot of it – you will learn to maneuver more confidently and then to judge exactly when the conditions are right for some more ambitious aerobatics.

Bringing the glider back in to land also needs plenty of practice and before even launching the model you should pick out at least one likely landing spot. This will be an area which is out of the lifting air current. The glider can be navigated out of its final downwind zigzag leg into a crosswind and away from the lift to head towards the chosen landing spot. As it loses height, turn it into the wind over the landing area and allow it to settle.

Some of the points to remember about radio-controlled gliding are that there is a strong chance that other operators will have selected the same area in which to fly and you must expect to take your turn. You should always watch out for people and animals in the way of your flight path and avoid traffic routes: a glider, however beautiful to its owner, becomes an ugly beast when it appears in a motorist's windshield without warning.

Because of the accuracy of control which good radio control gives to a glider, competitions are held in which the models are required to perform strictly defined 'tasks' within a given flight time and to land precisely on a marked spot. Scoring is for the accuracy with which the tasks are performed, the closeness of the landing to the spot and the adherence of the flight's duration to the set time. There are then two further stages which will call upon the pilot to fly his glider as far as possible in the zigzag pattern between two base lines in a given time and then to fly at speed from one base line to the other in the fastest time.

Success in such competitions depends upon the pilot's ability to make the maximum use of the up-current (he is given time to find it) by climbing swiftly to gain height which will give him speed as the glider adopts its natural tendency to return to earth.

The other form of radio-controlled gliding which we have mentioned, thermal soaring, is probably the best first stage for someone who is switching from free-flight gliding to radio-control. As with the basic slope soarer, it is usual to have a simple rudder and elevator control system, although a third control to release the tow hook on the thermal soarer can be included. (With aerobatics slope soarers, aileron control is also necessary.) That is not to say that you should necessarily start by investing in a two-channel system; since one would expect that you will progress to a thermal soarer with flaps, a better buy might well be a four-channel system which can be transferred to a more sophisticated model when you feel ready.

Right and far right

Fridolin Fritz with his Werner Sitars F3B model. The photograph on the far right shows the model being launched.

Below
Herbert Sitar and Fridolin Fritz with an F3B model at the International Gliding Championships in Oxford, England in 1977.

04122

Though the thermal soarer can be hand launched it is better to persuade an experienced hand to assist you with a tow launch. If you have a model of about 100in (254cm) wing span, a tow line of around 35lb (16kg) breaking strain and about 150m long is ideal. It should be pulled steadily so that there is even tension on the line – *not* so that the whole thing develops into a race between tower and launcher. Unlike the slope soarer's nose-down launch, the thermal soarer should be released with its nose up by between 25 and 30 degrees. A difference compared with free flight is that the controls will have been set at neutral before launch so that the elevator lines up with the tailplane and the rudder is not offset but lines vertically with the tailfin. Once the glider is airborne the necessary adjustments in trim are quickly made, depending upon the way the model is performing and its relation to the all-important thermal you will have detected.

All of what has gone before in this chapter is the merest hint of the world of radio-controlled flying, its delights and its pitfalls. To experience its many delights to the full requires a close study of one or more of the many books devoted entirely to the subject. Above all, it requires the participant not to be afraid to ask and to feel free to mingle with the inevitable group of experts who will gather at any popular flying spot and will exchange information and advice.

Provided you have not barged in as a newcomer and caused chaos by failing to show your frequency color coding on your aerial or by monopolizing someone else's airspace, you will be as welcome as any convert who is prepared to listen and learn.

Far left
An elegant 120-inch span Vee-tailed open-class soarer, very reminiscent of the full-size 'Orlice.'

Above
A Veron Cobra scale glider for slope or thermal being launched at one of the 1977 thermal events.

Left
Sean Bannister launching his model Algebra.

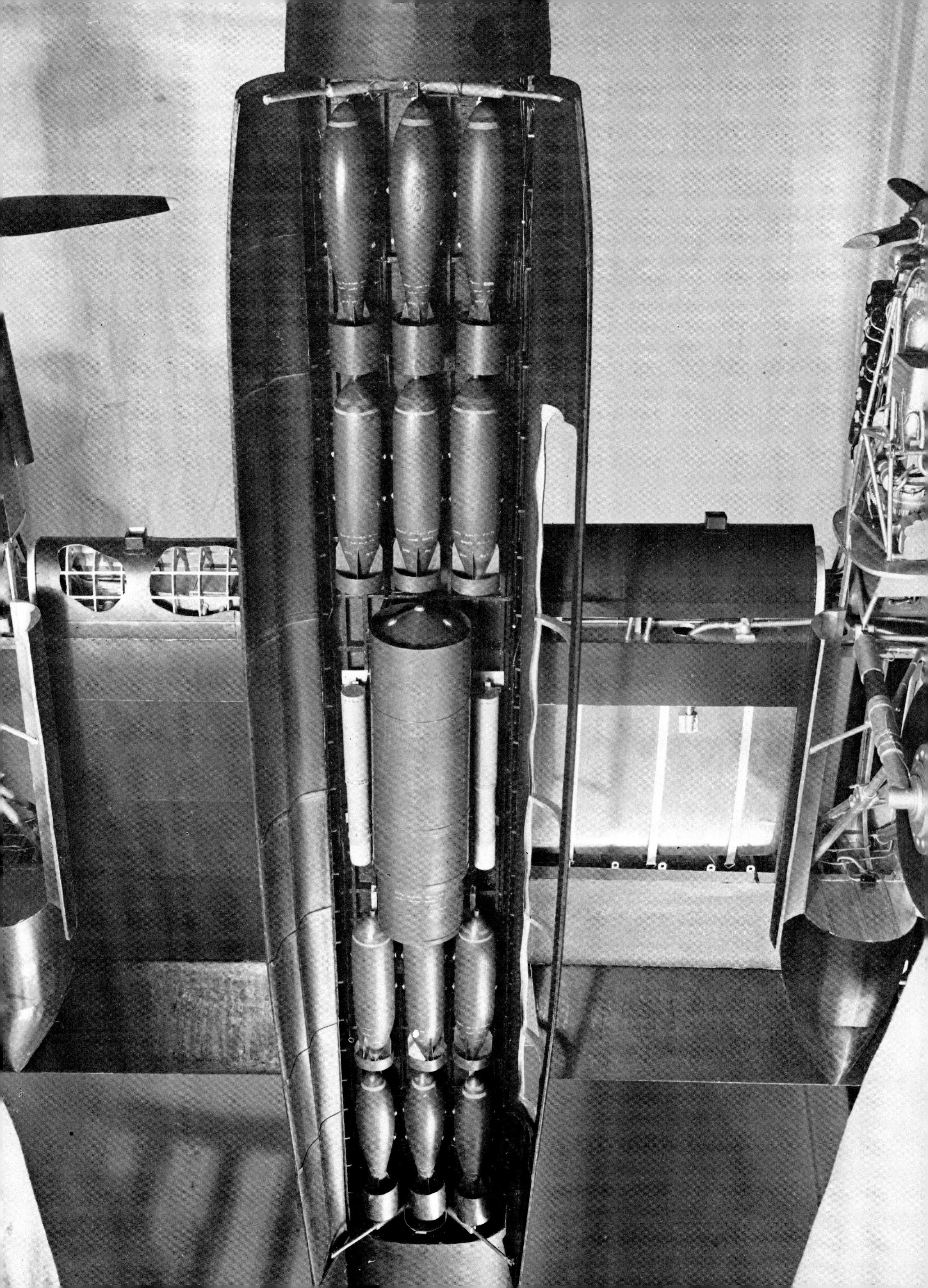

The Final Effect

Whatever type of model you are interested in, its finish will be of primary importance to the success of the project. This final stage of making a model is the one which will decide whether it looks like the 'real thing,' whether it flies moderately well or excellently, and whether it is a durable object capable of withstanding crashes or a flimsy toy which collapses at a touch.

These factors apart, there is also what we might call the 'decorative' finishing stage in which your model is given its own particular touches of individuality. This may be to mark it out as an aircraft of a certain squadron or pilot or it may be simply a matter of providing it with distinctive coloring for spotting purposes.

As far as static models built from kits or from ingenuity are concerned, the modern airbrush has made a vast difference to the standard of finish which can be imparted to a model, spraying on the paint in a fine film which can be increased in thickness by repeated applications. This is, in fact, an exact duplication of the way in which full-size aircraft are painted and it has the great advantage of avoiding the risk of leaving bristle marks in paint applied by brush.

However, not all pockets are going to extend to even one airbrush, let alone the ideal of a selection of them. If paint brushes are going to be used there is no point in spoiling the model to save money; buy good quality brushes which will not deposit their bristles or score the paint and which are soft and well shaped. Always wash the brush in warm water after it has been purchased; this will remove dust, grease and any loose hairs. While the head is still damp, smooth it to the finest point you can achieve and stand it on end to dry to this shape. Remember to repeat this procedure each time you have used the brush, first cleaning it thoroughly in turpentine or white spirit, followed by soap and water. In this way you will prolong the life of the brush – and also give yourself the best possible start to achieving a good finish.

Left and below
This is one of Cyril McCann's 'built-for-the-fun-of-it' models, a Mk 1 Avro Lancaster which was completed in 1954 and is also on show in the Imperial War Museum, London. Much information about the 'Lanc' was still classified when he started building, working from official photographs and an Avro handbook. 'In my view it falls short because of what we now know about the "Lanc," ' McCann says. Even so, note the fine detail and workmanship in the bomb bay.

Choice of paint for a plastic model can be confusing because of the number of brands which are available. Of one thing you must be certain: *do not* apply dope or laquer directly to a plastic part since these will 'eat' at the plastic, destroying the surface. Use either a water soluble paint, which gives an excellent finish and can be easily thinned, or an enamel paint, which is less easy to thin but provides an excellent, tough final shell.

In plastic kits you will normally be provided with at least an indication of the *basic* colorings for various parts and in some cases with fairly detailed instructions or even a choice. However, it is entirely up to you whether you follow these or elect to use your own coloring. If this is the case we will assume that you are keen enough on maintaining realism to have chosen particular markings which you have accurately researched. Use the plan or draw a separate color chart so that you know before you even pick up your brush exactly where each color is to be applied. Remember, too, that if you are using a camouflage finish this is not just a random application of earth brown and green but should conform to the design pattern set down by the service concerned. Before you apply those colors, first check that the model's surface really is ready to receive paint, that excess cement has been removed, blemishes polished out and cracks filled in.

Some parts of the model which would be inaccessible or difficult to reach after completion will have been painted during assembly. These parts and areas such as the cockpit canopy, windows and gun turrets which all need to be free of paint, should be masked, preferably using masking tape made specially for the purpose with light adhesion so that damage to delicate parts is avoided when it is removed. If the tape which you are using seems to be too sticky and there is a likelihood of damage to thin struts when it is pulled off, the adhesion can be reduced by lightly dusting the tape with talc or simply by rubbing your fingers over the sticky side.

Canopies can also be protected by brushing on a masking fluid which sets to a thin skin. This is peeled off when the painting is finished. However, difficulty

can be experienced in lifting the edge of the skin to obtain leverage for peeling it back and there is a danger that the canopy can be scratched as you attempt to slide a blade under the protective layer. For safety it is best to use very narrow strips of masking tape around the edges of the cockpit and over any sections which will be painted later to represent framework. Then brush on the fluid, taking care that it is not allowed to stray over the edges of the outlining tape on to parts which are to be painted. To provide a good base, give the model an undercoat of grey or white matt. This fulfills a number of purposes: it provides an excellent and sound base for your final colors and it also serves both to show up any faults which still require treating and to seal areas on which body putty has been used.

Before applying the top coat make sure that the paint is thoroughly mixed. In the case of enamels, this will involve stirring the sediment at the bottom thoroughly into the base liquid to ensure an even distribution of color. If it is necessary to mix two or more colors, use a

Seen by many thousands of visitors to the Imperial War Museum, London, this model of Gloster Gladiator 'Faith' was made for enjoyment by Cyril McCann in about 1952 and later presented to the museum, where he now works. The original was fitted with a variable-pitch propeller from a Beaufort.

separate mixing jar or pot and transfer the colors to it, cleaning the brush well before putting it into a different color and adding thinner if necessary.

The ideal in painting with a brush is to apply the coats thinly and evenly. There is a terrible temptation to return to a spot already painted just to add that extra touch of paint. The result can be a catastrophy, particularly with quick-drying paints on which a skin starts to form as soon as they are applied. Application of a fresh spot of paint on to a partly set skin will cause 'dappling' and wrinkling. It is also easy to be deceived into thinking that a coat of paint is completely dry when, in fact, only the outer surface is hard and the inner is still spongy. Always allow the recommended time for each coat to dry and take into account high humidity.

If you do make an error and your paint strays – which is particularly likely if you are using freehand to paint straight lines – on no account should any attempt be made either to wipe off while the paint is wet or to cover the mistake by thickening the line. Instead, wait until the coat is thoroughly dry ('crisp dry' is the best description). Then take a cocktail stick or matchstick fined to a point and thoroughly soak the tip in thinner. Delicately apply the tip to the point of error and work at it slowly and gently to remove the offending spot.

Airbrush painting has become increasingly popular in recent years – originally for the wrong reason that people believed it would, without fail, givé a perfect finish no matter how inexperienced the user. In fact, as with everything about model aircraft, the best only comes from experience combined with care. The greatest advantage of airbrushing is that it does give an authentic look to the finish and it is the best means of applying a smooth finish.

Essentially the airbrush is a precision instrument which produces a fine, variable spray of paint emitted under pressure, usually through an adjustable nozzle. The type of finish which can be achieved can vary depending not only on the fineness of the spray but also on the distance the nozzle is held from the object. The necessary air compression used to force out the paint is achieved by a variety of means, depending not just upon the particular model of airbrush being used but also on the ingenuity of the user. The ideal but also the most expensive method is to use an electric compressor attached by air hose to the airbrush to give an instant and constant supply. Cost will be in the region of $80 (£40) but becomes worthwhile if the modeller is reasonably productive. Less expensive than the electric compressor, the foot-operated compressor has an air reservoir which is kept topped up by operating a foot pump. The aerosol can, connected by adaptor to the airbrush, is the commonest source of air supply but is by far the most expensive since one can spray only about five models. The aerosol is also unsatisfactory in that there is little warning that the supply is about to run out. Many cans are not able to sustain long bursts of spraying and will lose their power.

An alternative involving ingenuity is the use of a primus cooker. This is 'primed' by pumping air with a built-in injector pump. The air supply is emitted through what would normally be the fuel nozzle, suitably adapted to take an air hose. Like the foot compressor, the reservoir has to be topped up and the disadvantage is that both hands are needed for the purpose. Yet another method is to make use of a spare tire fitted with an adaptor which is commercially available and which controls the release of air through the valve.

If one airbrush is used for a variety of colors always ensure that it is thoroughly cleaned by spraying thinner through it before refilling with a different color. When you have finished painting or are taking a long break, give the airbrush another clean, making sure that not even the smallest amount of paint remains. If strong paint cleaner/stripper is used, be sure to wash the airbrush through thoroughly with thinner afterwards.

Airbrushes can use matt or gloss paints, water based or enamel. If gloss paint is used – because the full-size version was so finished – there is a danger that it will collect dust particles from the air as it dries. For preference I would use a quicker-drying matt which is less likely to collect the dust and can be lightly rubbed, once it is thoroughly dry, to remove any that may have settled lightly on the surface. The gloss finish is then achieved by airbrushing with gloss varnish.

Whatever type of paint is used, be sure to read the maker's instructions – you would be surprised how many people do not – not only regarding thinning or drying time but also about any possible dangers in using the paint in an airbrush in a confined space. It is a wise precaution to use a face mask since the very fine spray carries easily in the air, will settle on your skin and is easily drawn into your nostrils as you breathe. Prolonged airbrushing can also cause eye irritation and if eyes are your weak point a pair of goggles may be necessary. Make sure that wherever you do your airbrushing is well ventilated.

Filling the airbrush is a simple enough operation but still requires care. The selected color should be dropped into the color container or cup using a well-loaded paint brush. Thinner will need to be added to give the smoothest-flowing consistency and this can be done either with a different brush or by using an eye dropper.

Before starting to paint a model by airbrushing a beginner would be advised to carry out some test spraying using a sheet of plastic card to discover the different effects which can be obtained by varying the nozzle spray aperture and the distance the instrument is held from the object. The beginner will quickly discover that it is essential to keep the brush moving evenly across the surface in a smooth-flowing movement, otherwise the finished coat will vary in thickness. Something else the novice will discover is that a certain amount of the sprayed paint inevitably misses the target. It is, therefore, a good idea to use a simple three-sided spraying box, placing the model on the base and towards the back. If you cannot run to the luxury of a turntable a useful expedient is to make the back of the box removable – hook-and-eye fastenings on either side are simplest – so that when you have finished spraying from the front, the back is taken off, rehung in the eyes provided at the front and you can move round to complete airbrushing.

If the objective is to paint the model in camouflage you should first determine the correct pattern and then cut thin paper masks to the required shapes and fit them to the model. In the case of small models this can be a somewhat awkward job but for the beginner it does ensure clear demarkation lines between the colors. Later the modeller may feel confident enough to dispense with the patterns and work freehand. Where fabric or tissue covered models are concerned a completely different set of rules apply both to the application of the 'skin' itself and to the way in which it is treated.

The lightest form of covering for outdoor model flying is Japanese tissue which, as we have mentioned previously, is available in a full range of colors. Before it is applied to the framework of the model, the wood should be thoroughly sandpapered and dope, thinned to about 50 percent, applied to all the surfaces which the tissue will touch. When the dope is dry it is sanded lightly again and a second coat applied.

The purpose of this undercoat of dope is to provide a keying base to which the tissue will adhere. It also serves to seal the wood and strengthen it.

When the second coat is dry, sand it and then lay the tissue over the frame, making sure that the grain for each matching or adjacent piece runs in the same direction. Now the tissue is given a coat of thinned clear dope at all those points which lie over the previously doped areas and to which it is to adhere. The thinned dope will seep through the tissue and dissolve the surface of the undercoat of dope on the wood surface, combine with it and bond firmly as it dries. Always start at one end or edge and pull the tissue evenly over the frame, little by little. Do not attempt, for example, to lay the tissue on the leading edge of a wing and straight across to the trailing edge: the result would be creasing and sagging and an unsightly mess. Instead work outwards from a center line in a herringbone fashion. Do not attempt to make the tissue absolutely

Left and right
A classic example of a model built for display purposes, McCann's Mosquito FB Mk VI in the Imperial War Museum, London, with cut-aways designed to show detail of the construction methods and equipment in the original. The model, presented to the museum in 1958, exhibits supreme attention to detail and can stand up to the closest scrutiny, as the undershot (below) indicates.

taut as there will be shrinkage at a later stage.

If the fuselage is a simple box shape it will usually require just four pieces of tissue with holes cut accurately for any protruberances such as dowels, struts or undercarriage legs. However, if the fuselage is circular or of a varying profile, it is essential to use a series of narrow strips of tissue. Where the tissue is applied wet, it will begin to shrink quite quickly; if dry tissue has been used, this must be sprayed or lightly brushed with water to the extent that it is damp, not wet. The tissue is then left to dry thoroughly; do not attempt to rush this stage by applying a source of heat but allow the drying to occur naturally over several hours.

The tissue will shrink quite appreciably and it is therefore important not to complete just one surface of a wing and allow shrinkage before starting on the other surface. This will tend to induce warping whereas treatment of both surfaces will produce similar tensions on each and lessen that risk. Where a particularly light frame is involved an added precaution against warping is to pin it to a flat surface as it dries.

When the tissue is thoroughly dry apply the first overall coat of clear dope and allow it to dry before applying the second. The purpose of these coats is to seal the tissue not only against moisture but also against penetration by air which could alter the flying characteristics of the model. A further function is, of course, to give the tissue strength. Three or four coats are usually sufficient to fulfill these requirements without adding appreciably to the weight. Because dry dope in several layers tends to be somewhat brittle, there is some advantage in adding a few drops of castor oil or banana oil to the dope – four or five drops to the ounce – to act as a plasticizer and make the finish very slightly elastic to resist shattering.

An important point which must not be overlooked involves tissue or fabric covered models which are engine powered. Fuels for glowplug engines – and to a lesser extent, for diesels – dissolve ordinary dopes. A fuel-resistant dope must therefore be used and this can either be used throughout, in place of ordinary dope, or as a couple of fuel-proofing topcoats, depending upon the maker's directions.

On larger models fabric coverings are treated in almost the same way as tissue except that they are *always* applied wet and attention must be paid to the different 'shrink qualities' of the various fabrics. Terylene, for example, is highly shrink-resistant while silk shrinks quite considerably. Another difference is that rather than treating the frame with dope which has been thinned to 50 percent, dope with practically no thinning should be used and the fabric applied before the coating is fully dry. The fabric is pinned in place over the doped starting point, pulled taut and pinned at its other edge. For example, pin the fabric at the top center of the nose and at the tail end; then work from nose to tail, pinning liberally and smoothing out as you go before applying the topcoat over the fabric at its points of contact on the frame. Take care not to allow dope to collect on the pins, run down and dry in blobs.

It will be found that most fabrics will seal satisfactorily with three coats of dope, though the lighter weight silk will require only two. Open weave fabrics will need more unless they have first been dusted over with talc to seal the weave. A point to remember in using any fabric is that the warp and weft should always be kept in straight lines. These also provide a useful indication of points where there is overstress since the lines will be distorted by the extra tension.

Though transfers are nowadays available for a very wide range of national service and civil airline markings, the range of sizes is not as wide and it is, of course, not commercially viable for manufacturers to market all individual squadron or personal markings or

decorations. However, this need not present the modeller with any problem – nor with any excuse not to have the right markings in the correct scale! Making your own transfers can be a most satisfying exercise not only from an artistic point of view but also because you can ensure that the colors incorporated are not prone to the variances which sometimes occur in commercial transfers and are mixed exactly to your requirements.

The homemade transfer is best produced from a well-gummed label. Add a couple of drops of castor oil to some clear dope and brush or spray this on to the gummed side of the label, allowing it to dry. Then the required marking can be drawn on in outline using soft pencil or chinagraph and painted in with colored dope. Achieving the perfect circle for roundels of the right scale can present problems. One method is to scribe a set of patterns on stiff cardboard or plastic card and cut them out for use whenever required, simply holding them in place while you draw round them or using double sided tape so that both hands are kept free. This method, though not as satisfactory as using a compass direct on to the gummed label because of the risk of movement, avoids making a hole in the transfer with the compass point. It is, to the writer's mind, more advantageous when the modeller is painting directly on to the aircraft instead of using transfers.

If a compass is being used, its pen is loaded with thinned dope of the correct color and the compass point is rested lightly on a small center 'base' of three or four layers of Scotch tape to avoid damaging the surface. Some practice is required in achieving the right amount of thinning to give a free flow of dope on to the surface: if it is too thick it will drag and make an irregular line with a ragged outer edge; if it is too thin not enough color will be deposited.

When the outer lines of the circle or insignia have been drawn the painting in follows and the transfer is allowed to dry before being cut out of the label. When cutting out, a margin of about ⅛in (3mm) should be left around the insignia to aid handling and peeling off. The addition of those drops of castor oil will ensure that it retains a sufficient degree of flexibility for it to be slid on to the receiving surface comfortably after being soaked in luke warm water, as is done with a commercial transfer.

Freehand lettering can present problems when it is done directly on to a model's surface which is not flat and therefore will not make an acceptable base for a ruler. The only answer is practice and still more practice. Stencils, either homemade or one of the wide range of commercially-produced, can be a useful aid but great care must be taken not to allow seepage of the color under the edges, producing drag lines. Thin strips of double-sided adhesive tape are an answer here, even if the job of sticking it down to the under edge of the stencil does prove tedious. It is, at least, a good test of that most important quality for any successful modeller – patience!

A great aid to success is the range of markings introduced by Letraset some twelve years ago, thanks to the initiative of the Canadian modeller, Alan Breeze. The Letraset system of transferring designs, patterns, shadings and letters does not require water or any other liquid or adhesive. Markings come on transparent sheets and are simply cut out, placed in position and lightly rubbed over with a soft pencil.

Care must be taken to position the markings exactly, as they cannot be moved once they are rubbed down. In addition, it is important to cover the whole of the marking when rubbing down to avoid the risk of cracking or crinkling as the facing paper is removed. The risk of cracking also increases with the age of the sheets, which should not be stored in very dry atmospheres. If a mistake is made in positioning, or if the transfer does crack and cannot be successfully mended the only answer is to use a strip of adhesive tape such as Scotch tape to lift the offending piece away. Then start again. On no account should you attempt to scrape the Letraset off as this will only mark the undersurface.

In recent years many other companies have entered the field of specialist decal sheets for modellers and the range of markings has become vast. Competition has ensured that the quality of the decals is generally excellent though to date the larger scale model tends to have been somewhat overlooked.

The introduction of any new range of parts or aids for the modeller tends to be greeted with a certain amount of skepticism on the part of purists who believe only in building from scratch using their own ingenuity. Such was the case with plastic kits, with nylon propellers and with airbrushing and now with the widespread use of decal sheets.

Built as a stripped-down display model by Cyril McCann, this Hawker Typhoon Mk IB is also on show at the Imperial War Museum, London.

Sadly there is a degree of snobbism which creeps into every branch of aeromodelling and nowhere is it more pronounced than in 'scratch-building,' whose purist practitioners take upon themselves the role of arbiters of what is 'good' and what is not, and who lay down an unofficial list of dos and don'ts.

Yet modellers will agree that they took up the hobby for pleasure and have found themselves caught up in the pursuit of 'perfection' only after their first, fumbling attempts. As they progress so 'perfection' seems perversely, to be that little bit harder to achieve. They will also discover that what is 'perfection' in one person's eyes is not in another's.

The art and craft of aeromodelling is so much a matter of individual ability and ingenuity, of personal choice and of home economics that it seems a pity to allow these notes of carping criticism to enter an arena which should be one of pleasure. That having been said, it is also true to say that within its various 'branches,' aeromodelling includes the friendliest of people and a feeling of comradeship which it would be hard to equal. There is always someone at hand to offer advice, to lend equipment and even give away a spare part.

If you have decided to take up aeromodelling, in whatever form, you will have opened the door to a lifetime of friendship as well as to hours of patient hard work which, in the end, bring the most delightful of rewards.

Bibliography

Clément Ader - his Flight and his Place in History, Charles H Gibbs-Smith, (HMSO)
The World's First Aero'lane Flights, Charles H Gibbs-Smith, (Science Museum)
Sir George Cayley's Aeronautics, Charles H Gibbs-Smith, (HMSO)
Modern Aeromodelling, R G Moulton, (Faber and Faber)
Flying Scale Models, R G Moulton, (Model and Allied Publications)
This is Model Flying, Martin Dilly, (Elm Tree Books, Hamish Hamilton)
Aeromodeller, (MAP Ltd)
Making Model Aircraft, Bryan Philpott, (Patrick Stephens Ltd)
Airfix Magazine and Airfix Annual, (PSL)
Scale Models, (MAP Ltd)
Flight International, (IPC Ltd)
Aircraft, John W R Taylor (Hamlyn Publishing Group Ltd)
The World of Model Aircraft, Guy R Williams (André Deutsch)
Scale Model Aircraft in Plastic Card, Harry Woodman (Argus Press Ltd)
Radio Control Models, (MAP Ltd)

Index

Numbers in italics refer to illustrations

Picture Credits

Aero Modeller
Front jacket, 1, 2 (top left and top right), 27, 28, 32 (both), 33, 34 (top), 35 (both), 36/37 (both), 44 (both), 45 (both), 46, 47, 96, 97, 100, 102, 108, 109, 110 (both), 111, 112, 113, 114 (both), 115, 116 (all three), 117 (all three), 118, 119, 120/121 (all three), 122/123 (both), 124, 125, 126/127, 128 (all four), 129, 130/131, 132/133, 134, 135 (both), 136, 137 (both), 138/139, 140/141, 142, 143 (both), 145, 146/147 (all three), 148, 149 (all four), 150 (both), 151 (both), 152/153 (both), 154, 155 (both), 156, 157, 158/159 (all three), 161, 162/163 (all four), 164/165, 166/167 (all three), 168/169 (all three), 170 (both), 171 (both), 172/173 (all three), 174 (both), 175, 176 (both), 177 (both), 178 (both), 179, 180, 181 (both)

B Bettany and H Woodman
90/91, 92/93 (right), 94/95 (both)

Crown copyright, Science Museum, London
6, 7, 8/9, 10, 11 (both), 12/13 (both), 14, 15 (both), 16, 18/19, 20/21 (both), 22/23 (both), 24/25, 29

Imperial War Museum, London
4/5, 182, 183, 184/185, 186, 187, 188/189

Mat Irvine
78/79

Doug McHard
43 (both)

Ray Rimell
34 (bottom), 40/41, 48, 49 (all three), 50 (both), 51 (both), 52/53 (all five), 54 (both), 55 (both), 56/57 (all four), 58 (both), 59 (both), 60/61 (both), 62 (both), 63 (all three), 64 (both), 65 (all four), 66/67 (all three), 68/69 (all three), 70 (both), 71 (both), 72/73 (all three), 74 (both), 75 (both), 76/77 (all three), 80, 81 (both), 82/83, 88/89.

Ripmax Ltd
98 (all four), 99, 101 (both), 103, 104/105

Royal Aeronautical Society
(lent to the Science Museum, London)
17

Peter Russell
106/107

Scale Models
2/3, 79 (top)

Vic Smeed
Back jacket, 2 (center), 160

Bill Stone
All line illustrations

N Whitcomb
84/85, 86/87 (all three)

H Woodman
92 (both)